The Bill

the first ten years

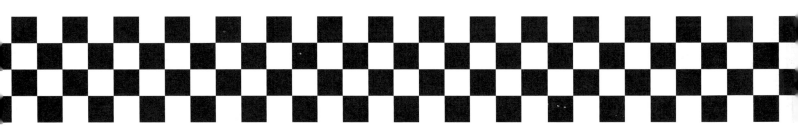

The Bill

10

THE FIRST TEN YEARS

HILARY KINGSLEY

B⬤XTREE

THAMES TELEVISION

Dedication

This book is dedicated to the memory of Geoff McQueen, creator of 'The Bill' and Micky Moynihan, the programme's long-serving location manager. Both were inspired, enthusiastic and wonderful company; both sadly died during the summer of 1994. They are much missed by all who knew them.

First published in Great Britain in 1994 by Boxtree Limited

ISBN 1 85283 911 2

A CIP catalogue entry for this book is available from the British Library.

Designed by Millions Design
Printed in Scotland by Bath Press Colourbooks for

Boxtree Limited
Broadwall House
21 Broadwall
London SE1 9PL

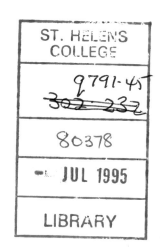
Acknowledgements
I'm grateful to many people for help in writing this book. The cast and production team at 'The Bill' were without exception patient and forthcoming. Mariette Overeynder, in the Press Office, was an excellent fixer and go-between. Nigel Wilson, 'The Bill's Project Co-ordinator who works longer hours than a junior doctor and is always answering at least four people's queries at once, tolerated my quizzing and allowed his busy room to be my frequent meeting place. Tony Lynch's reliable earlier book on 'The Bill' was useful. Frank Jeffery contributed thoughts and words. Copy editor and 'Bill' fan Edward Leeson endured pestering about who did what to whom when and compiled the Casebook.

Picture acknowledgements:
Photographs pp. 2, 7: Mark Bourdillon, courtesy of Carlton Television. Other photographs by: Pat Dyos, John McDonald and Stan Allen.

Every effort has been made to obtain permission to reproduce the pictures which appear in this book. The publisher apologises for any regrettable omissions which have occurred at the time of going to press.

Contents

Preface   6

1   Ten Tough Years   7

2   Sun Up on Sun Hill   24

3   The Making of an Episode   34

4   Identity Parade: The Stars of Sun Hill   48

5   All Right on the Night   82
    Teach Yourself Billspeak   85

6   Closed Files: Past Stars of Sun Hill   90

7   Casebook   105

Preface

The fact that 'The Bill' is ten years old in October of 1994 is both gratifying and remarkable. Gratifying because success in the world of entertainment is much sought after and hard to find. Remarkable because no matter what experience, effort, money and any other attribute or skill you care to think of is brought to bear on the subject, the presence or absence of one indefinable factor is what makes the essential difference. Call it luck, magic, happy accident, it is what turns a single play into a short series, and a short series into a regular appointment at 8pm, three times a week.

'Woodentop' was a play in a Thames Television season of single dramas, and was aired on 16 August 1983. It was about a young policeman's first day at a police station in the east end of London. Shortly afterwards Thames took the decision to develop that single play into a thirteen-part series of one-hour episodes which went out in the autumn of 1984. From then on the programme has gone from strength to strength, becoming a regular twice-weekly half-hour series in 1988, with a third half-hour being added in January 1993.

I think what gives the programme its particular character aside from such stylistic considerations as every scene always having a police presence in it and rarely if ever going into the domestic backgrounds of our regular characters, is its presentation of human situations seen by the public through the eyes of the police. In the sense that 'The Bill' provides the audience with a window through which to look on to other people's worlds, the programme is as much as anything a play series, since the stories are largely self-contained and the continuity elements really only the regular police characters, otherwise it is about other people's lives.

This book shows how we juggle thirty regular actors and three teams of producers, directors, location managers and so forth to provide these dramatic insights three times a week. We hope you will continue to enjoy the programme and that you will enjoy this account of how we go about making it for you.

Michael Chapman, *Executive Producer of 'The Bill'*

Ten Tough Years

The five 'old timers', with Executive Producer Michael Chapman

SGT. BOB CRYER

Sergeant Bob Cryer is an old-fashioned copper who has kept up to date. Rock-steady Cryer has the old virtues of humanity, dedication to duty, and complete loyalty to the men he works for and those who work under him. But his sharp intelligence has made it possible for Cryer to adapt to the big changes in policing brought in by PACE (Police and Criminal Evidence Act).

Some people feel Cryer's natural fair-mindedness is a bit too much in evidence when he's dealing with villains, but the man will not change. A spell in the Army as a young man gave him a feeling for discipline, but Cryer has always been a pragmatist and finds a way to make things work.

As Duty Sergeant, working some of the time in civilian clothes, Bob Cryer is a sort of adjutant to Brownlow and Monroe, and a kind of buffer between the blokes and the brass. He's always willing to listen to both sides of an argument, will go out of his way to help anyone.

But he can't take being lied to, and a copper who tries to con him is in for trouble. Cryer will probably never be promoted; he's far too valuable doing the job he has. The nick would find it tough operating without him. Here's how he sees ten years at Sun Hill.

Bob Cryer's Ten Tough Years

I know some of the younger men see me as a father figure, and I've no quarrel with that. So long as they realize a father has to be obeyed – most of the time, anyway.

I hope I'm a friend to everybody at Sun Hill; I get along pretty well with most of them. I hope I've still got a sense of humour after all these years in the Job. It helps when times are tough, which they are quite a lot of the time.

It's been said I don't suffer fools gladly, and I suppose I don't – though I do try to remember that grey matter wasn't dished out with total equality. We get quite a lot of customers at Sun Hill who are in trouble because they are simple rather than evil. I keep that in mind.

My home life helps me keep a sense of proportion after a day of near-Bedlam at the nick. My wife Shirley and my two sons Daniel and Patrick are as important in my life as my work. I've had a few problems with Patrick, the older boy. He's not always kept the best of company, and I can't help blaming myself for that.

I suppose the worst night of my life was when Patrick was brought into Sun Hill and charged with causing a girl's death by dangerous driving. The case was thrown out on a technicality when Ted Roach took it to court, and my mind was in a terrible mess. What they call conflicting emotions, I think. Patrick and I grew apart after that. When he was at university I hardly spoke to him. But I still think about him all the time.

I suppose at the start I didn't have much time for Chief Superintendent Brownlow. I saw him as too much of a ducker and diver, too interested in playing golf with the right people, too concerned with police politics. But I've learned to respect him more over the years. He's always willing to listen to what I have to say, or to anyone else. And that's not as common as you might think among men who run police stations. I've come to understand a bit more about the problems men like the Chief Super face. The job has changed a great deal in a decade. It's his job to make sure those changes operate at all levels, and that's not always easy.

I've had my share of problems at the station, too, of course. When Sergeant Alec Peters got stabbed on that housing estate, I was . . . well, gutted. He was a shadow of his old self when he came back. He's driving a desk upstairs now, and I hardly ever see him. It's a shame, because I used to think of him as my best mate at Sun Hill.

Bob Cryer guides young George Garfield round the Sun Hill filing system

Well, let's put it this way, I always tried to get on with Alec Peters, considered him a good mate; but, you know, he was a funny bloke at times. I think I got on his nerves. He'd look at me sometimes as if he found me a bit of a pain in the arse, too good by half. That's where the bit of friction came in. I used to say, 'Alec, let's talk about it,' but he just couldn't accept my support. Funny, that. But there you go.

Then there was Sergeant Tom Penny. He wasn't what I'd call a bundle of laughs, old Tom, and he took a few pops at me in his time. But he did his job, and I respected him for that. I think he drank a bit on the quiet – those Canley Fields child murders played on his mind a bit. None of us forgot them in a hurry, come to that. But when he got a bit squiffy at the party to celebrate my twenty years in the Job, and was then stopped in his car and done for drunken driving, I was sorry for him. Was it a fit-up? No one could prove it; no one ever can with the Barton Street operators. But it was a bad business and it leaves a bitter taste even now.

Then, there's a lot

Sergeant Cryer shoots but regrets

about my fellow officers I don't understand – especially some of the younger ones like Loxton. They seem to be in it for the buzz. I'm a bit uneasy about the thrills of our job. I'm not sure about this trend towards more coppers carrying guns. Not sure at all. I have a firearms certificate, which means I can carry a gun on duty if authorized; but I've never liked guns, and I think that if the day ever comes when the copper on the beat is routinely armed that will be a sad day for the force.

The first time I was on an operation that involved firearms was when some looney with a gun snatched an old lady. I tried to talk him into letting her go but before I managed it Galloway, Roach and Dashwood burst in. The bloke was shot dead in front of the old lady. I still think that if I'd been given the time I could have ended it peacefully.

There was a time when I myself shot a robber who pointed a shotgun at me. It turned out his gun wasn't loaded, which made me feel terrible. Everyone told me I had no choice, but it didn't make me feel any better about it. Still doesn't.

I can't say DI Burnside and I were great mates from the start. There were rumours that he was bent, and there was no doubt at all that he didn't always go by the rule-book. But the man earned my grudging respect because he did his job so well. And by the time he mysteriously left Sun Hill I didn't believe he was bent – even if the man was a bit of a maverick.

There was a time when Ted Roach and I were fairly close mates. We were both sergeants and around the same age. But I couldn't approve of his drinking, though I understood why it happened. I think that opened up a bit of a gulf between us.

I've got a lot of respect for June Ackland because she does her job so well and manages to remain a human being. Of course she should have taken stripes. I haven't given up on her doing that. There are extra problems for women police officers, I know that, including the odd sexist pig of a male copper making life difficult. I've always stamped on that when I've seen it, even though male chauvinism is an attitude someone of my age and background can easily fall into. I was totally devastated when Viv Martella died; so was everyone else at Sun Hill.

I've come to tolerate Reg Hollis rather better than I did. I've known Reg a long time, and I've been close to clocking him one on many occasions, but I've come to appreciate that he's a bit more than the station clown. Which doesn't make him any less irritating at times.

I like it when Sun Hill does things together –

cricket matches, fishing trips, snooker tournaments, that kind of thing. (We had an Open Day at Sun Hill once, and the Snooker Cup got nicked – which amused them no end down at Barton Street.) I usually have a hand in setting up these sporting and social occasions. Somebody has to.

Eric Richard

Eric Richard, who plays Bob Cryer, sees himself as a typical South Londoner. He was born in Margate but brought up in Brixton. Unlike your typical South Londoner, he'd moved north of the river and was living in Hertfordshire when he was called up for 'The Bill' ten years ago.

Eric always does a lot of research for any part he plays, but he didn't have far to go to find out what makes Bob Cryer tick. He had a neighbour in the Thames Valley force, and Eric spent a lot of time finding out why the guy had become a policeman.

'The very essence of the man was to do a job he thought was necessary for society and to do it well,' Eric says. 'That gave me the key to Cryer. He does think his job is necessary. We need policemen, and I'm going to be a good one – that's the way Bob thinks.

'I got to know Bob well. He was working class, a Londoner, he'd joined the Army as a young man, but when he was married with young children Ulster had started to happen. He thought that with those responsibilities he'd better get out, and the Met was where he went.

'The role of sergeant suits him. He has the good NCO's ability to liaise with the officers and the other ranks. Good man-management in both directions, that's Cryer's skill.'

Cryer is now in his late forties. Eric Richard is fifty-four and he came to acting quite late. One of three brothers, he hated school, had a tough time of it. Just one teacher caught his interest for a time. She told the English class stories and got them to act the tales out. Something stirred in Eric Richard; there was an actor in there trying to get out.

But Eric was twenty-eight before the actor escaped. He was married with two children and managing a motor accessories business. Through work he met a man involved in amateur dramatics, and this led to him joining the South London Theatre Centre in Norwood.

After a couple of months he knew that acting was what he wanted to do full-time. With a young family he realized he couldn't afford to go to drama school, so he hustled around for work in the theatre, joined fringe groups, and gradually infiltrated his way into the profession.

But it wasn't until 1972 at the Liverpool Everyman that people began to notice Eric. Jonathan Pryce was in the company; Eric shared a pokey dressing-room with Anthony Sher. He began to play bigger roles, moved to the Crucible Theatre in Sheffield, started doing the odd commercial.

But he didn't really work in television until 1978 when he played a nasty little villain in 'The Onedin Line'. Then he was in 'Angels', 'Shoestring' and 'Juliet Bravo'.

The 30-million-dollar 'Shogun' series was the biggest thing he'd been in, even if work was limited to one month because his character died of gangrene. After that television alternated with theatre work. He was touring with a play called *Red Saturday* with John Salthouse in 1983 when the casting director of 'The Bill' saw the show. Result: Eric became Bob Cryer, and John became DI Galloway.

Eric loves his part, has no fear that Cryer might typecast him as a good-guy copper for ever. He has made sure that Cryer isn't too good to be true, which makes the character more interesting for both the actor and the viewer. Cryer is a fair-minded policeman, mainstay of Sun Hill; but if Eric showed him as endlessly sweet-tempered, fault-free, we'd soon get tired of the man.

Eric has been married, divorced and is now remarried. His grown-up son Richard is a travel writer and his grown-up daughter Frances is reading Law at university. And son Jack is just two years old.

Eric has always been mad about motor-bikes, and he still is. For a time he was keen on getting Bob Cryer astride two wheels, but it never happened.

Currently he owns ten bikes, ranging from a 125 Honda to a Honda Goldwing with a sidecar. (Don't mention Harley-Davidsons to him; he thinks they're for posers.)

In 1990 he took his second wife, Tina, to see the famous Daytona 200 race in Florida, and his interest in bikes also got him fascinating spots touring for 'Wish You Were Here' and testing two-wheelers for 'Top Gear'. Tennis and badminton are other interests.

So, still, is the theatre. Eric has managed to get time off most years to tread the boards again. (He played Enobarbus in *Antony and Cleopatra* for Birmingham Rep.)

But most of the time he's happy playing Bob Cryer, especially in the twenty or so episodes a year in which Cryer has the heavyweight role.

'But', he says, 'I could never really be a policeman. Couldn't take the discipline. One of the happiest days of my life was when they abolished National Service. I missed it by nine months.'

CH. SUPT. CHARLES BROWNLOW

Chief Superintendent Charles Brownlow is a complex man. He seems a bit remote when you first meet him, a bit conventional, bordering on the

A sunny smile from Sun Hill's CID team – but are they always under Brownlow's command?

At fifty-four, Charles Brownlow does not feel ready for the scrap-heap, and there is wife Marjorie and their two children to think about. Here he gives an overview of the last decade at Sun Hill.

Charles Brownlow's Ten Tough Years

I suppose you could say my job was man management, and if that sounds to you a long way from the policeman's task of keeping the peace and catching villains . . . well, you're right.

But running a large Metropolitan station in a high-crime area has become almost entirely an administrative job. It's not often that I get involved in day-to-day policing matters. I have to think about policy, adapting the way we do things in the light of changing laws, Home Office directives, the word from on high – which usually reaches me via a phone call from the Deputy Assistant Commissioner.

I have so many people to keep happy: the Metropolitan hierarchy, what you might call the officers and the troops below me, then all kinds of local groups like Rotary clubs and influential politicians and other individuals in the community of Sun Hill. I perform a sort of juggling act to keep friction low. To tell you the truth, I was happier a couple of promotions back from my present exalted position, when I was more in what you might call the thick of things.

I have of course seen a great deal of change at Sun Hill. For a start, more women officers and more women in senior positions. I welcome this. I'd go so far as to say I'd like to see the day when we had a woman Commissioner in the Met, but I don't think I'd bet my pension on it happening in my lifetime.

We have had some very able ladies at Sun Hill. I think of DCI Kim Reid, who did not have an easy task controlling a somewhat chauvinistic department. She managed it by being better than they were at any job and by having a sharply humorous tongue. Kim is going to be a very high flier.

I think of DI Sally Johnson, who has surprised quite a lot of villains with unexpected physical strength and not a few detectives with an ability to outguess them. I think of our well-liked WPC June Ackland, who has steadfastly refused promotion and a move to CID, although her team spirit in the burglary initiative team Bumblebee has shown her commitment. She is one of the most skilled and intelligent officers at Sun Hill.

The refurbishment of the station at enormous cost – I was informed of the development at a

stuffy. But you don't get to run a major London police station without having formidable talents, and Brownlow is a sharp operator. He has come up through the ranks, and he misses the hustle and bustle of everyday police work. Which is why he likes a yarn with one of the men or women he commands: he can experience their lively world vicariously.

Brownlow has always been a bit suspicious of his CID officers. He sees them as mavericks, chancers sometimes, and he's not always sure they're really in command of their investigations. He's not always sure he's really in command of them. Burnside he treated with special caution. He had a well-concealed admiration for the man, but he was always worried that Burnside would drop him in deep trouble.

Brownlow has had to become a bit of a politician as he has been promoted, both with local pressure groups and with the top brass of the Met. He doesn't much like this but feels he has no alternative. He plays a lot of golf, often with people who might help promote his career. And that's another worry.

After the Sheehy Report it seems likely that the ranks of chief superintendent and chief inspector will be abolished, but for Brownlow, future promotion (to Commander) is a distinct possibility.

Commanders' Strategic Planning Meeting – has made our job easier in many respects. I am not one of those who think that computer systems will one day replace good policemen, but they certainly make our job easier. But the people I work with are more important than any electronic wizardry.

I confess I was quite shocked to discover when I came back from a week's leave that I was losing Chief Inspector Derek Conway, who had been appointed Community Liaison Officer in my absence. Not losing him entirely, of course, for Derek works from Sun Hill. It is just that the man I trusted as my deputy was moving out of my orbit. I understood

Brownlow views his new deputy, Philip Cato (left), with concern.

that Derek felt frustrated that his route to further promotion seemed blocked, and that perhaps to some extent he blamed me.

If that was a surprise, his replacement could be called a shock. Chief Inspector Philip Cato from Barton Street, a neighbour station of ours, is not universally popular, perhaps because he often gives the impression that the only way to go is by the book. Indeed, DI Burnside, I understand, called him 'that bald-headed bastard from Barton Street', though I'd prefer it if you didn't repeat that outside these walls. But Philip has proved himself an efficient and scrupulous officer.

I have always had loyal and helpful support from Inspector Andrew Monroe, with whom I sometimes feel rather more rapport than with Philip. Again I'd ask you not to repeat that.

There have been dramatic incidents in the last ten years – affairs the tabloid newspapers were keen to report. A man died in a street fight and one of my PCs, young Philip Loxton, had to explain how blood was found on his truncheon.

Two PCs, Stamp and Hollis, discovered human skeletons in a flat. It turned out that they had been imported for medical students and were not evidence of a serial killer on the loose. Stamp and Hollis seemed a little disappointed.

Then there was that business when DC Dashwood was held hostage on a rooftop by an armed robber. Some sharp observation by PC Quinnan led to a child-murderer being apprehended. Quite properly, young David received a commendation for this work.

PC Tony Stamp was shot and wounded, and Sergeant Bob Cryer managed to shoot the assailant. I lost a good officer in PC Ken Melvin in a bombing incident. Sadly, I may have been partly responsible for his death. But I don't want to dwell on that. Does no good.

PCs Melvin and Quinnan stopped a Jaguar that was being driven dangerously. A check showed the car was stolen, and Melvin drove it to Sun Hill, parking it rather carelessly. I ordered him to park it again, and while he was doing that a bomb planted in the vehicle went off. Along with others, I was slightly injured. Poor Melvin was taken to hospital but died soon afterwards.

We had trouble proving that the driver of the car, a man called Wilkes, was a member of a terrorist organization. The press wrote about stories like that, but they represented a tiny fraction of our work at Sun Hill. I think we continue to do a good job in protecting the public in this area of East London.

Personally I have problems with my future with the Met – or lack of it. The future does look bleak for many senior officers in London's police force. And, indeed, for other forces.

I have sometimes been accused of being overkeen on keeping my nose clean, of not speaking my mind strongly enough to my superiors. I find this criticism unfair. At an important meeting at Scotland Yard I spoke forcefully against some Home Office policies, and I know for a fact that certain views I expressed on national housing policies – views that some might think radical – got back to the top echelon at the Yard.

I do not regret this, for there are times when a

man must speak out. Though I have always endeavoured to do this with politeness and without undue heat.

Peter Ellis

The first thing you notice about Peter Ellis is that he looks a lot younger than Brownlow, the man he plays. Then you discover he's fifty-eight, four years older than the Chief Super.

Peter is amusing, charming, imaginative – a long way from the stuffy top cop. He has three grown-up sons by his marriage, now ended, and a one-year-old son named Sam, whom he had with actress Anita Parry, twenty years younger than himself. They met in a touring version of *Educating Rita*, and live together on the Isle of Dogs. Peter had the Michael Caine role, Anita the Julie Walters part.

Peter's a bit sheepish about being a dad again in his late fifties, but see him 'off duty' in a sweater with young Sam on his shoulders and you see a besotted father. 'It's not something I'd planned, but it's great,' he says. 'When you're older you want to do things right. I may be too old to be a real copper but I'm not too old to enjoy Sam.'

He's had a fascinating life, this shy, smiling man. He was born in Bristol in 1936 but was brought up in Aldershot and Devon. Left school at fifteen, did a number of jobs, including merchant seaman. But an apprenticeship at an aircraft factory took him into a flying scholarship with the RAF and then a degree at Ruskin College, Oxford.

And university life brought him into contact with theatre. He got a part-time job as assistant stage manager at the Oxford Playhouse, then began to act with Peter Hall's Elizabethan Theatre Company.

But he was not yet completely hooked. Peter worked as a civilian flying instructor before training at the Central School of Speech and Drama. After that he was rarely out of work, with stints with the Old Vic company, important companies like the Nottingham Playhouse and the Leeds Playhouse and then the Royal Shakespeare Company.

Television intruded from time to time – he has played eight different roles in 'Coronation Street', which was a record at one time; was in various prestigious Wednesday Plays; appeared in both 'Dixon of Dock Green' and 'Z Cars'; and won a part in the wonderful soap spoof 'Acorn Antiques' after appearing in a play by Victoria Wood, the soap's deviser.

If all that isn't enough, Peter has worked for Arnold Wesker's Centre 42 and for various community arts projects. He still does community work of this kind in the East End.

He loves playing Brownlow, though he almost missed being in 'The Bill'. He auditioned for one of the CID parts and didn't make it. 'I was probably too old,' he says. But as he was walking out of the door the casting people realized he was exactly right for Brownlow. He's been running Sun Hill ever since.

How would he like the Chief Super to develop? 'I'd like to play him with more humour. Brownlow makes jokes but usually he doesn't do it with much skill. Probably chief supers are only funny with other officers of the same rank, and there aren't any at Sun Hill. And I'd like him to get out of the station more, like he did when he calmed a near-riot in a housing estate. But I know that's difficult.'

Could he be a cop in real life? 'Never. I'm much too disorganized and probably not brave enough. I'm capable of jumping in and helping someone in trouble – I have actually done that – but if I had time to think I'm sure I would be a coward!'

Unlike Brownlow, Peter Ellis doesn't play golf. But he likes cricket, gliding, walking and 'a bit of climbing'.

He likes spending time, too, with the grown-up sons: Chris is a musician/actor, Hugh is a writer ('Ben Roberts, who plays Conway, and I appeared in a film he wrote') and Charlie is a stagehand. What with home life with Anita and little Sam, that community work and the non-stop demands of playing the Chief Super, Peter Ellis hasn't got time to think about retirement. Unlike Charles Brownlow.

PC REG HOLLIS

We all know someone like PC Reg Hollis. A bit of a nerd, a bit of a clown, not above creeping to his superiors on occasion. Reg's whiney voice, silly jokes and odd ways make him the butt of much Sun Hill humour, but the older hands have a lot of respect for Reg. They know that in spite of everything he's a good copper. Those who suggest he doesn't always have the stomach for a rumble should remember that more than once unarmed Reg has tackled a gunman. And Reg has more sympathy and understanding for crime victims than some of his more gung-ho colleagues.

Reg Hollis's Ten Tough Years

I've seen a lot of changes in my decade at Sun Hill, and I'm a man who understands what's going on in this particular nick. I should do. I was Federation rep for five years – sorting out the problems of policemen in bother or having some sort of dispute with the brass.

I think I can say that I carried out those duties to the best of my ability – even if I did lose the job when I came up for re-election by fifty-eight votes to two. Obviously my colleagues felt that I'd given service enough and should not be asked to make more sacrifices which might affect my career.

Reg, the Federation rep, points out the problems to Garfield, Quinnan and Stamp outside the locker room

But no one can say I didn't put up a good case for the lads when it came to talking to Mr Brownlow and Mr Monroe about overtime, Sunday working and – perhaps most important – a coffee machine in the locker room. I do feel that machine was a real triumph for my negotiating skills.

And don't forget my time as Collator at Sun Hill. I did that responsible job well, though I was not sorry when I was asked to give it up. I like to be out and about, not stuck in the station all the time. In the same way, I wasn't upset when Chief Superintendent Brownlow decided to replace me as Local Intelligence

Officer. No, I didn't mind the jokes that my intelligence was so local that they couldn't find it. I can take a joke – and I'm quite good at making them, too. Anyone will verify that. I keep the lads laughing, helping to keep up their morale.

The thing about Sun Hill is that it's a very friendly nick. Of course, you get little disagreements between colleagues – bound to in a stressful job like ours. There was a time when I thought that DI Burnside and DS Roach overdid it a bit with what some people called a feud. Came to blows once, so I've been told; but, as I say, this is a stressful job.

Most people rub along pretty well, though. I've got some real friends at Sun Hill. I've known June Ackland and Bob Cryer a long time, and we respect each other, I feel.

And most of Jim Carver's years in uniform, before he went to CID, were spent alongside me. People have asked me why I've never gone in for promotion or wanted to become a detective, and I always say the same thing: I'm happy where I am, thank you. The copper on the beat is the mainstay of the police force.

I went through the great upheaval in 1990, when Sun Hill was modernized and refurbished at a cost of £1.3 million. (Mr Brownlow explained to us that this was to make the old place into 'a station for the twenty-first century'; though, of course, he'll be drawing his pension by then, as I jokily pointed out. He didn't seem too amused.)

Of course, it was money well spent. We certainly needed modern communications, and I will never speak against the age of computers. All the same, a few of us felt that some of the money could have gone on improving the canteen food, but you can't have everything.

There have been personal high points for me. I'd never claim to be a hero, of course, but I didn't do too badly the night I heard a gunshot in a shop. I went in and found the manager with a shotgun at his throat. I had to talk the gunman into surrendering without getting the manager or me shot, and it took some doing. But I managed it.

On another occasion I was called to a disturbance in a Social Security office which turned out to be a bit more than a disturbance. Some poor, crazed, unemployed nutter had failed to get his Giro on time, so he'd gone down to the office to collect his money in person – with a gun.

A woman with a baby was being threatened, and I managed to get her out of harm's way without provoking violence. One or two people accused me of being smug about this little episode, but I think that was unfair. I had to tell other people what happened, didn't I? Knowing how I dealt with a tricky situation could be helpful to less experienced officers.

But I suppose what I'm most proud of is the way I saved a twelve-year-old boy from suicide. It's hard to believe a kid of that age would want to slash his wrists, but it happened. I'm not a trained psychologist or anything but I did manage to make him see that life's worth living. Things like that make all the stress and worry and danger of the Job worth while. Any copper will tell you that.

There was another occasion when I was reading a porn magazine – purely in the course of duty it was! – when I realized that one of the models was a fourteen-year-old girl I had seen about Sun Hill. Because of my sharp reaction CID were able to catch the man who was exploiting her. Of course, a lot of people say I should have been a journalist, and I won't argue with that: I do have a way with words. I have edited various station newspapers and contributed to other police journals.

Bob Cryer wasn't too pleased when I printed a cartoon of him as Cyrano de Bergerac. I mean, he could do a fair impersonation of Barry Manilow, so why should he be so sensitive about it?

I did suggest to Mr Brownlow once that my time might be best occupied in producing a Sun Hill newspaper full-time, but he felt my experience and undoubted talents would be better used in more bread-and-butter police work.

Though he does tend to single me out when a little public relations job needs doing, I notice, like the time he sent me to a local school to talk about police work. He wasn't to know that I'd have so much trouble with a gang of teenage hooligans who wanted to spoil things for the younger element. But at least I got my message across to some of the kids – that the policeman is your friend. It's just that not everyone reciprocates.

You do get some surprises as a copper on the beat. Like the time I discovered a fifteen-year-old boy was having an affair with a thirty-five-year-old woman. It's not our job to adjudicate on private morals, but when the law is broken like that we do have to act. I'll confess I was a bit disturbed by that episode, and so were most of my colleagues.

I suppose you could say I was a bit of a loner, in a way. I've never quite found the right girl, though I haven't given up hoping. There was a time when I thought June Ackland and I . . . but never mind. I live in the section house, though I have ambitions one day to buy a flat. I went into it seriously once, but the economics were against me. And, anyway, there's something to be said for living close to your mates.

I have had my moments with women, you know. A stripper in a pub once cut my tie off for a joke. I had to speak to her sternly, and we ended up in an intimate situation. And a traffic warden once took such a fancy to me that she invaded Sun Hill more than once. She was a trifle on the hefty side, I must admit, and some of the lads suggested I'd had a lucky escape. I said she was just a flatterer, and they thought flattener might be a better word. I have a serious hobby: an interest in building model railways. I regularly read *Railway Modeller* in slack times at Sun Hill, and when I do get my flat I know exactly how I shall construct my layout.

That will surprise a few people. There are depths to Reg Hollis they don't suspect.

There have been a few sad occasions in my time at Sun Hill. The shooting of Viv Martella affected us all for months. The tragedy of DS Ted Roach, a good man wrecked by drink and bitterness, gave some of us a lot to think about.

Policemen get treated like rubbish sometimes . . .

And, of course, my good friend Sergeant Penny having to retire 'on medical grounds' when he was charged with drink-driving. That was a lesson to us all. I don't run a car myself, preferring to do my bit for the environment by cycling.

Jeff Stewart

At thirty-eight, Jeff Stewart, who plays Reg Hollis, seems a lot younger than the comic copper. Acts it, too. And you're surprised to find the Stewart voice is nothing like Reg's nasal whine.

'We call it acting,' says Jeff in perfectly pleasant tones.

He was born in Aberdeen but spent his childhood in Hampshire. He went to art school, drifted through various jobs and then decided he wanted to act. Got himself into drama school, found it too boring, left and by a chance meeting in a pub landed a job as an assistant stage manager in the West End. A year later he had his Equity card and was a working actor – though, like all beginners, he was a non-working actor for long periods.

He got jobs in beer commercials, played small parts in television drama – notably a nasty piece of work who ran over poor Benny with a Cortina in 'Crossroads'. Gradually things improved, more work was offered, though when 'The Bill' began Jeff was having a thin time again.

The fascinating thing about Reg Hollis is that he made an offscreen appearance before 'The Bill' proper began. In the pilot play, 'Woodentop', PC Hollis was on the other side of the gasworks, out of radio contact, and the squeaky voice was never heard. When 'The Bill' proper was being cast Jeff was seen, with half the young actors in the country. At first he didn't seem right for any of the parts, but when it came to bringing the unseen Reg Hollis to life Jeff was suddenly seen as the perfect performer.

At first he was hired for just one episode, but Jeff had made Reg such an individual figure that Hollis began to appear more often.

'I love the man to bits,' says Jeff. 'I enjoy being the underdog; and, though he's a bit of a clown, he never completely messes up. He does the job. I get quite a bit of fan mail, largely from people who think poor Reg is put upon. The silly jokes are Reg's way of coping with stress. Other people – Ted Roach, for instance – coped with the same problem by taking to the bottle.

'From my point of view he's a wonderful character to play. A man who doesn't realize how funny he is must be a gift to an actor.'

Jeff Stewart is an interesting man – bit vague sometimes, with conversation that goes off at surprising tangents. He's intelligent, a bit arty perhaps. He likes staying in bed late when he's not working; clubbing late, too; drinking coffee in King's Road cafes where the talk flows as free and frothy as the cappuccino.

In one of these, the Dôme, he met his girlfriend, Katy Kass, five years ago.

'It was a great coffee bar then,' he says. 'The old crowd included Adam Ant, Naomi Campbell and Kylie Minogue. I was sitting there one day, killing time until I left to work on a "Bill" episode, "They Also Serve", directed by David Hayman. A superb episode, it turned out, with all of us sitting in the back of a police van for most of the time, waiting to deal with a demo.' (He's off on one of his tangents, but stick around.)

'Then it ended up all action, with a riot scene and a fire. Reg had brought his portable telly along because there was a Test match on. Anyway, there I was in the Dôme having a late breakfast at 2.30 p.m. I knew I had to leave for work by 3.15. In walks this girl with jodhpurs and a marvellous orange jumper and a plastic bag full of books and pens. I couldn't stop watching her. She was writing something, and I turned to my friend and said how pretty she was. I kept trying to talk to her, though she said she was writing poetry.

'When it was time for me to leave I finally managed to arrange to meet her in the same place a few days later. She turned up, and we went to see the Doors movie and had a meal. She dropped me off at my home, and I still didn't really know anything about her.

'We went out a few times, and I realized she hadn't asked me about my job, what I do. She said she wasn't working at the time, just living with her mother.

'I asked about her mother, and she said she was an actress and I might know her. I said there were thousands of actresses and it was unlikely. So I asked her mother's name, and she said: "Joan Collins." She had to pick me up from the floor.

'Much later Joan asked me if I'd known Katy was her daughter when we first met. I said if I'd known that I'd have run a hundred miles in the opposite direction! I'm glad I didn't know. If I had, Katy might just have felt I wanted to be in with her because of who her mother was.

'Katy and I don't live together. We might as well, because we see each other every day and spend every night together, but we enjoy our independence.'

Jeff's a bit of a foodie – loves Italian, Thai, good English cooking – and he's becoming a bit of a cook himself in the new kitchen in his London flat. He'll always be skinny, though. Worrying sees to that.

His other love is a battered Suzuki jeep, which he's had for more than eight years. 'It's like a pet, really,' he says. 'When I get a new car I'll still keep the jeep.'

He cares about his clothes – his over-all style. But don't ever ask him the time. 'I never wear a watch. I used to find myself looking at it every five minutes. It's just a nervous thing. So I've stopped.

'Reg would never be without one, of course.'

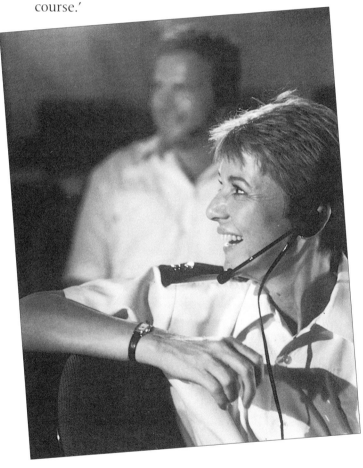

WPC JUNE ACKLAND

There are two mysteries about WPC June Ackland. One is why this efficient and dedicated officer isn't a sergeant at least. The other is why this attractive blonde woman doesn't have a steady boyfriend. There's a two-word answer to both questions: Sun Hill. The nick has become June's life. She'd deny that, of course, but it's true.

She may have lost some of her early idealism, she may have been made a little cynical by the gritty realities of a policewoman's life and by working in a force which is not famously unchauvinist. But she still gives 110 per cent to the Job, worrying away at details some coppers might forget, determined that if criminals get fair treatment so must victims. Blonde June is a fair cop in more than one sense of the word. If she 'went in for sergeant', she'd have to devote time to study, and suffer a lot of hassle and perhaps even resentment. There's no doubt that she's more than got the smarts for it – but not the heart. And she would have to be transferred from Sun Hill. And Sun Hill, as we said, has become her life.

It's the same with boyfriends: they can never be as important as her work. June fancies the occasional bloke, and a whole regiment of them – including most male Sun Hill coppers – fancy her. But any kind of steady relationship just wouldn't suit her lifestyle. A decade ago she had a solicitor boyfriend who treated her appallingly, and sensible June thought she was well out of it when that relationship broke up. Then she had an affair with married DCI Gordon Wray, and that was a disaster. He was transferred, his promotion prospects blighted, and June was left with an unfairly blackened reputation – and a determination that she'd never again get involved with anyone in the Job.

At forty, she doesn't meet many unmarried males in the right age group outside the force. There's a kind of sadness, a resignation about June Ackland. It comes partly from the feeling that, however hard she works, she's never going to solve the problems of mankind, or even of her tiny Sun Hill patch of it. And perhaps from her feeling that women in the Met will never truly get the same opportunities as the men.

June has never quite got over her father's death. He was a teacher, and they got on really well. She looked after him as an invalid, and when he died in hospital there was some sense of release for her. But she rarely felt guilty about that. The real problem for June is that her standards are too high for her own good. But, like her good friend Bob Cryer, she is almost the perfect copper. This is her view of Sun Hill in the last decade.

June Ackland's Ten Tough Years

I puppy-walked Jim Carver on his first day at Sun Hill. He was a new boy, just finished training, and I had to show him how a real bobby behaves on a real beat. He seemed nice enough but clueless – like they all are.

It wasn't an easy beginning; we ended up finding a body – an old lady had died in her bath. We should have had some help from Reg Hollis, but Reg's radio mysteriously wasn't working. God knows what he was up to.

Jim's done all right for himself since that day. Doing well in the CID with some prospect of becoming a detective sergeant.

I suppose I can't truly say I taught him all he knows – he learned most of that from Burnside and Roach – but I think I gave him a good grounding.

A lot has happened in Sun Hill since that day. Murders, terrorist attacks, rapes, and more bread-and-butter crime – shoplifting, vandalism, small-scale burglaries, drunken violence – than I can remember.

Except that nothing is small-scale to the victim. I always try to remember that.

What keeps you going in this job is support from your mates. All right, you get your petty jealousies, your personality clashes, your odd bloody-minded colleague in the police, as in any job. But at least in mine you know that when some nutter's coming at you with an iron bar you'll get real help from a brother or sister officer.

I got support of a very different kind when my father died. I got drunk on duty – or, rather, I came on duty drunk and I could have been in deep trouble. Bob Cryer and Tom Penny covered for me and eventually got me into a sauna to sober up before anyone higher than the rank of sergeant spotted me.

In a way that feeling of friendship and support keeps me going. Though I did feel let down when I got punched and kicked while trying to arrest a drug pusher on the Jasmin Allen Estate. The estate's 'community representative' Everton Warwick perpetrated the assault, and when the force refused to prosecute him for local political reasons I took out a private prosecution myself. I lost, felt terrible and ended up broke.

Of course I get days when I despair. Don't we all? I look around my house – Dad's house. But, then, I get other days when I feel – I don't want to sound all moral – that I'm actually doing a job that's worth while, that helps society. Though I wouldn't want you putting that about in the canteen.

People say I should have taken the CID route, and in the early days I did help that bunch of cowboys with their enquiries quite a lot, when they needed an undercover woman. Then Viv Martella started to do those jobs, and eventually they got genuine girl detectives on the staff and sometimes in charge of the staff. I didn't mind dropping out of the plain-clothes work, though I am still attached to the Bumblebee team. What I enjoy is a wide variety of

Anxious Ackland waits and watches with Loxton

policing work. I don't mind collecting the odd shoplifter held at a supermarket. I don't mind the occasional domestic, though I had to put my sensibly shod foot down when all domestic problems, anything to do with children, were down to me. I'm not that fond of kids, to tell you the truth.

I suppose I usually do what I'm told, though I've been at Sun Hill long enough to have my protest listened to if I don't agree with the orders. One I disobeyed without a second thought was on the day Viv Martella got shot. Steve Loxton had to hold me back when I wanted to run to her body. And when I went after the bastard who shot Viv I was ordered to discontinue pursuit by Philip Cato. I did not discontinue, and when Cato had a go at me for disobeying orders I told him straight: 'If you'd known Viv, you'd know why I went on.'

You're not supposed to speak to a chief inspector that way, but I didn't care. Not that day. I've got a bit of a reputation for being brave at Sun Hill, though I could do without it. I have been knocked about, punched, kicked. I've ended up far too often with cuts and bruises all sustained while just trying to do my duty. The truth is I'm often scared, and I don't look for trouble but I have to be prepared for it. Every police officer does.

I'm pretty good at dealing with male coppers who get patronizing or downright nasty about being paired with a girl in uniform. Though I did have a really tough time with a particularly awful military policeman. I was helping him look for a soldier who'd gone AWOL, and he tried to treat me like a sergeant-major treats a new recruit. I wasn't having that and gave him as good as I got, though it was a bit of a strain. I came out on top, though, when we finally located the squaddie. He had a gun, and

Conscientious colleagues, not exactly friends: Ackland and Johnson

Rambo was all for bullying and blustering and beating. But I tried the softly-softly approach and talked the kid into surrendering his weapon. I felt fairly good about that.

I haven't got anything against working for a woman, either. I think we all had our views about Inspector Frazer. I'd better not go into mine. Sally Johnson is another kettle of fish. She let us down over that gang of muggers preying on casual labourers, and I was furious. I told her exactly what I thought of her high-handedness. Mind you, she laid into me when I failed to persuade that ex-copper to give evidence in court for her. I dare say she'll hold that against me for some time.

But, when I get fed up with this job, I remember my little triumphs. Like when I pestered Mr Brownlow into getting compensation for a bloke who'd been burgled and beaten.

I suppose that's what I remember most of my time at Sun Hill. Small victories, the few times I've managed to help someone a bit. Most of all I enjoy being part of a team. Not always a winning team but at least one which tries its best.

Trudie Goodwin

Trudie Goodwin is like June Ackland's younger, slimmer and more bohemian sister. She's also a lot jokier than June is allowed to be.

That blue serge uniform gives Ackland bulk, and that awful jammed-on hat gives her height. Trudie hates the hat. 'You have to wedge it right down on your forehead to keep it on at all,' she says. 'It must have been designed by a man.'

The hat probably accounts for June Ackland's super-stern look in the front of a police car as that familiar tune plays over the opening credits.

Trudie admires June enormously. 'She's the kind of police officer I'd like to see on the streets, and I try to play her that way,' says Trudie.

Trudie's a couple of years older than June. She has a full life, unlike her character. She's married with two daughters, Jessica, aged twelve, and Eleanor, aged six. They live in South London.

She almost missed out on playing June – the best part so far of her career. 'I was still breast-feeding Jessica and I had to trek right across London for the audition for "Woodentop", the play that preceded the series, and I didn't think I was going to get the part anyway. I thought I wouldn't bother going, just sit in the garden by the paddling-pool instead.

'In the end I left Jessica with my mother and went to Teddington. But I was sure it was a waste of time. I was a bit overweight, and I didn't look quite like my picture in the casting directory, so I was amazed when I got the part. I'm even more amazed that I'm here ten years later.'

Trudie was born in Eltham, south-east London, and wanted to perform in some way from the age of seven. An older couple who lived next door encouraged her to read poetry and plays. She went in for school plays and finally decided to become a drama teacher. She went to Exeter University and then settled down to teach drama in schools.

But all the time she knew she wanted to do it rather than teach it, so she started to work for a group that took plays into schools, then moved into rep. At Leicester rep she met an actor called Kit Jackson, who was going to become her husband. Kit still acts but is working most of the time now as a comedy scriptwriter.

They had some tough times, with Kit working on a building site and Trudie doing a spot of barmaiding and waitressing when the parts weren't coming. At other times she has worked as a supply teacher – so she's glad she gained those qualifications, and when she talks to girls at schools and youth conferences, which she's often asked to do, she stresses this.

Trudie did the odd commercial, played tiny parts on television and then got her first real break in the series 'Fox', which was about a criminal family. She played the girlfriend of one of the villains; and Mark Wingett, who was later to become Jim Carver, was also in the cast.

The two of them came together again in 'Woodentop' and have been partners in crime-fighting ever since as Ackland and Carver. Trudie understands why June can't seem to form a long-term relationship with a man, thinks this gives her character extra strength ('Though I wouldn't say no if they came up with an episode where June meets a toyboy,' she giggles).

Trudie sometimes wishes she could have the film-star treatment. 'They want gritty realism – I want the make-up, the jewels, the glamorous clothes, the soft-focus lens!' she moans. But she understands this would be quite out of character for Ackland.

She had every intention of leaving when she was pregnant with her second daughter, Eleanor. 'By the time we finished that series, I was six months pregnant, and for the last episodes June was in plain clothes – so luckily it didn't show. But I couldn't see how I could manage to carry on. But I was persuaded that it would be possible, that I could feed throughout the first year and that, if necessary, I could bring her and the nanny in to work with me. I was so lucky. But that next year's episodes went past in a blur. I was so tired, so stressed. It's not surprising, really: there were five of us, with the nanny, plus a dog, two cats, a rabbit and a guinea pig living in a tiny three-bed cottage!

'Since then I've thought hard about my life. My family comes first, my work a close second. Kit has decided to write and – I know this sounds like the usual moan – there are not that many great parts for women, especially women of my age, forty-three.

'Anyway, who'd want to stop playing a character this well written in a series of this quality? I can't see playing June all my life, until she collects her pension, but I've certainly no plans to give her up. Especially as the series gives me time to be with my family.'

Trudie is still studying June Ackland, still working out what makes her tick. 'I know she joined the force for the right reasons. Not for money, not for excitement, not for ambition. She thought she could help society, and she's right. That's what she does. Playing her has given me a new respect for police officers. It's also taken away that slight fear I used to feel when I saw one. I understand how the police often feel threatened. If you're in a crowd wearing the uniform, you can somehow be the focus, the target, of the crowd's anger. That's terrifying.

'Though I know I couldn't be a copper in real life, even if the public does sometimes confuse me with June. I've been taken for her on holiday in France

and Italy, and a woman once came up to me and asked me to put in a good word for her son, who'd been arrested for something or other.

'The most embarrassment June ever put me through was when I'd just had my second daughter. The doctor who was doing the stitches looked up and said: "Aren't you that woman in 'The Bill'?" '

DC JIM CARVER

Detective Constable Jim Carver has a nickname for himself: James 'Moral Dilemma' Carver. It is a wry acknowledgement of the way his ethical scruples can get in the way of his police work. Burnside was always making fun of Jim's rectitude.

The two men became angry at each other because Burnside often thought Jim was behaving like a prat and Carver often thought Frank was an unprincipled chancer. It all came to a head when Carver refused to lie in court when Burnside ordered him to. Jim Carver is a serious young man.

He wasn't sure whether to become a policeman or a social worker and, although some of his ideals have been bashed out of him by a decade of tough police work, at first on the beat, then in the CID, he is still a man of integrity. He is a clever intuitive thief-taker, often jumping to the right conclusion on not much evidence, but making his fair share of mistakes.

He has other faults. A quick temper sometimes leads him into inappropriate physical action. On his first idealistic day on the Sun Hill beat, the greenest of new bobbies, he spoiled everything by giving an insolent young yobbo a clip round the ear. He went for Burnside when he thought Frank was being callous about Viv Martella's death, and the two men had to be pulled apart. But most people understood when Jim threatened to kill Phil Young for a sexual attack on WPC Norika Datta. Jim had carried a torch for her for years. But she doesn't want to know.

Jim was glad when he moved from uniformed work into the CID, because life was more interesting for him. If he had stayed in uniform, though, he would probably have been a sergeant by now. Bob Cryer spotted his potential early on. At thirty-two, Jim has discovered that he's tougher than he thought he was, that tea tastes better with three lumps of sugar, and that life is just as real and earnest as he always thought it was. Which probably explains why he doesn't smile much.

Jim Carver's Ten Tough Years

People sometimes accuse me of taking my work too seriously, but I don't see how a police officer can take it any other way. We are responsible for keeping the public safe and for dealing with criminals in a scrupulously fair way.

I'll always admit to being a bit bull-headed sometimes, for going straight in when waiting a bit and thinking about it might be better tactics. But I want to get on with things. I don't want to waste time.

There have been occasions when I have been a bit insensitive, maybe. When DCI Kim Reid was leaving, DI Burnside detailed me to buy her a leaving present. All right, a silver tankard maybe wasn't quite right – she didn't drink too many pints of beer – but they didn't have to go on at me. And a tankard's traditional, isn't it?

But not too many have criticized my dedication to the work, either as a beat officer or as a detective. I do resent the way some people in the CID – I won't mention names – have cut corners, ignored the rules if they could get away with it. I suppose I resented the way Mr Brownlow was so welcoming of DC Woods when he joined us. Not all of us play rugby – or 'the gentleman's game', as he'd call it.

But there have been times when what I see as

Getting it done – Carver and dependable Tosh Lines

dedication is seen as something else by others. I had four complaints of harassment lodged against me in one week, and I got a semi-official warning not to collect any more. Tosh Lines suggested I was going for a Sun Hill record; but, then, he will have his little joke. Too many little jokes sometimes. Tosh will be Tosh.

But I do have a sense of humour, contrary to common report. When I look back over the ten years in which I've helped solve major crimes – murders, rapes, big bank raids, illegal arms-dealing – it's the silly little things that stick in my mind.

Like the time I had to take an escaped pig back to its farm. Like the time a pickpocket stole a pen my aunty gave me for my birthday. (And that was inside the nick.) Like the man I had to arrest for holding up petrol stations – in the nude. (Him, not me.) Like the time Burnside made me go through about fifty-eight rubbish-bins to find some briefing papers I'd mislaid.

People stick in my mind, too. A bloke named Thompson I brought in for possession of marijuana. He thought it was all a giggle – who cares about a little thing like that? And then he was quite willing to shop his suppliers because it would help him keep his job with a merchant bank. I despised him for that. I suppose I expected law-breakers to have principles, too.

I remember a man whose terminally sick wife had died of an overdose. For a while it looked as if he had given her the drugs. I tried to make Burnside see that euthanasia might sometimes be justified, but to Frank murder was murder and that was that.

I remember getting a black eye trying to arrest a

drunk in a pub called the Lord Duncan. And a number of rather worse injuries I collected from serious villains intent on doing me down or in.

On the whole I think I've done a good job in my years at Sun Hill. I've tried to be a good member of the team. I've kept quiet about some things. You have to. But there have been times when I couldn't. Like when DC Boulton from Barton Street arrested some kid he believed got off a charge of mugging some pensioner. But he wasn't arresting him; he was knocking six bells out of him, claiming that he was committing criminal damage and resisting arrest. I turned a blind eye to the assault – but I couldn't stand by and see the kid go down for something I knew he hadn't done. No doubt Boulton hasn't forgotten.

I can't say my life outside Sun Hill has been that brilliant. Let's just say I've been unlucky in love, shall we? There was Sonia, of course. We tried living together, but it didn't work out. She expected me to be home for my supper at set times. I ask you! All right, I admit it, she threw me out and there are a few things I never managed to collect. Like my watch. Burnside put me back in the section house. I knew he'd smirk – the swine.

Surprisingly, I didn't get much flak over Norika Datta. Really I did what anyone would do. Young was capable of anything. I don't care if he was bonkers – he had to be stopped. When we found out he'd committed suicide, I can't pretend I was sorry. Of course, I didn't expect anything in return from Norika. Yes, I would have liked our relationship to have changed. Of course, I would. She's brilliant. But she has a relationship, and I've had to accept that we'll only ever be colleagues. I'll probably meet someone some day. I hope so. Till then the lot at Sun Hill are my family. And they're a good team. Mostly.

Mark Wingett

Mark was born on New Year's Day 1961, an easy birthday to remember unless you have a hangover from New Year's Eve. His father was a naval officer, and the family moved around – Malta and Singapore to name but two exotic places – but spent most of their time in and around Portsmouth. (His sister Fiona is a magazine journalist in Australia, his younger brother Matthew, until recently a student at Durham University, has written television scripts, including some for 'The Bill'. He used a fake name when he submitted the first, 'Thicker than Water', to make sure he didn't get favourable treatment as Mark's brother.)

Mark always wanted to be an actor but was put off by a school careers officer who decided zookeeper was his best bet. But he joined the National Youth Theatre at sixteen and he was playing a lead role in his second year. Because of that he was cast as a Mod in the Mods-and-Rockers movie *Quadrophenia*, though he was only seventeen when the X-rated film came out and wasn't old enough to see it. So Mark missed out on the traditional drama school route and began to do a fair amount of television work – including the 'Fox' series with Trudie Goodwin. He was seen in a stage-play as a nutty soldier and was remembered when the pilot play 'Woodentop' was casting.

Mark likes Carver, admires his seriousness – 'Can't quite manage that degree of it myself' – and is never unhappy when the scriptwriters make the DC screw up. Unlike some actors who want to be perfect heroes all the time, Mark understands that faults and flaws and doubts deepen a character.

On the whole he's glad that his character moved into plain clothes – 'The uniform's uncomfortable and it seems to take you over when you put it on' – but enjoyed playing the young Carver, too.

Woodentops Dave Litten (Gary Olsen) and Jim Carver

When they were making 'Woodentop' it was a new thing to have an actor walk the streets dressed as a policeman. Mark as Carver had to walk by a spot where a man was packing meat in a lorry, and the scene was reshot several times. Eventually the packer got fed up and said something unprintable to the 'copper'.

During a break in filming 'Woodentop' Mark took

Mark Wingett takes his own tumbles: no stuntman necessary

off his helmet and smoked a quiet cigarette. 'An unmarked CID car drew up, and a bloke leaned out,' Mark recalls. 'He gave me a rollicking for smoking on duty, and I said: "Sorry, mate, I'm just an actor." He saw the Thames TV van, accepted this, but said: "I'm going to complain about this." He did, too. So Carver really did start off with a black mark.'

There have been times when Mark felt like hanging up his handcuffs and giving Jim Carver the elbow. 'But', he says, 'where else could I get the acting experience I'm getting here? I'm working with nine different directors, I get twenty to thirty good scripts a year, I'm playing with a team of real professionals and some brilliant guest artists. I wouldn't find opportunities like that if I left.'

But he's had to take some knocks playing Jim the jump-in-feet-first copper. 'I was working on two episodes in one week. In the first story I was Action Man, jumping over fences and walls, leaping in and out of moving cars, and I didn't get a scratch. In the second I was doing a simple arrest scene. I had to hold someone, do a little turn and get into a small tussle. We fell over, and I broke two vertebrae.

'It meant I lost an episode. Kevin Lloyd – or, rather, Tosh Lines – had to take over my part in the story.'

The fall means that Mark has to be a bit careful with his back these days, but it hasn't stopped his scuba diving. He's an expert at this sport, a qualified instructor and technical adviser for 'The Bill' when an episode calls for divers. Three so far: in the Thames, a canal and a park pond.

Mark does most of his diving around Littlehampton, an area rich in wrecks, which fascinate him, but he has also been to Ireland and the Orkneys to dive.

Diving in Weymouth bay he was allowed to keep one silver piece from a coin hoard – most of them went to museums – from a wrecked ship called The Earl of Abergavenny. 'Fascinating, that one,' says Mark. 'The captain of the ship was the brother of William Wordsworth the poet, and William's fortune went down with it. So did three hundred people.'

Sharon doesn't join him in diving. 'She'll come along if there's a nice warm beach nearby. You have to have the right temperament to go out into a Force Five gale and be swung about in a small boat so you can dive for an hour round some grubby wreck.'

Apart from his family and his diving, Jim Carver is Mark Wingett's main interest in life. 'I get to know him better and better all the time. And I feel "The Bill" itself has improved enormously since the early days. They've got the technique exactly right now.'

Sun Up on Sun Hill

The most successful continuing drama series about the police began almost by accident. No one at Thames Television, then one of the five major independent television companies, was looking for a cops-and-robbers show in 1983. Quite the contrary. Michael Chapman, then a Thames drama producer, was casting a net to find ideas for 'Storyboard', a series of plays, any of which, if liked well enough by viewers, might become a six- or ten-part drama series.

He was open to suggestions but knew that he wanted one of the plays to be set in London. He didn't want another 'Minder', the Thames comedy drama that was slowly becoming a hit. But he'd been impressed by two drama series on 'the other side', BBC1, which explored similar territory. One was 'Give Us a Break', about the wheeler-dealer world of snooker, which had starred Robert Lindsay and Paul McGann. The other, 'Big Deal', had followed the fortunes and misfortunes of a small-time gambler, played by Ray Brooks, and his disapproving girlfriend, played by Sharon Duce. In both the writer showed that he knew London 'with the lid off', knew the lingo, knew 'what went down'; and he loved it, litter, layabouts and all.

So he should. For Geoff McQueen had grown up in the East End and had worked around London as a semi-professional footballer and a carpenter for many years. Michael Chapman tracked him down and asked him if he had any other good ideas.

McQueen, who had begun writing in his thirties when hard-up, certainly had. His favourite, 'Old Bill', was a project about life in a police station which he'd submitted a few years earlier to the BBC. They'd been running 'Juliet Bravo', their drama about a Northern force headed by a woman officer, at the time and had thought his idea too similar.

In McQueen's revised plan, 'Old Bill' had developed into three plays, each about an officer of a different rank. Michael Chapman liked the basic outline, saw that it was sufficiently different from 'The Sweeney' and other fast-action crime-busting series running at the time, and asked him to condense his idea into a single script.

The title became 'Woodentop' (the nickname that plain-clothes police give their uniformed colleagues), and the story was of the first day on the beat of a probationary constable called Jimmy Carver. Out and about with WPC June Ackland he discovered the decomposing body of an old woman in a bath. Later his first day in the job almost became his last when he clipped a cheeky teenager around the ear. He might have been disciplined but for the fact that the

First day on The Job for Carver (left) while Taffy Edwards (Colin Blumenau) and June Ackland take notes

boy's father was in favour of Carver's short sharp shock, and the matter went no further.

The play was directed by Peter Cregeen, who knew a bit about cop shows: he'd worked on 'Z Cars', 'Softly Softly', 'Juliet Bravo' and 'The Gentle Touch', the London Weekend Television series starring Jill Gascoine as a woman police detective inspector. Cregeen, who was to rise to the position of Head of Drama Series at the BBC, admitted later that he worried about ways of making 'Woodentop' different. Then he watched Roger Graef's award-winning BBC series, 'The Police'. This was a fly-on-the-station-wall documentary which went a long way to opening our eyes to how the real boys in blue – those in the Thames Valley force, at least – worked, thought and swore. Cregeen decided he could nick a few tips from that series. So he copied the free-wheeling style, used one hand-held camera and kept the lighting to a minimum.

Trudie Goodwin and Mark Wingett were supposed to fit in a moment in which their typical coppers' sensibly shod feet, plodding along Bow Road, could be filmed for the opening and closing credit sequences. They were too busy, so two extras on location that day were grabbed. The feet seen then and ever since at the end of every episode belong to Karen England and Paul Page Hanson.

The result of everyone's efforts was a play screened on 16 August 1983. It was so well received that within a month a twelve-part series was being planned. Mark Wingett, who had played Jimmy Carver, and Trudie Goodwin, who was Ackland, would return. So would Gary Olsen as PC Litten. Peter Dean, who'd played Sergeant Wilding, and Gary Hailes, who'd played the boy whose ear had been clipped, were to go on to another marathon-runner: the BBC's new soap 'EastEnders', which went into production the following year and on screen in 1985. Dean was to play Pete Beale, and Hailes was to come in as gay barrow-boy Barry Clarke.

Thames's new series would not have the cumbersome name 'Woodentop' but instead would take McQueen's first title, 'The Bill'.

Early Days

Geoff McQueen died suddenly in July 1994 aged 46. He was happy to give these comments only weeks earlier

Geoff McQueen's idea was that everything should be seen from the point of view of the police.

'We talked about it at length and we agreed that it would always be the police officer's story, that nothing should be shown without one of our police men or women being there. So you'd never see two villains talking, planning a job. You'd never see a man beating his wife in their house or see an accident or a fight happen on the streets unless one of the police characters was passing by or knocking at the door or trying to make an arrest.

'We also agreed to keep out of the police officers' homes. If they had problems at home, I wanted to see how it was affecting their work at the station rather than how the work at the station was affecting them at home. Immediately you go into the police officers' private life, it's the kiss of death to police series, as I see it.'

Geoff, who lived and wrote and fished in a quiet corner of the countryside in Mulrose, Scotland, said that he had a hunch 'The Bill' would last – but he hadn't dared to hope it would reach its tenth birthday.

He agreed to let his 'baby' be chopped in half to allow 'The Bill' to switch to half-hour episodes in 1988 – on certain conditions.

'I wanted new writers to have a chance to cut their teeth on it. I wanted new directors to be hired and as many new actors as possible. I think we've managed to use more newcomers than any other series.'

He also insisted that 'The Bill' kept its large policeman's feet on the ground. 'It was important to keep a balance between life on the streets and the politics of policing. I'm actually far more interested in the beer-and-darts set than the white-wine-and-soda set.'

Geoff, who wrote several of the earlier short episodes but then became too busy with other projects, including Yorkshire Television's 'Stay Lucky' series, added that he was tremendously proud to have fathered 'The Bill'.

'I'm very pleased with the way my characters came to life. Tosh is terrific, and I always felt Burnside was very powerful. But the big achievement is the teamwork in keeping the standard up. Michael Chapman has done a marvellous job in holding it all together. It's looking as fresh now as when it first came out.'

Geoff was busy developing a comedy drama to feature actress Pauline Quirke for the BBC and two other dramas for ITV, including a new police action drama called 'Rules of Engagement'.

THE IMPOSSIBLE JOB

Police dramas have been around since the beginning of television time. We seem to need them. Perhaps they bring us reassurance that, despite all that we see and all that we think we know, someone somewhere in the threatening carparks, the suburban sprawls and the unwelcoming hillsides is still striving to keep law and order for us.

There have been milestones: Dixon of Dock Green, a salt-of-the-earth old-time copper on the beat; Lockhart of the Yard, in 'No Hiding Place', a gentlemanly but tough detective in a hat solving any crime in thirty minutes; 'Z Cars', with its folksy car-cops in Liverpool; 'The Sweeney', featuring Regan and Carter, a couple of Flying Squad heavies sometimes behaving like their thug adversaries; and 'Juliet Bravo', a succession of spikey lady-boss cops policing the Dales with a posse of stage Yorkshiremen. The Americans have come up with their own classics: gritty 'Hill Street Blues' and grittier 'NYPD Blue', set in cities with more and more violent crime than anywhere here, thank heavens.

When 'The Bill' switched on its blue lamp for the first time at Sun Hill, East London, a decade ago, something new was added to small-screen police fiction. For we got the strangest feeling that this wasn't fiction at all. The actors didn't seem like actors; they seemed like real bobbies patrolling real streets, chasing real villains, helping real victims. For the first time policemen were shown as ordinary people. Trained, yes; but not supercops, not

The 'boys and girls in blue' – Sun Hill's uniformed officers take policing seriously

aggressive toughies who'd sooner batter down a door than ring the bell.

Instead of heroes, a bunch of everyday men and women in the Metropolitan Police were busy doing an impossible job as best they could, and we were tagging along behind them, craning to see over their shoulders. They were men who worried like the rest of us about keeping up the instalments on the Escort and getting off duty in time to watch the football on television. They were women who had moody menfriends to cope with and a bit of shopping to collect at the end of the shift.

The impossible job was keeping law and order in an underprivileged patch of London with about half the resources they needed and within the constraints of a book of rules so scrupulous that half the time an eleven-year-old could run

Routine inquiries with a suspect

rings around them and they seemed powerless to act.

What these ordinary men and women did was simply get on with the job, or 'the Job' as they call it. They got on with it with humour, with an understated integrity, with hard work and with real expertise.

If you told them down at Sun Hill that they were a dedicated bunch of professionals, they'd come over all embarrassed and tell you to leave it out. But that's what they are.

Rarely do they have to tackle big-time crime; there aren't too many major bullion raids in Sun Hill. Most of the time it's some kid nicking videos or flogging hookey jeans down the market. There's a lot of car crime, a fair share of domestic punch-ups, the occasional arrival of a bigger criminal fish in this small urban pond. Of course, from time to time there's a rape, or a murder, or a gang of villains with shooters who

PC Loxton has a truncheon ready, PC Garfield has a pen. But who knows what the witness really saw?

need stopping. The men and women of Sun Hill just deal with problems as they occur, the way the real Met does, in a day-to-day way.

Just as we switch on not knowing if we'll see a car chase or a cot-death, it's as though these people also have no notion of what's coming next. Unlike Inspector Morse, for whom a complicated serious set of crimes and a cerebral puzzle are always waiting, the Sun Hill people have no idea when they start their shift if they'll be called out to sort out a disturbance in a pub, look for a twelve-year-old kid on a shoplifting spree, or face an armed robber with no more than a truncheon, common sense and a line of talk. As for intellectual satisfaction – a day without indigestion would be a fine thing!

If we feel 'The Bill' is almost 'as-it-happens' drama, that it's just another day for the team, clocking on for work hoping it's a day when no one is sick on their shoes, the trick has worked.

Most of the time the Sun Hill officers do what they set out to do. There are cock-ups, of course. Sometimes the Met's own rigid code of practice gets in the way of booking the bad 'uns. Much of the time these ordinary people are frustrated, puzzled by laws that seem to favour the villains not the victims.

The characters in 'The Bill' have never been shown as perfect policemen or women. But just how much reality there can be in a half-hour popular show screened at eight in the evening is a complex question. Some critics will argue that no black youth has ever been beaten up in the cells and no black

police officer has quit and sued the force for racial discrimination (as several real ones have done, winning substantial damages).

In fact, in its ten-year life, racism has often raised its head in the neatly resolved stories. But confronting big issues head-on has never been the show's style. On the other hand, the black officers at 'The Bill' have never been more noble or more knowing than their white colleagues. The creation of DI Sally Johnson to succeed hard-nut Frank Burnside was not a flashy gimmick. Nor was it falling in with the American fashion (most recently displayed in 'Homicide' and 'NYPD Blue') of making every television police precinct's captain black and saintly. 'The Bill' is jumping the factual gun in that no black policewoman in Britain has yet made the rank of inspector. (Of 3,897 women police in the Met only 152 are from ethnic minorities; and the highest rank achieved, by four of those officers, is sergeant.) But the Met will surely soon catch up – there has been no squeal of 'cheats!' from Scotland Yard.

But, then, except for a few predictable tut-tuts, the sort you'd expect from any group portrayed in fiction, the real police have held fire. They have not tried to shoot 'The Bill' down, perhaps because it was always more than just telly coppery. As its everyday story of policefolk continued to attract a large and loyal audience, the Met realized that the show was helping its officers and those from all the other constabularies. That is not and never has been the producers' intention, which is to provide an entertainment, an alternative to the soaps and the glossier drama series on the airwaves. But they're not knocking it.

We are all of us a little ambivalent about the police. If we get burgled, we dial 999 before we sweep up the broken glass. But if we're told by someone in a blue uniform we can't park in a particular spot we whisper 'Officious bastard' under our breath.

What the series has done is to show us that the long arm of the law can be very comforting and that when it comes to footing the bill for the 'Bill', whatever the police service costs our council tax, it's not money wasted.

PLODDING ALONG VERY NICELY

'The Bill' came to the screen in a year when few people were neutral about the role the police were taking in society. The service lost popularity, seeming to be no more than a tool of the Tory government when riot police charged against demonstrations by striking miners. But incidents such as the shooting of WPC Yvonne Fletcher outside the Libyan embassy in April and the terrorist bombing of the Grand Hotel, Brighton, during the Tory party conference which occurred only four days before the first episode of the first series in October perhaps moved public opinion in the other direction.

It seemed very much the small change of police work that was counted in that first episode, called 'Funny Old Business – Cops and Robbers'. Sergeant Peters and Sergeant Cryer conducted the morning parade and reminded the team about the spate of pickpocketing, car theft and burglary. But that first run of episodes covered subjects including bomb-hoax phone calls, indecent assault, drug dealing, pornography and murder. It also brought out the slight distrust Cryer's uniformed people had of Sun Hill's CID, led then by bad-tempered DI Roy Galloway (John Salthouse). By the time that series

Easily ruffled – that was DI Roy Galloway

ended in the New Year of 1985, a new series had been ordered by Thames and Peter Cregeen had taken over from Michael Chapman, who went off to develop 'Mr Palfrey of Westminster'.

The series hadn't pleased everyone. Alan Coren, then reviewing it for the *Mail on Sunday*, objected to 'warts-only copperdom, presenting the police as a bunch of hamfisted dimwits'. A writer in *Today* said the show portrayed the police as 'Neo-Nazi jobsworths'. The real Bill wasn't keen then, either. Commissioner Sir Kenneth Newman 'deplored' the programme for 'projecting attitudes and actions which are thoroughly unprofessional and not even true to life', and the editor of the *Police Review* wrote that the show went 'out of its way to paint a force virtually at war with society'. This was possibly how a majority of the public saw the police then, but the force didn't like television to rub it in. Most people agreed that the series which began in November 1985 was altogether more entertaining, and plans were soon made for a third series to launch the all-important autumn schedules in 1986.

The first two series had been made, not at Teddington Studios where 'Woodentop' originated, but in a set of buildings in Artichoke Hill, Wapping, East London. It was this address that had established Sun Hill as 'somewhere in the East End'. Unfortunately, next door to that 'somewhere' was the new and controversial base for News International's printworks where several national newspapers were to be produced without recognizing the traditional power of some of the print unions. During the winter of 1985-6 the strike by printworkers at what was known as Fortress Wapping brought police again into confrontation with the public. Not only were actors in police uniform not welcome in and around the district in this highly charged atmosphere, but also driving to and from the base was increasingly difficult. Eventually work on the third series was abandoned. As the television cops moved out of Artichoke Hill the real ones moved in, using it as a base for the duration of the strike.

By the following autumn a former record company distribution depot in Barlby Road, North Kensington, had been found as the new Sun Hill, and designer Robin Parker began to create a 'cop shop' there. Shooting began in March 1987 for screening that September. The episodes were to end on a cliff-hanger: Sergeant Tom Penny was shot in the stomach by a mad old woman protecting her flat against her wicked landlord. The reason for this was not that Roger Leach, who played Penny, had a deathwish. It was that Thames had already made an

Sun Hill in Wapping – too hot a spot for filming in 1985

violence, and it defies belief. You should see what a face looks like after being slashed with a Stanley knife. It isn't a pretty sight.'

The shorter episodes were made with two teams, the Red and Blue units, working in tandem. When screening began with Geoff McQueen's episode 'Light Duties' showing Tom Penny trying to get back into the swing of things, concealing his physical and emotional weakness, it was clear that John Salthouse and other prophets of doom had been wrong. Inspector Christine Frazer (Barbara Thorn) arrived in that episode, too, in plain clothes – only to have the terminally macho Roach try to chat her up. With devious and dodgy Frank Burnside in Sun Hill's CID, there was no whitewash of the police. Quite soon the Police Federation leaders were up in arms. An episode screened in August 1988 featured the arrest of a teenager after being smacked in the face by an officer. Then Burnside and his boys spent the afternoon drinking in a strip club. Alan Eastwood, then chairman of the Federation, said angrily: 'I have ordered my men not to have any contact with the show. The more distance we put between ourselves and that rubbish the better!'

Audiences clearly enjoyed 'that rubbish', and the switch to half-hours was declared a success. In the following year Peter Cregeen left to join the BBC and Michael Chapman returned to take the helm. His first problem was Sun Hill itself. The owners of the Barlby Road buildings wanted to redevelop them and gave 'The Bill' its marching orders. The move was to be made in March 1990. For a while, it seemed as though a base in Clapham, South London, would be its next home. That fell through, and a wine warehouse on an industrial estate further south in Merton was chosen. It had the space to house a third unit which had been assembled by then: the Green team. This team began work to produce twenty extra episodes which would cover the show for the weeks when they were moving house.

The Merton Sun Hill would not look exactly like the earlier police stations. But the imminent departure of Mark Powley, who played Ken Melvin, provided the perfect opportunity to explain the change. The station would be damaged and rebuilt and refurbished. Melvin was blown up while parking a suspect car in the station yard. He was right to suspect it: in the car's boot was a bomb. Meanwhile the making of the show went on with parts of some of the episodes being made in Barlby Road and other parts made at Merton. Painters, decorators, carpenters and electricians could sometimes be seen in the background – and why not?

important decision: 'The Bill' had become so popular that they wanted it to compete with the soap operas and win audiences for ITV on two of the nights not then dominated by 'Coronation Street'. Viewers were to get two smaller episodes of 'The Bill' on Tuesdays and Thursdays from July 1988. But the change that was probably more important than the halving of the screen time was the change in timing. Instead of its nine o'clock 'grown-up' slot, 'The Bill' would now be seen at eight.

Fear that the show would be watered down was a factor in the decision of John Salthouse – with his ginger hair one of the show's most recognized and popular performers – to quit. 'I am sure police flinch every time I appear on screen. A lot of coppers are like him, but it isn't the image they want the public to see even if he's not bent and is good at nicking criminals. I believe that to change the format would obviously mean that "The Bill" would lose that rawness, that immediacy which was essential for its success,' the actor, then thirty-four, said. 'You can't make a contemporary series about the police without including some violence. When you go into a police station, as I have, you see the ugly consequences of

of football hooligans. The episode, the police protested, might prejudice court proceedings about to start involving the West Midlands police and Birmingham City fans.

But these objections were few and far between. The show's police advisers were having no trouble in sending writers and actors into real police stations to research the truth. And the short snappy episodes were enjoyed by viewers so much that an extra helping was soon being discussed. The switch to three episodes a week meant an investment of £750,000 on additional sets and new characters. The Green Unit, up till then a stand-by team, would grow into a fully fledged partner.

The system was perfected. A minimum of nine directors work to three producers who work to Michael. Each episode has four weeks' preparation, five days' shooting, ten days of editing and four days of dubbing the sound. Each is shot using lightweight Ikigami cameras and recorded on half-inch tape, and the recorder can be clamped on to the camera. All the equipment fits into one small van – usually an unmarked van so that the camera man or woman may move almost unnoticed around the streets. There is no scanner and only minimal lighting.

The network put in the order during 1992, and Michael Chapman's team went to work, stockpiling the extra episodes for a starting date in the New Year. By February 1993 the third episode, shown on Fridays, had clocked up a record audience of 17.5 million. If anyone thought that was easy, they had only to consider the BBC's thrice-weekly effort that year. 'Eldorado' was struggling to keep audiences of 5 million.

By October of 1993 it was announced that the ITV network had placed an order for a further three years of three episodes of 'The Bill' a week. By then the show was being seen in thirty-five other countries, and early episodes are hits again now on UK Gold. In 1994 the annual advertising revenue that 'The Bill' is believed to generate was calculated at more than £59 million.

Geoff McQueen's hunch that there was room for another police show had turned out to be worth playing.

The Bill's `studio' on wheels: it looks like an ordinary van, but it's full of valuable equipment

The half-hour format seemed to provoke fewer criticisms from the real Bill. An episode in 1991 in which two male detectives laughed off a prostitute's rape ordeal was singled out by the Met Commissioner as a 'disservice' both to the police and to rape victims who might be dissuaded from reporting their cases. A Derbyshire DS was intrigued to know how a Sun Hill DC whose finances were under scrutiny could afford a wardrobe bulging with designer suits and shoes. He presumably hadn't heard about Dashwood's family background. Hotly contested was Thames's decision to screen a 'red card' episode showing detectives infiltrating a gang

NOT REALLY A NICK – WHEN YOU LOOK CLOSE

The Sun Hill station that was ordered for the new twice-weekly series was a modern, bright, efficient building, and that's what designers provided at the current real address, the former wine warehouse on an industrial estate in Merton, south-west London.

After the first few episodes were made there, everyone from the executive producer down hated it. An SOS went out to top designer David Marshall.

'It was an excellent design, but the effect was something which wasn't "The Bill". So I came over a long weekend and generally made the set look messier, to give it a bit more "texture". When the next lot of episodes went out, no one had noticed – which was a huge relief to us.'

What David did sounds simple, but of course it took an experienced eye. He ordered dirty patches, scuff marks and chips on the paintwork. He made the furniture look dirtier and older. He added posts in corridors, which made it difficult for people to walk down them. He added what looked like skylights. He put scruffy furniture, cardboard boxes, odd gym shoes and piles of paper in inconvenient places.

'What I was really doing was bringing it back to the look of "The Bill" that Robin Parker created right at the beginning. He set up the whole thing with very little money when no one much wanted to do it, and the result was brilliant,' say David, who now runs a design service for other designers.

'It isn't quite realistic because most police stations now have far larger main rooms. But the slightly claustrophobic feel to the place at Merton is good for the action.'

The real change which came with the move to Merton's Sun Hill (which is neither sunny nor on a hill, but who cares?) is that it's not just a dull old nick with cells and interview rooms and the usual police rooms. It's also a hospital, several courtrooms, and everything the cast and production teams need from dressing rooms and canteens to the editing facilities all on one site. Around 200 people, including the cast, work there at any one time.

There were also spaces into which to expand – which proved ideal when the ITV network ordered three

Sun Hill puts down roots in South London, with the help of guest star Dorothy Tutin

episodes per week and new units such as the Community Liaison Office were required. It's this and the scheme for using the site which makes 'The Bill' the envy of the television industry.

Having everything at hand means that no time need be wasted preparing and 'dressing' a studio set or making elaborate arrangements to use space in hospitals or courts at weekends when they weren't required by the authorities.

Instead the sombre wood-panelled place where the 'accused' of Sun Hill face their doom would fool the Attorney-General. It takes time to spot that the 'oak' benches and seats of Canley Magistrates' Court

Swearing to tell 'nothing but the truth' in a fine fake of a courtroom

(which, with a quick change of the crest on the far wall, doubles as Canley or Rushmead Crown Court, too) are plywood painted in a specially dull varnish. Only if you look up at the public gallery might you suspect that there's something fishy. The warehouse ceilings being lower than most court buildings means that anyone over three feet tall would have difficulty standing up in it.

In the corridor outside, the Old Masters painted by several of the designers with an hour to spare are pleasing if hardly Royal Academy material. The Roll of Honour to Sun Hill's 'Glorious Dead' begins with the name of the far from late Robin Parker and continues to include several still healthy members of the design team. In the police office by the court is a hideously grotty fridge, courtesy of David Marshall, and there's a jacket he found and hung up. It has been there for years. A door from there marked 'Toilet' actually leads to the Collator's office, on whose walls are pinned photographs and details of locally active criminals. These are strangely familiar: one is the show's accountant, another is one of the chefs, another is a lighting man.

In the CAD room the real computers have been adapted so that a stage manager may sit in another room of the building and key in information which then appears on the screens. When it's known that the screens will not be on camera, actors may find the information riveting for other reasons – it may be football results or bits of 'Bill' gossip, for example.

There are doors to seven detention cells, each with a bed and a lavatory, although three of the cells are dummies. Keep this to yourself, but you wouldn't need to be Houdini to escape from a Sun Hill cell. The thick metal doors are in fact grey-painted plywood closing on ball catches because the locks do not turn. The 'clunk' closing noise you hear has been dubbed on afterwards.

'It makes hammering on the door to get out a bit difficult for the actors,' says David Marshall. 'On occasions the doors have been nailed closed to stop them flying open – so you could say those actors were really nicked.'

The cups and trophies in Brownlow's office are left to tarnish so as not to make reflections, and there are no golf clubs. Michael Chapman isn't keen on scenes of his top cop teeing off with the local bigwigs. So clubs are hired for any golf scenes that writers squeeze in.

David Marshall also introduced St Hugh's Hospital. This has an accident and emergency ward, a waiting area, a four-bed ward using beds which were surplus at Hammersmith Hospital a few years back, and a corridor with waiting trolleys and bags of linen.

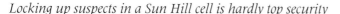

Locking up suspects in a Sun Hill cell is hardly top security

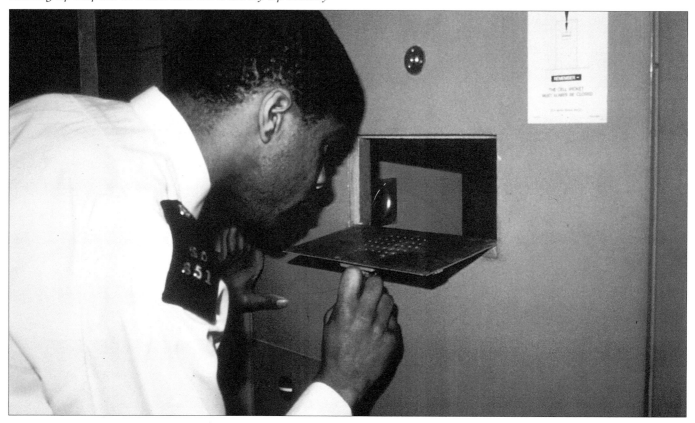

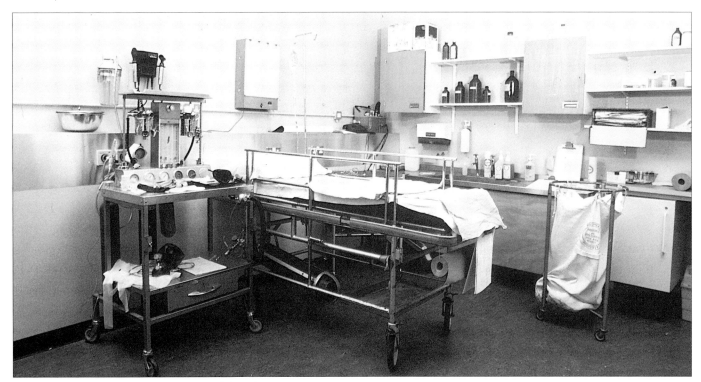

St Hugh's Hospital has never seen real blood

There's also an intensive care ward, a recent addition, in the only space available: next door to the senior officers' dining room – which would be handy in cases of food poisoning, if nothing else.

All these rooms so familiar to 'Bill' viewers are kept suitably untidy by Dave Hodges, the show's props master, and his team. He is based in a large store-room, the 'engine room' of the show, and works closely with current head designer David Ferris, the team of location managers and the stage managers who take care of all the props handled by the artists in a role.

The Engine Room contains all the articles needed to 'dress' the set's rooms or the rented homes or other locations. These range from bottles of tomato ketchup, prams, curtains, doormats, lampshades, ornaments of every description. He also keeps supplies of fake snow for the occasions when changing weather could give the game away on screen that a few minutes' action has taken days to shoot. He also has stocks of glasses made of sugar which may be broken over heads without danger; smoke machines which make a pub look puffed in, and steam wallpaper-strippers which, placed under the bonnet of a long-dented car, make it seem as though the dents were made seconds earlier in a crash.

For each day a team is out on location, Dave's props assistants pack a list of requirements into the team's vehicle. His carpenters and painters are on hand to prepare special windows, install whatever is needed for safety and, when the shooting is over and the crew move on, to restore the location to its former state.

His other responsibility is to put out the large blue lamp and the 'Metropolitan Police Sun Hill' sign over the entrance when external shots are needed. They are taken down as soon as possible to stop local people calling in convinced that this is the place to take driving documents or ask after lost property or missing persons. He must also arrange for the sign for a nearby Saab garage to be covered. This is not because they object to advertising the garage – they simply want to conceal the tell-tale word 'Wimbledon' on the sign.

And, if he has a moment to spare after all that, big Dave will pop down to the recreation room and beat any of the actors at table tennis.

World Beat

'The Bill' is now seen in Australia, Bahrain, Barbados, Brunei, Bulgaria, Canada, China, Denmark, Dubai, Eire, Finland, Germany, Gibraltar, Greece, Holland, Hong Kong, Indonesia, Israel, Italy, Jamaica, Kenya, Malaysia, Mauritius, New Zealand, Norway, Saudi Arabia, Singapore, Spain, Sweden, Thailand, Trinidad, Russia, Zambia, Zimbabwe.

The Making of an Episode

Edwin Pearce, a journalist on the *Sunday Telegraph*, first wrote 'Domestics', an hour-long episode for 'The Bill', in 1987 and has written many of the half-hour episodes since then as well as contributing scripts to other television series. Where do the ideas come from? Anywhere. He spots beggars on the street and wonders what the police should do about them. That becomes an episode called 'Beg Borrow or Steal'. Sometimes one detail from a newspaper story such as a man taking slates off his roof to torment his wife intrigues him. That became a part of 'War of Nerves'.

THIS IS THE STORY OF 'A TOUCH OF BRAID'.

Thursday, 17 February. Idea comes from a half-serious thought at a meeting between writer Edwin Pearce and script editor Rob Pursey. Poor Chief Superintendent Brownlow rarely escapes the office. Can't we get him out on the beat? The image of the Chief Super strutting his stuff – in full uniform (with braid) on the streets of Sun Hill like a five-star general – is a very seductive one.

Edwin talks to police contacts about when and why a chief super would go public. The most promising occasion dramatically would be in response to a public-order emergency where it would be down to him to go out, cool tempers, talk to leading citizens, councillors, etc., and risk eggs or worse being thrown at him.

Edwin decides to make the public-order emergency a potential riot on a housing estate. This would be caused by a CID raid for stolen goods that goes badly wrong.

The raid would take place on a third-floor flat. A teenage boy – a talented runner at a local running track – would try to escape, fall from a window and be seriously injured. The estate would be up in arms at police 'brutality', and Brownlow would have to go out and try to mend fences – risking the wrath of the residents. At the same time the episode would tell the story of the teenage boy, his mother and the uncle – a receiver of stolen goods – who lives with them and ruins their aspirations.

Monday, 21 February. Edwin delivers the nub of the idea – a single-page story premise – to Rob Pursey, the script editor. He calls it 'Running Scared' because the plot turns on the teenage boy being bullied by his uncle who makes him hide a batch of stolen pocket televisions in lockers at his running track.

Wednesday, 23 February. Story premise is passed at the full weekly editorial meeting. Edwin moves on to the storyline stage – a synopsis of three or four pages outlining the episode in more detail, with Brownlow's visit to the estate not only keeping the peace but providing a clue to the whereabouts of the pocket televisions and nailing the wicked uncle.

Wednesday, 2 March. Storyline passed and script commissioned under the title of 'Running Scared' with the proviso that – as the housing-estate riot develops, hoax calls come in and officers are attacked out there – we stay inside the Sun Hill 'pressure cooker' and follow the reverberations through the ranks as uniform bears the brunt of the CID 'cock-up'.

Friday, 18 March. Script delivery date is 25 March, but Edwin finishes an early working draft and meets Rob Pursey to discuss how it is shaping. A key point is firmed up. Brownlow's role in helping to crack the case must be crucial to give us the best dramatic pay-off – that the old man can still do the business when the rest of his Sun Hill team cocks things up.

Edwin includes a 'defenestration' joke – suspects falling out of windows – by one of the Sun Hill PCs to show coppers' black humour. The joke goes down well.

Friday, 25 March. First draft delivered and passes the meeting with comments and suggestions from the producers and the show's police advisers. It is pointed out that using lockers to hide stolen goods may be impractical. Edwin decides to ditch the running theme and have the boy hide the stolen pocket televisions in a cello case at his school.

Edwin feels the script would be more powerful if the boy was not so much scared of his uncle as being his willing tool. This would intensify the dismay of his mother, who wants the boy to better himself and rise above the surroundings of the estate.

Thus both the 'running' and 'scared' elements of the story are lost. This means a new title. Edwin decides on 'A Touch of Braid'. It reflects, after all, the original idea!

The once important role of a councillor is cut down because it slows the pace of the story. Another idea disappears: Brownlow will not get eggs thrown at him when he visits the estate. Rob Pursey feels this just wouldn't work. The defenestration joke stays.

Monday, 4 April. Revised draft delivered and accepted for production. Richard Handford to produce.

Monday, 11 April. Edwin, Richard and Rob meet for final brainstorming session. Richard thinks some of the outside estate rioting scenes (youths attacking police and cars, etc.) are too good for us not to see. He decides he'll film them.

The script is long. Edwin comes out with the writer's age-old plea not to cut the jokes. Defenestration hangs on in there. Richard and Rob feel the role of the councillor can be dropped altogether. Councillors tend to be boring.

We are still long. Director Frank Smith comes in, the latest and freshest eye to it. He says that our 'key' interrogation scene of the uncle at Sun Hill actually holds the drama up and gets in the way of an emotional climax involving the boy's mother. The fresh eye is right. We ditch the scene.

We are still a bit long. More trims. The defenestration joke finally goes. We now have a lean, mean and hungry script ready to go, timed correctly at 24 minutes 30 seconds.

Head of design David Ferris reads draft script and discusses details with designer Peter Elliott. Will scaffolding be needed for proposed stunt of fall from balcony? Three front doors to be ordered in case of retakes. Hires vehicles.

Monday, 18 April. First production meeting with Red Unit producer Richard Handford, director Frank Smith, production manager Derek Cotty, Peter Elliott, costume supervisor William McPhail and location manager Micky Moynihan.

Micky immediately begins to research the necessary twenty locations. Finds a council estate, a third-floor flat with a suitable balcony, and a school with a suitable music room. Micky begins to make telephone calls to residents and the headmaster. Offers a donation to the school music department in return for the disturbance.

Groundwork - nothing glamorous as one of The Bill's newest directors, Sam Miller (who used to be Sgt John Maitland), monitors outdoor filming on a typical location shoot

Nigel Wilson, project co-ordinator, begins to fit a jigsaw of actors and scenes from different episodes in which they are required for the week of 16 May. Derek and James Corbett, first assistant director, begin to work out a schedule on a time basis, scene by scene, allowing enough time for short rehearsals and unforeseen problems with the weather, with the aim of making the shooting week about forty-two hours.

Friday, 22 April. Preliminary budget meeting for Red Unit. Derek Cotty reckons this is a fairly simple episode. They're using a location which is only a short distance away. They don't have to blow the whole estate up or set fire to buildings. They are not planning a car chase and multiple crashes. There is nothing so expensive that money has to be 'pinched' from others episodes' budgets. Makes first estimates of cost of cast and crew vehicles needed, catering, portable loos, etc.

Casting director Irene Cotton begins to audition child actors for the roles of two teenage boys. She asks agent Sylvia Young for suggestions. Of the six young actors who read for the main role, she thinks Kristian Wilkin, whom she recalls from the children's series 'Hangar 17', conveys the right sense of vulnerability. (Licences have to be sought from the local authority for child artists, and those can take about three weeks, so they can't dither.)

Monday, 25 April. James Corbett begins sorting out the schedule in association with Nigel Wilson, who must fit the Red Unit's requirements of the regular cast into those of Blue and Green. Nigel points out that Ben Roberts, who plays Conway, is available for mornings only because of the stage-play in which he is appearing.

Are there alterations to be made to the script? Thankfully, no.

Irene begins to see adults for the parts of the boy's mother, his uncle, the other boy's father, a teacher and a resident. Irene sees about six artists for each role. She is delighted that Irish actress Veronica Duffy is available and keen. She also likes the 'quality of cockiness' Andrew Clover shows when he reads some of the uncle's lines. She and director Frank Smith make choices.

Friday, 29 April. Rachel Rolfe, booking assistant, arranges guest artists' contracts.

Tuesday, 3 May. Micky writes to the headmaster outlining what they had agreed. He also writes to

Anyone fancy a pint? Garfield, Lines and Bostock (Carl Brincat) with one of the show's more unusual vehicles

agents for a building site nearby with details of the indemnity 'The Bill' would provide as insurance against any damage.

Thursday, 5 May. 'Release' letters sent to all parents of children who may be in the background of the shots at the school. Explains arrangement with the headmaster, etc.

Monday, 9 May. After visits and talks, Micky writes to the neighbour next to the flat to be used, outlining request to use access to the balcony. Small disturbance fee agreed.

Tuesday, 10 May. Second of many letters sent to local police informing them where and when the crew would be shooting. Letter to local council agreeing payments to film on the estate and letters sent to all residents warning them.

Micky also checks the safety certificates of the scaffolding that the design department has ordered for the stunt where the 'boy' falls from the balcony.

Wednesday, 11 May. Production meeting in Derek Cotty's office. Frank Smith decides that a milk-float on the estate will set the time as early morning. Orders a milk-float for one day. Discussion of the riot and the paint-spray assault on Garfield. Jo Ingerson, the stage manager, confirms that the paint-spray will be a harmless aerosol; the yellow paint will be supplied afterwards. Frank also asks that enough sugar-glass bottles and fake bricks are available for the riot. Micky warns that they will not be able to film inside the music department of the local school until after exams there have finished. He also warns about the local children who are sure to gather and must be handled firmly. Derek asks how much blood there is likely to be on and around the young actor after his 'fall'. Make-up co-ordinator Gilly Holmes says there will be only a trickle of blood from the boy's ear. Producer Richard Handford sighs with relief. 'The death rate in Sun Hill is already too high!' he says.

Friday, 13 May. At coffee morning, guest stars briefly meet the regulars and some of the

PC Stamp (Graham Cole) 'tests' one of the sledgehammers with which hundreds of doors and dozens of fences have been tapped in ten years of `The Bill'

production team. They also have photographs taken to place in frames in their screen home. Carpenter John McNamee visits flat on housing estate to measure the front door for the replacement(s) which will be smashed with a sledgehammer. He also puts a Rawlbolt on the wall on the back balcony so that a safety harness can be attached for the young actor and the stuntwoman if she requires it.

Monday, 16 May. Shooting begins of scenes within the police station. Actors playing Carver and Woods must work with Blue Unit after 4 p.m. Meanwhile Dave Hodges' painters and carpenters are 'dressing' the location flat, changing a girl's bedroom into a teenage boy's, with new paint and wallpaper, laying new carpet in hall and living room, moving in bed-settee. They'll have spent around £1,200 on the job by the end.

Tuesday, 17 May. Cast and crew leave base for Mitcham location at 8 a.m. Frank Smith says the boy's bedroom looks far too new – orders marks and

tears on the wallpaper for a more realistic look. Jimmy Corbett hushes everyone gathering outside the flat. One of the neighbours is a sick man. In small kitchen sound and lighting directors work silently with ASM who checks the scripts and prompts. Occasionally they talk on walkie-talkies to colleagues in truck in carpark. Actress Veronica Duffy begins her scenes in a nightdress and dressing gown. It's a cold, wet, windy day. With the flat doors open, everyone is freezing except her. She has a thermal vest. ' "Terminal vest", as we say in Dublin,' she jokes. Stuntwoman Tina Maskell decides that the wet weather makes the balcony fall unsafe. She, Frank and Derek agree to reschedule it for 7.30 the following morning if Mark Wingett is available then. He is. Irene Cotton arrives to tell Frank that they need to recast one of the minor roles in a hurry because the actor needs to be on stage. They agree on an alternative.

Wednesday, 18 May. Tina falls off the balcony with perfect timing, then goes off for breakfast. Michael Keane, one of the team that controls traffic and security for the unit, is shot in the rear by a local child with an air-rifle. He reports it to the real police. His colleagues sympathize. Later Peter Ellis and Ben Roberts as Brownlow and Conway tour the estate. Later Huw Higginson as Garfield chases youth, who squirts him with a paint-aerosol.

Thursday, 19 May. Afternoon filming in local comprehensive school after exams have ended.

Friday, 20 May. Final scenes shot in police station.

Monday, 23 May. Editing begins.

Another local resident allows her home to be invaded – this time by Johnson and Skase for 'A Touch Of Braid'

Rough Stuff

Tina Maskell, who doubled for Kristian Wilkin for the balcony jumpin 'A Touch of Braid', used to be a nursery nurse and became interested in children's theatre.

'I kept getting cast in physical roles, and I thought I'd like to learn to do them properly. So I became a member of Equity and became proficient at several sports, such as fencing, trampolining and some of the martial arts. It takes about seven years to be accepted on to the Equity Stunt Register. You have to keep a record of your work in scenes involving fire, water or cars.'

Tina persevered, learning as she went on from experienced stunt co-ordinators. She also fitted in having two children. She continued to be in demand not only to double actresses but also, at only five feet tall and weighing little more than eight stone, to double children and teenagers of both sexes.

Jumping off the third-floor balcony of this block of South London flats held no terrors for Tina. She has jumped twice as far – 82 feet – for the final scene of the BBC's 'House Cards'. Then she doubled actress Susannah Harker, who was pushed from the top of the House of Commons by evil politician Francis Urquhart (Ian Richardson). That tumble – actually from the top of Manchester Town Hall – was all in a day's work, too. The hard part is supervising and checking the rig, which for 'A Touch of Braid' was four layers of mattresses at the bottom of three layers of cardboard boxes, tied into a firm rectangle. Concerned that constant rain would soften this structure, Tina and Derek dropped the plan to shoot the stunt on Tuesday.

So before breakfast the next morning she was dressed in the same jacket and tracksuit trousers that Kristian wore in the part, with a brown wig to match his long hair; she checked the newly assembled and dry rig; then at the director's signal, while the crew watched in silent awe, she fell backwards with the required yelp.

Seconds later she popped up like a jack in her big cardboard box, smiling. Soon she was picking up her holdall and heading for her next death-defying leap: in a scene from 'Heartbeat'.

Now you see him... Carver and the boy Colin Price (Kristian Wilkin) on the balcony in 'A Touch of Braid'

... now you don't: stunt arranger Tina Maskell takes over for the fall from the balcony, flanked by (l to r) Rob Wahl (sound), Frank Smith (director) and Andy Parkinson (camera)

Wheels

It's not unusual for as much as £12,000 to be spent crashing cars in one episode of 'The Bill'. More than £30,000 was spent on the car crashes in Viv Martella's farewell episode. It wasn't a record. Derek Cotty believes that may turn out to have been set by 'Instant Response', about a teenage joyrider. In this, twelve cars including two Jaguars were bought from a scrapyard to be rewrecked.

Action Vehicles is a specialist company which supplies 'The Bill' with its vehicles. They have an office on-site at Merton. As soon as designer David Ferris reads a script he lists the vehicles needed. All specialized vans, flash cars, old bangers or vehicles not even Arthur Daley could flog (because they're ready to be wrecked in spectacular screen collisions) are on their hire-lists.

The programme has its own pool of fifteen police vehicles which includes Area Cars and Pandas, a black Ford Scorpio, black and white Marias and an

PC Stamp, Sun Hill's Nigel Mansell

MS15 vehicle. The police officers' private cars are privately owned vehicles which are hired by the day when needed.

THEY WHO MUST BE OBEYED

Pat Sandys, one of the three producers of 'The Bill', says: 'Keeping to Met practice is the great strength of the programme. It's like writing a sonnet. There are rules, and you don't break them. When one of our police advisers writes "Oh, no!" on a script we would never ignore it.'

Brian Hart and Trevor Hermes are the real 'Old Bill' at 'The Bill', and their word is law. Brian, whose wry smile is hidden beneath a bristling moustache, retired after thirty-one years as a chief inspector at Leman Street, East London, in 1989, and joined the series soon after as an adviser. Trevor worked under him as an inspector until, after twenty-two years' service, he foolishly drove his car after taking a drink. He was breathalysed, found to be over the limit and, as is automatic, lost his job. Though he still kicks himself, and would love to be back in uniform, he describes his work in jeans and T-shirt behind the scenes at Sun Hill for the past two years as the next best thing.

Trevor, patient but direct, and a bloke you'd never try to rugby-tackle, was already a fan of the series when he joined. 'Everyone inside the police wanted "The Bill" to get it right because it was the first series about uniformed officers since "Dixon". I did a stint as a recruiting officer, and I used to ask the applicants if they were watching "The Bill". If they said "no" but they loved "Hill Street Blues", I'd say that maybe the British police force is not for you.'

What Brian and Trevor do is to arrange for all new actors to visit police stations and shadow real versions of their character. They do so under the Old Pals' Act. 'We haven't had a refusal yet,' beams Trevor. They read all the scripts at the first-draft stage and point out any glaring inaccuracies or areas of potential problems. Then they divide the list, each taking reponsibility for checking future drafts of about twenty episodes at any one time.

Sometimes they draw blood when they pick holes in a writer's idea. 'I can understand how they feel,' says Brian. 'A new writer has probably put up about a dozen premises before he actually gets a commission for a script. The thought that he will be losing an idea because Trevor or I is being difficult panics him. But the Met can't change its attitude to fit a script. We always try to give alternatives. They always exist because any situation, absolutely anything and everything involving people and the police, has happened before, so there are always answers.'

Writers soon learn that these two slightly forbidding men know the characters of Sun Hill well. Brian says: 'We know them through and through. After all, we share their attitudes and mannerisms.'

One recurring mistake is that writers give the coppers too much to say, especially when talking over the radio. They are also corrected if they use

Quinnan radios 'in' briefly

surnames – it's always first names or numbers.

But, even when a script has been cleared, small errors may creep in through a misinterpretation of the notes by a busy director out on location. 'It's usually something no ordinary viewer spots, but I'm sure to have a phone call from someone I used to work with to say, "Well, you made a pig's ear of that, didn't you?" ' Brian sighs.

General advice to actors who ask is that they should not appear too confident about their work. 'Most young officers are really scared about doing it wrong and making fools of themselves,' says Brian. 'They are more worried about letting their mates down than letting someone poke them in the ear with a stick.'

Neither Brian nor Trevor believes that 'The Bill' whitewashes the image of the real officers. 'We do show bent coppers, but they usually come from another station because these days the police find the rotten apples and throw them out of the barrel.'

Both say they miss the buzz of excitement and real satisfaction of nicking villains. Trevor thinks working with actors and writers has broadened his outlook,

liberalized him in some ways. 'I might have referred to a woman officer as a "trout" when I was in the Job. Now I know that that is really offensive to women, so I'd never use the term here. But the police has changed so much in the last couple of years it would probably not be tolerated in the Job today, either.'

Brian thinks today's policewomen simply would not stand for any put-downs by their male oppos. 'They're not weak little flowers. Their language is as salty as the men's, and in some ways they're tougher,' he says.

The changes for him have been external ones, embarrassingly. 'It was very hard to leave my suits and ties in the wardrobe when I started here. But I had to, because everyone in television is casually dressed,' he says. 'Now, if my ex-colleagues see me as I'm travelling across London to "The Bill" in what must look like gardening clothes, they assume I've gone to the dogs!'

WHAT GOES DOWN: WRITING THE STORIES OF SUN HILL

A woman who knows more about the cops at Sun Hill than they do themselves is Zanna Beswick, the series script editor. Her job is to make sure everything we see happening involving the police characters could happen in a busy British city in the 1990s to real police officers.

'We work closely with the Met police, but we have to be careful that we're not just putting out their propaganda. Our stories aren't always exactly what they want to hear,' she says. 'Our officers aren't perfect. When the police themselves decided to clean up their act and outlaw certain practices, we followed. We didn't show Burnside shoving a man's head down the toilet, but we still showed him being devious and cunning.'

The Met is very keen that the 'Bill' writers 'get it right' because their surveys show that the public gets most of its information about how the country's police works from watching this one television series.

'It means we're hoisted by our own petard,' says Zanna. 'Because we started off as a down-to-earth realistic police drama, and that proved successful, we've had to stick to that. So that we're never allowed to forget that we're based on fact. It's a hard discipline but a good one.'

So all 'Bill' stories follow three rules: they must be authentic in terms of what the police do; they must be right for the early-evening viewing slot; and they

Datta and Jarvis work just as well in civvies

must be possible – that is, the actors and the crews must have had the time to film them, bearing in mind that they must produce three episodes a week.

'We do sometimes write episodes which make a point the police have asked us to make,' adds Zanna with a smile, 'so long as we think it's interesting. For instance, the Met asked us to do an episode to show that uniformed officers were not less important than plain-clothes CID people. They'd had victims of burglaries getting cross because the investigating officer sent to them was in uniform, and they thought they were "entitled" to a detective. So we included the Bumblebee initiative in our stories. This was intended to put the fear of crime in the home back on the villains and off the victims. It also let viewers see that some officers – Ackland and Quinnan, for example – worked in and out of uniform.'

'We also helped the Met with their Doorstoppers campaign to make the public aware of people who'd get into the house by pretending to be officials from the Gas Board or something. We created a story called "Gift of the Gab" featuring Pearce and Croft,

and it was shown to coincide with the launch of Doorstoppers. The campaign cut the practice down by about 45 per cent, and I think we contributed to that.'

Zanna and her colleagues are not so comfortably 'in bed with' the Met that they sacrifice elements of the series they know viewers love to the Met rule-book. 'In reality many of our long-term officers would have been promoted by now. Carver and Ackland certainly. Cryer might have become an inspector and Tosh Lines a sergeant,' admits Zanna. So why haven't they?

'Because the rules are that no officer when promoted would stay in the same station and give orders to his former equals. There would be resentment. The officers are always transferred to another station. So we'd have to lose some of our best actors. We'd never do that willingly!'

If the first guv'nor of 'The Bill' is fact, the second guv'nor is the audience – an audience which at eight o'clock at night includes lots of children. Because of this, and the Independent Television Commission's guidelines about what can be shown before 9pm, too much violence, blood and gore, swearing, or scenes of sex or talk of it, and anything which might prey on a young person's mind are never included in the writing. If anything which may be dodgy or disturbing creeps in, it's escorted off the page sharpish.

'That isn't to say we avoid crimes such as rape of prostitutes or paedophile rings or baby-battering; it's just that we have to be subtle and hint at what has happened. No one would watch "The Bill" for a quick thrill. And, of course, you would never see the sex attack or the baby-battering because we never show anything unless a police officer is present, and they're almost always there after it has happened.'

For this reason the writers are asked never to give the characters gruesome injuries; never to turn a plot on a hacked corpse. If there are weapons, these must never be 'glamorized' by the camera; guns are not the 'stars' of any sequence, knives are never brandished above a character's waist or held anywhere near a character's face.

'We had a story about the rape of a prostitute which we were going to turn into a two-episode story,' says Zanna. 'Then we decided that that would soften it. We decided to have Burnside and Ackland argue about it. Burnside regarded the rape as par for the course for women who were on the game. Ackland said that a violation without consent was still rape.'

Zanna has been responsible for 'feminizing' Sun Hill to some extent, for including more regular female characters and introducing more women writers to the pool of about fifty writers who supply the all-important ideas for the life of Sun Hill.

'It hasn't meant we've gone soft and soppy,' she says. 'In fact the woman writers often write the toughest episodes and they write sassier dialogue, especially for women criminals. But there are more women in the police now, and promotion is getting slightly easier for them. I know there is no black woman DI in the Met. We just thought when Jaye Griffiths came in as a guest it was too good an opportunity to miss. If we'd considered it academically, we'd have run a mile!'

As for the show's third guv'nor – the art of the possible – it is only occasionally a restricting factor. If an actor simply cannot appear in a plot line that has been written for him, such as making an arrest, because he or she is involved in scenes for other episodes being pelted with stones in a riot or having a row with a colleague at the station, the script must be rewritten to include a different actor who may be free at that time.

These problems are mostly avoided when the scripts are first discussed. This is the way it works.

The script editors of the three production teams (Red, Blue and Green) each have a 'stable' of writers at any one time. Every writer will have studied the 'Bill' rules, will be familiar with police procedures and will have 'loitered with intent' around police stations in the name of research.

'So if a writer comes to me with an idea my first question is "Who is it about?" The writer may say Datta. I ask how it would work. The writer may say: "It's about a child-molester; it arose after a talk I had with one of the police advisers." I'd then ask for a very short summary explaining how the police break the cycle of a child-molester. I'd then put this premise to the people at the script meetings we hold every Thursday. If Michael Chapman, our executive producer, likes it, I'd then tell the writer to do a three-page "storyline", which would be discussed at the next meeting. If the storyline is liked, we commission a script and give the writer three weeks to come up with a working draft. At this stage our police and legal advisers may send notes to the writer. Nigel Wlson, our project co-ordinator, is very important at these meetings. He advises us if we're getting too heavy with CID or if we haven't featured certain subjects or characters for a while. He'll also shout out if he thinks we may have done too much on one theme – domestic violence, for example.

'We look at the scripts at different stages and ask the writers to include humour if we feel we haven't had enough lately, or a reference to something political within the police. We try not to nitpick. The

Four-legged 'suspects' aroused viewers' sympathy

individual script editors keep a check on the scripts being the right length – that's about twenty-four minutes of screen time.'

Zanna has come to know which subjects are likely to be more popular – those with car chases and a lot of exciting action – but she has been surprised.

' "Sleeping with the Fishes", an episode in which a boat was found and it turned out that some boys had drowned, proved hugely popular,' she recalls. 'We also had very high ratings when an off-licence was stormed. But adult viewers enjoy our stories when there is some real insight.'

Subjects they don't consider? Bomb stories, too alarming at eight o'clock, are definitely out. 'Any involving animals tend to provoke complaints,' says Zanna. 'We had one which briefly showed Rottweiler dogs being let out of cages. The story was about a mother worried about the safety of her own child. We had a tremendous number of complaints from Rottweiler-owners!' When we tackle the subject of child abuse, no one turns a hair. The merest hint of criticism of dogs, and people are up in arms!

'We do take complaints on board, though. For instance, we are often asked why we don't include a gay police officer. The answer is that we may already have a gay police officer. We don't know if an officer is gay or not – and we don't go into their private life. But we are thinking about it – just as we are always thinking about racism within the police.'

The co-operation with the Met is a two-way deal. While the series writers try to reflect the current concerns of police men and women with stories about the effect of the Sheehy recommendations to

A real officer shows Dashwood (Jon Iles) how to cuff 'em and keep 'em

abolish certain ranks and make policing not a job for life but a job for the length of a contract, the police assist the programme.

They allow writers to talk freely to serving officers and enable them to use real police dogs and use real police equipment, such as the new-style handcuffs. The show was also able to use a police helicopter for an episode and borrow some of the 'compressors' which blast doors open.

Zanna has tasted police work herself, and still shudders at the shock she received.

Burnside chooses a chopper

Subjects Tackled

Totting up the Sun Hill 'crime' figures earlier this year, Ruth Parkhill, the show's archivist, found that by far the most common offence was that of assault, including mugging. Her total of stories on that theme was 98. There had been 78 murders, 59 fires some of which were arson. There had been 26 suicides, 17 rapes, 16 cases of serious domestic violence, 14 cases of armed theft, 12 cases of racially motivated violence, 10 cases of hijacking, 9 cases of forced evictions involving bailiffs, 8 stories of business corruption, 6 pornography cases, 6 cot deaths, 5 stories of illegal immigration, and a sprinkling of animal cruelty stories, euthanasia, bigamy and other less common offences.

'I went out in an Area Car on a chase,' she says. 'The police were raiding the flat of a suspect known to be violent. I was trying to stay invisible but not succeeding. Suddenly I was pulled down and pushed back by a policeman as I walked past a window. The suspect had just grabbed a knife he kept in a door-jamb.'

THE CLOTHES

When Pauline Daly has a few hours free in Kettering, where she lives, she often spends them in charity and secondhand-clothes shops. She's looking for a 'new' mac for Tosh Lines.

'He has had one since he arrived and he adores it, but it's falling to pieces. He really needs a replacement, but a new one would be wrong for his character. Even then, they don't make them the same now. So I have asked everyone to keep an eye out for me at their local Oxfam shop.'

Tosh needn't feel he's the only 'second-hand Rose'. Pauline and her team are often out shopping in markets for the outfits needed for residents of Sun Hill, who are mostly hard up and keep clothes for years. 'We are very good at tramps and brilliant at prostitutes,' she says. 'I make mental notes about tramps' clothes whenever I see one in the street. And I went out with the Vice Squad recently to see what most of today's tarts wear. They're not "Irma La Douce" types; they tend to wear very few clothes, and they're of pretty poor quality. We can easily find them or get them made for us.

'The hardest things to get right are very ordinary people's clothes. On television even dull old things can look bright and new.'

Consequently Pauline's team are constantly busy 'spoiling' clothes. On a wall in the warehouse can be seen what looks like the efforts of an uninspired graffiti artist.

It is in fact an execution wall against which a stream of garments have been pinned to be sprayed with aerosols of paint or hairspray. They may then have been attacked with a cheese-grater to produce the 'loose thread' look; buttons may be tugged off, and cardigans and jackets may be hung up with heavy objects in the pockets to produce the 'stretched-with-wear' misshapen look.

Perhaps the cruellest treatment is meted out to supplies of dazzling white shirts destined to be worn by the Sun Hill police officers. They are no sooner taken out of their wrappings than they are washed in a hot cycle of the washing machine – with a couple of black socks! This process – most people's idea of a laundry nightmare – is in order to 'tone them down' or to stop them distracting the eye. From then on they join the usual washload of the wardrobe department: up to sixty whitish shirts are processed each day.

The police uniforms used in 'The Bill' are the real McCoy, bought from the Met's own suppliers after the show's producers and police and Home Office representatives met to discuss it. There are approximately twenty regular uniformed officers and about the same number of 'walk-ons' – police who are seen in the background. 'We agreed to keep our uniforms locked away when not in use because they can be very valuable to criminals. And our actors don't hang around on the streets in them. When they are not actually shooting scenes, they put anoraks over their police jackets. We don't want to mislead the public.'

When Pauline first reads a script she begins making notes and lists. At any one time she may have eighteen episodes 'on the go'. She also writes herself a mini biography of the 'visiting' main

Tosh's mac makes Columbo's look smart

Exactly how long is the arm of the law? 'The Bill's wardrobe assistants are precise

characters to give herself an idea of how they would be dressed. She attends meetings with the designers, location managers and directors, and submits her budget for each episode. Even if very little would seem to be needed, Pauline is aware that fight scenes and other action scenes may require doubles and trebles: fresh, clean or dry copies of a garment which may be soiled in a scene which may need several takes to get it right. Doubling is always necessary, of course, when stunt artists replace actors for dangerous scenes.

The non-uniformed officers present different challenges. June Ackland's plain clothes are just that. 'They mustn't make any statement or be distracting,' says Pauline. 'Sally Johnson's clothes have to be functional but of good quality.' The men's clothes are similarly low-key. But ties have to be numbered and the dates they were worn noted down, both to maintain continuity on an episode and to make sure that Carver, for instance, doesn't wear the same tie for weeks on end.

CASTING 'THE BILL'

The actors who become police officers have to fit in; they have to get the hang of the show's unique way of working and the speed of it all. Rehearsals? A few run-throughs on the set or on location, if you're lucky.

Tony O'Callaghan describes working on the show as like waiting for a bus. 'But it's a bus that doesn't stop. You have to run with it and jump on it.'

Pat Sandys, one of the show's three producers, says: 'When a new regular joins, he or she is given the character's professional background – then that actor is left to find his own space.'

'You are always taking a chance because the newcomers tend to make existing actors redefine their characters.

'Eventually the way a regular character turns out is a cross between what was first imagined and what the actor has put in himself.'

As far as guest performers are concerned, 'The Bill' has a high reputation. James Wilby played a uniformed PC before becoming the sensitive hero of several films. Gary Olsen played PC Dave Litten before becoming well known in situation comedy. Dorothy Tutin, Roger Lloyd Pack, Danny Webb, Sorcha Cusack, Ann Mitchell, Brian Glover, John McArdle, Louise Lombard and many other highly experienced actors have been happy to take small roles.

In its ten years 'The Bill' has employed more than 70,000 people in walk-on roles and 10,000 guest artists. Pat Sandys says: 'This show eats up actors. We try not to use them within a year. We don't use smart "Equity" villains. We hardly ever go for a bravura performance. We prefer to cast someone with street cred. It's a shame, but there are just not enough actors of quality who can play villains. '

Brian Glover plays a pained customer at Sun Hill, in 'Broken'

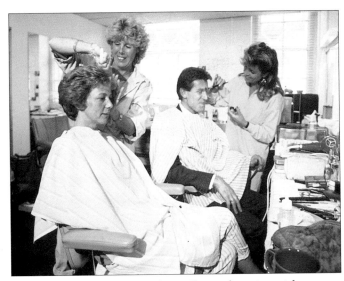

Trudie Goodwin won't get the Hollywood treatment here

MAKE-UP

Gilly Holmes and her team of make-up artists have a rotten job. On most television series they would strive to make the stars look flawlessly attractive, help the audience believe in a world which is larger than life and build up the artists' confidence. On 'The Bill' they have to 'break the actors down'. That means making the women look as though they have been working flat out for ten hours, removing any trace of glamour and never letting lovely hair fall loose. That applies to some of the men, too.

'Iain Fletcher looks like a fashion model with his thick floppy hair,' says Gilly. 'So we have to stick it back with hair gel. In general with the men, we just have to keep their hair cut short, which they never like. But we have to strike a balance. We like the show to look like a documentary, but we don't want our stars to look too dull and boring. So we have to touch up some of the grey from time to time. And we're there to touch up bags under the eyes, de-shine noses and cover up the odd spot or blemish.'

When Chris Ellison, who played Burnside, was there Gilly's work included removing the traces of the actor's suntan. 'Chris loves the sun and goes very dark, especially when he'd been to Spain. So we were always "washing him out" because Burnside probably hated fresh air.'

Apart from the day-to-day grooming, Gilly's team also provide the blood and gore for the show. Gore may include vomit: 'We always have tins of vegetable soup handy,' she says. It may mean sickly foam around drug addicts' or glue sniffers' mouths. For

A touch up for Lynne Miller as she pounds the beat

ALMOST THERE: EDITING AND CHECKING

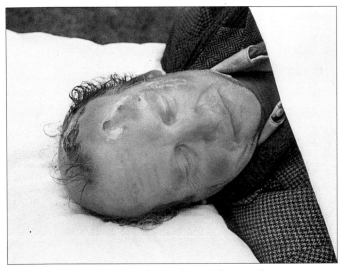

A bit of blood and gore – but this isn't `Casualty'

this Gilly would send out for a carton of eggs.

'We whisk up the whites of eggs and stand by to spoon it on,' she laughs.

They study medical textbooks to research wounds and make 'scars' and 'burns' with layers of fine latex, gelatine and glycerine. 'And we try to keep up with the new ways of stitching used in hospitals whenever we have a scene in our St Hugh's.'

Professional fake blood is kept in large containers. But Gilly regrets that viewers sometimes do not see their best Technicolor glistening creation.

'We often make what would be dreadful wounds, and they look so realistic you flinch. But when the producers see the shots they fear that viewers will be too upset. So they are cut out, which is a shame for us.

'We always underplay injuries so as not to upset people. For instance, if I read in a script that someone is going to be shot in the face at close range, I know that in fact that person wouldn't have any head left. But I interpret that as a lot of blood. I'd love to go to town and do a realistic job, but I can't in a show which is seen at 8 p.m. But when Viv Martella died this was such an important episode that they did let us show a realistic wound.'

When Melvin was killed by a car bomb the problem for the make-up people was to keep the stuck-on wounds stuck on with five people squirting fire-hoses at the 'corpse' of Mark Powley. 'We tried every sort of adhesive and plastic spray, but they kept being washed away,' she laughs.

And Tosh's punched lip caused headaches. 'We had this swollen cut attached to his mouth, but he had to keep it on for days as the episode was shot. Every time he took a sip of tea, the injury miraculously healed – because our effort fell off!'

They've devised a system of editing and finishing the episodes on 'The Bill' to cut out time-wasting. This is roughly how it works. The director and his or her team work on two programmes at a time. After four weeks of preparation, the team begins filming for two weeks on their pair of episodes. The director and crew view each day's tapes with their editor as they go along to check what they have and how it may best be edited.

When all filming on the episode has finished, 'post-production' begins in one of four editing suites. Over his first four days the editor makes a 'rough cut'. Generally this involves two days on episode 1 and then two days on episode 2 (in the same order in which they were shot).

The director joins the editor in the second week to produce a 'fine cut'. The producer takes a look and may request changes. When the producer is happy a fresh version, the 'edit master', is sent to the dubbing suite. There, one of our dubbing mixers together with the director and production assistant refine the sound which accompanies the pictures. This may involve adding sounds from those held on computer

When the actors think it's all over, the fiddly stuff starts

or lifting dialogue from other takes, adding incidental music from compact disc or making new sound effects.

It is usually three weeks before the tapes are assessed by the executive producer, legal advisers and the producer at one of their weekly sessions. Only when an episode has cleared all these hurdles is it ready for screening. That master tape is sent to Thames Studios in Teddington to be copied on to the various formats for showing overseas and on Carlton Television in Britain.

Friday, 1 July, 8 p.m. 'A Touch of Braid' transmitted.

Identity Parade: The Stars of Sun Hill

SGT. MATTHEW BOYDEN

Sergeant Matthew Boyden seems to have enough conflict in his private life for all the officers at Sun Hill put together. For 'private' read 'sex'. But it's the effect of his relationships with women and with the people he meets on the street on his professional life that makes compelling viewing. Boyden's bothers, like Roach's revels, delight us as they horrify his senior officers. Unlike Roach, he actually *likes* women, too.

Born in Margate, his summer jobs on a funfair for holidaymakers allowed him to polish his patter and showed him that making girls laugh paid dividends. He left school at seventeen, wasted time in a couple of clerical jobs before joining the force in 1975. Transferred twice as a PC, he took his sergeant's exams twice and passed them in 1985, aged thirty. By then he was happily married with a young daughter, but on a training course at Hendon he had an affair with a woman officer. It put the kybosh on his marriage and his chances of further promotion for a good many years.

In his years stationed at Romford, his sparkle returned and he became a popular colleague, a charmer of the public. His smart appearance owed a lot to careful planning. There was always a clean shirt in his locker, and a shaver, toothbrush and breath-freshener in his drawer. He made his peace with his ex-wife, who remarried. But a foolish affair with a WDS, which soon became public, meant that his Romford days were numbered. Early in 1992 he arrived at Sun Hill, full of good intentions. His superiors had been given the nod, though. They knew his style of policing didn't fit the newer rules. He's an opportunist. He's not dishonest, but if someone wants to buy him 'a drink' he doesn't say no. So when, at Christmas 1993, his quick action

trapped thieves who had just raided an electrical shop, and the owner offered Boyden a CD player as a 'thank-you', he said to himself: 'Why not?' He placed it on the back seat of the Panda where, as luck would have it, the Inspector saw it and was suspicious. As soon as he could, Boyden was back in the shop asking for a receipt as proof of purchase! He got it, and his boss had to accept it. To Boyden it was a perk of the job.

This summer there has been more proof of Boyden's fatal attraction for women. It was nearly fatal to his career, when the affair with the wife of an officer at Barton Street almost led to a charge of accepting a £300 bribe. Luckily Boyden had been tipped off by yet another woman friend. He told Monroe in advance, and the handing-over of this

Boyden escapes from the station sometimes - to take charge of constables such as Jarvis

package of 'information' (the money) was seen for what it was: a trap. It did not stop Boyden from a thrashing by the woman's husband, who had beaten her, too. In another episode this year Boyden went to the aid of a woman whose husband had battered her. She, we gathered, was yet another of his 'old flames'.

Tony O'Callaghan

Tony O'Callaghan studied acting early – only he didn't know it. 'My mum was one of those ladies who wore maroon suits and carried a torch – a cinema usherette – at the Odeon in Golders Green,' he recalls. 'She used to sneak me into a seat on the back row, chuck me a packet of Maltesers and know I was happy while she worked.'

He certainly was happy as one of the few lads of his age who could 'do' scenes from *Lawrence of Arabia*, with music and sound effects. Or *Mary Poppins* extracts in a spot-on Dick Van Dyke voice. Or do anything else that had been playing the week before. He enjoyed school drama productions, but when a teacher offered to get him a part in a Watford Palace show he bottled out at the last minute. 'I just wasn't ready,' he says.

So he went to college and then to work in an architect's office, then in an engineering factory. But when his boss reprimanded him for returning late from a holiday he found himself saying: 'I was going to give my notice in anyway. I'm going to be an actor.'

It was, he thinks now, a bit of Boyden-style boldness and risk-taking. 'My boss looked at me as though I was a complete idiot. And when I began turning up at auditions at RADA and other drama schools with no preparation whatsoever I was behaving like an idiot.'

He got better at it, though. The Drama Centre at Chalk Farm accepted him, and he emerged to work steadily in rep for ten years. He played a policeman in 'Safe House', the BBC's drama-documentary about the Guildford bombings, survived four lines as someone's boyfriend in an episode of 'Terry and June' – even though, in his state of nerves, he pulled the door handle off the set door. He appeared in 'The Upper Hand' and the BBC's 'Children of the North' serial. He was also, briefly, Danny Moran, a would-be getaway driver waylaid by Viv Martella in 'The Bill'.

'I had such a good time then that I was delighted when two years later they asked me to join,' says the softly spoken thirty-eight-year-old bachelor whose spare time is taken up with tinkering with his sports-car, a vintage MGB.

His sack of fan mail may be heavy, but he denies that his private life in any way resembles his character's.

'My present girlfriend, who's a nursery nurse, and I have been together for two years. I wouldn't have the guts to have affairs at the rate he has them.'

CH. INSP. PHILIP CATO

They don't often go for 'bold strokes' when they create characters in 'The Bill'. But few who have seen Inspector Philip Cato forget the man they call 'the bald-headed bastard from Barton Street'. His strokes were legendary – but, then, Barton Street became by reputation television's answer to the once much-criticized West Midlands Police Force.

Legendary, too, were Cato's grudges against police officers he thought had worked against him. A Barton Street colleague, Inspector Twist, had a run-in with Sun Hill's former Sergeant Penny. Penny was then charged with drink-driving and dismissed from the force. At Sun Hill they believed Penny had been 'fitted up', and Cato had played a part in it. (Well, he had – for Philip Whitchurch, who now plays Cato, also played Twist.)

When Cato transferred to Sun Hill early in 1993,

he thought he'd have some allies there. But Sergeant Ray Steele distanced himself – he angered Cato by posting on the notice-boards a meeting-report including an off-the-record remark. Similarly PC Jarvis, who was also at Barton Street, has shown he is no Cato poodle.

Cato doesn't think he's abrasive. He'd describe himself as a no-nonsense person who has little patience with bureaucracy or sociological theorizing. But he's clever enough to disguise it in the company of his superiors sometimes. With others he doesn't put on an act. He's confrontational both on the street with suspects and in the station with Sun Hill officers. And what's wrong with that?

Philip Whitchurch

Actor Philip Whitchurch keeps a wickedly funny image in his mind when playing crabby Inspector Cato. It may be a slur on a fine woman who does charitable works, but it explains the man's bitterness. It's of Cato returning home each night to his lady wife – to find her slumped in her chair, drunk.

'I think of him as a man who doesn't have any friends; nobody likes him. And when he finally gets home, hoping for something of a welcome, his wife will have got fed up and hit the sherry. She's quietly sozzled!' says Philip with a twinkle.

'It helps to explain why he's a vindictive person, who can't ever forgive and forget. I've met people like him – not policemen – who won't let things lie and who have no respect for others. There's a dark side to Cato, and he's great fun to play. After all, there are a lot of nice guys in this station; they need a wicked uncle.'

Liverpool-born Philip, who now lives in Chiswick with his actress wife and his two-year-old son Matthew, may look similar to his character – they both lost their hair young – but the actor's quick humour would make Cato deeply suspicious.

He didn't begin his working life as an actor. He began and abandoned two apprenticeships before training as a teacher in English and drama. After teaching for a year in Manchester, he began working in community theatre, acting and writing children's plays.

'I enjoy acting, but it can be frustrating if you don't have much creative imput; that's why I've always written as well.'

In the early 1980s he began to appear more and more on television. In 'Coronation Street' he came to decorate Mavis's flat. He starred in the comedy series 'The Brothers McGregor', and in Alan Bleasdale's 'Scully' he was Castanets, the caretaker with rattling false teeth. In the same writer's 'GBH' serial, Philip played the council leader's chauffeur brother, the one in a permanent huff. He also appeared in a memorable episode of 'Casualty' as a farmer who has a breakdown and shoots his own child.

In late 1993 he was able to take a break from Sun Hill to appear in the period adventure series 'Sharpe', filmed in the Ukraine. His performance as officer Frederikson was screened in May 1994. 'Again I looked gruesome – false teeth, false eye, damaged jaw,' he says. 'You hardly recognized me – I hope.'

His wife Sally Edwards appeared in an episode of 'The Bill', "Sweetness and Light", playing a mother of a child in trouble. Philip hopes they'll both have time to do a stage-play together next year.

When there are spare hours, he tries to spend them in the attic, writing. 'I do what I can before Matthew climbs up the ladder to "help",' he sighs.

CH. INSP. DEREK CONWAY

Dogged Acting Superintendent Derek Conway may seem a straightforward old-fashioned copper, but he hasn't got where he is today without cunning. In his eyes real police work begins and ends on the streets – not behind desks or in the files of well-meaning experts. Dour, determined that none shall be promoted to a role that threatens his, that may be his style. But he has still been valuable to Sun Hill. His organizational abilities and his talents as a negotiator are second to none.

He has also been a means of bringing humour into the programme. For beneath that gruff exterior a prudish prat is occasionally to be seen. When he was determined to improve the station's reputation for orderliness, he went poking around looking for stashes of drink, which are officially banned from the premises. At one point he was caught searching in Inspector Christine Frazer's filing cabinet, and was found in possession of a pair of her knickers.

Last year it seemed that his boss Brownlow had no time for him and had put a block on his career. He got around that. He had a pal at HQ who wangled his name on to the shortlist when the new job of Community Liaison Officer was to be filled at Sun Hill. He hardly seemed the ideal candidate for the job, having never expressed an interest in race relations. But it became gradually clear that this was part of his plan. The CLO job was a route to

someone who found he really did care, and this surprised him and changed him. And when he suspected that he would get promotion I tried to play him with a sparkle in his eye. Mind you, if something happens that he doesn't like, he could easily revert to being an utter bastard.'

Unlike single-minded Conway, forty-six-year-old Ben, from Bangor, North Wales, dithered about his career.

'I left home at seventeen and ran screaming out of town. Some Welsh people are so narrow-minded. I can't stand them,' he says.

He went to London and studied catering; didn't like it and switched to a course training as an electrical engineer, like his father. Then he became friendly with a group involved in amateur dramatics.

'After some persuasion, I found I liked it myself,' he says. Aged twenty-five, he attended the Webber Douglas Academy and admits he was still messing around until the threat to throw him out concentrated his mind.

On leaving he worked as an assistant stage manager at the Pitlochry Festival in Scotland. While starring in his first spear-carrying role, he met his future wife, actress Helen Lloyd, playing the leading lady. 'It was love on opening night,' he says. They married in 1981; and he and Helen, who is now a producer with Central Television, have a son, Joe, aged nine.

It wasn't until he took the role of Conway in 1988 that his family in Wales considered that he had 'a proper job'. He jokes: 'They thought I must be gay to be an actor, especially as I got married late, at thirty-three.'

When not busy with scripts, Ben's favourite job is cooking and working on the family's Victorian house.

His favourite episode remains 'Beer and Bicycles', the snooping-in-colleagues'- lockers one. 'But that's still referred to here as a classic example of what to avoid because it's far too close to pantomime,' he chuckles. He also has fond memories of an episode when Conway as CLO dealt with a young single mother and her crying baby. 'We were up to our knees in mud one minute and off to court with the baby screaming non-stop the next.'

In May this year Ben took the role of a seedy, vacuous game-show host in the play *Blood Money* at Derby Playhouse, which is near his home in Nottinghamshire. 'It was exhausting but very exciting,' he says.

He usually commutes to Sun Hill's South London location several times a week. And, as he didn't stop filming the 'Bill' stories during the play's three-week

promotion to superintendent. And when he started to do the job he found to his surprise that it was interesting.

He also found that by giving up his membership of the Round Table and joining the Masonic Lodge his prospects improved. Certainly Brownlow, also a Mason, seems to have warmed to him.

Derek Conway's recent promotion to acting superintendent took most of his colleagues by surprise. It may not last, but he'll enjoy it while it does. But possibly it did not surprise his family. Perhaps his happy home life with his wife, two sons and a daughter, whose photographs appear in his office, is the basis of his success.

Ben Roberts

Ben Roberts is no fan of his character Derek Conway, but he can't fault the man's talent for survival. 'He has always been scheming and career-minded, resenting younger, better-educated officers. But it's been intriguing the way he developed in Community Liaison,' he says. 'He wasn't looking forward to it – he had felt it was a necessary means to an end. He seemed to understand the implications of the Sheehy Report faster than many at the Met.

'But, having got there, he discovered things about society. It re-educated him. I decided to play him as

run, it meant he had to leave home at dawn, speed south, pack his Conway scenes into the mornings and then dash to railway stations.

Conway would call that living dangerously. And disapprove.

WPC SUZI CROFT

Sparky WDC Suzi Croft is the first trainee investigator Sun Hill has had. But don't expect her to be grateful. She soon found out that the training was mainly in doing all the rotten jobs that the other CID officers could avoid when she was around. These ranged from fetching the tea to checking the files. She was rarely allowed to be present at 'the kill' and naturally could not share in the glory when a search or a raid was successful. Thank goodness for the courses she was sent on and on which she shone.

She never hid her forthright views and her disapproval of sexist remarks and attitudes – and Burnside and Woods, among her male colleagues, soon learned how to 'wind her up'. But she soon worked out what was happening, understood the politics of the station, persevered and proved she had a terrier-like toughness. What's more, unlike many of her colleages, she could whiz through the paperwork, writing reports with ease and style. This summer she attended the Met's interviewing course and had no hesitation in criticizing Woods's way of trying to obtain a confession.

Welsh-born, Suzi, now in her mid-twenties, had done well at school and had travelled. She had also had a couple of jobs before joining the police. She was a WPC for two years before applying for a move to CID. She was sent to Crime first, but now works on Bumblebee under the supervision of DS Grieg, whom she likes and – more important – trusts. You couldn't say that for Skase. He's a chauvinist pig in her eyes. They've clashed once. It's sure to happen again. If he can't attack her for her views, he could tease her for her bright fashionable clothes. She doesn't see why a detective should dress in that other dullest of uniforms: so-called good taste.

Kerry Peers

Kerry Peers first appeared in 'The Bill' huddled in an upstairs bedroom of a house, quaking after being raped and terrorized by a burglar. The producer liked that performance and waited for the right regular role to arise for her.

That was 1991. These days, we'd be surprised if she didn't grab any number of seven-foot brutes and reduce them to jelly with a sharp word and a shake of her blob of black curls.

The diminutive actress – she's five feet one and three-quarters – wishes she were more like her right-on character. 'I suppose I share her views, although I'm not fanatical. But she's far braver and smarter than I am,' she says. 'I decided to make her a real feminist, into women's rights and other liberal causes. I thought it would be difficult for her not to react in a male environment like the police force.

'I enjoyed one of my first episodes in which she hardly said anything but Burnside and Woods picked on her all the way through. But she objected to the way they'd treated someone and she was determined to let her views be known. It was quite nerve-racking for her.

'Then there was another episode in which the uniformed people were short-staffed and Croft had to get into uniform and go out with McCann. He assumed she was soft – so she had to prove herself by tackling this huge villain and fighting with him. She won, of course. She always does!'

Kerry enrolled on a beauty therapy course when she left school in her home town of Clwyd. 'That seems amazing to me now. I'd done drama at school

– well, the alternatives were games or typing – and I'd joined the local youth theatre and had good reviews. But I didn't have the bottle to take it further.

'My mother bought all the gear for me to go on the beauty course. But, just before I started, I met a couple of actors I knew from Theatre Clwyd, and they gave me that push I needed. My mother and sister were horrified when I told them I wanted to be an actress not a beautician – but they were incredibly supportive later on, especially when I was out of work.'

After training, Kerry spent two years in the theatre, played Bathsheba in *Far from the Madding Crowd* on stage in Bolton before her first television role came up. It was a dream of a job – three weeks of filming in Florence with actor Alfred Molina in a film called *The Marshall*.

A stint on an industrial estate in Merton – the real Sun Hill – may seem less glamorous. But twenty-nine-year-old Kerry, who lives in South London with her long-term partner, actor Patrick Bridgman, was delighted when the offer came through.

There was just one snag, though. 'I thought: Should I tell them how short I am – surely far too small for a policewoman – or hope they don't notice? In the end I said nothing. Much later I found out that they'd abolished the height rules as a way of recruiting more oriental women. So I needn't have felt guilty.'

WPC NORIKA DATTA

When PC Phil Young became obsessed with his colleague WPC Norika Datta, sexually assaulted her and confronted her again in her room, he made enemies of millions of male fans of 'The Bill'. For good-natured Norika, the cop with the super smile, has been a favourite since she joined Sun Hill five years ago.

During her ordeal with Young, Norika's nerve held, just as it has during all the sticky moments the scriptwriters have dreamed up for her. Perhaps that's because she learned to listen and be tactful as a junior in a hairdresser's before she decided to take on the challenge of police work. It has been a challenge to duck those occasional racist remarks from colleagues as well as to field abuse on the streets.

She isn't a flirt – that's why Young's approach came as such a surprise. And if she ever knew that Jim Carver had a crush on her she didn't let on. But, then, she's a confident woman whose home life with her parents, Kenyan Asians who run a newsagent's

shop in Uxbridge, has always been secure. She has a white boyfriend, Peter, who is a sports teacher. When they go out in his sports-car, the thieves, vandals, non-copers and no-hopers of the streets of Sun Hill seem a long way away.

This isn't her first posting and probably won't be

her last. At the start of 1993, she began working with the Domestic Violence Unit and has done valuable work, especially when Asian women are involved. She has learned to gain the trust of victims of abuse by never seeming to judge them – something which her boss Cato cannot master. Her male colleagues take her for granted sometimes – offloading matters they suspect will be tedious on the grounds that if they involve women they must be domestic violence. She's toughening up. So they'd better beware.

Seeta Indrani

Seeta Indrani would like the gang at Sun Hill to have more parties. It would give Datta a chance to dance. Who knows, a bit of flamenco in the force mightn't be a bad thing.

'We used to have more functions than we do now – leaving-parties, Christmas parties, those sorts of

Norika Datta, one of the lads, but not always smiling

things. It meant we could get dressed up – it was always fun,' says the London-born actress whose current passion is the exotic Spanish style of dance.

As it is, she has to make do with choreographing flamenco and other dance routines for others and giving brief but memorable demonstrations as she did for 1993's Children in Need appeal.

Sleek Seeta, who's in her late thirties, trained as a dancer at the London School of Contemporary Dance but decided to switch to acting, 'because it has a longer life', taking a year of intensive classes at the Actors' Centre. To widen it further, she took herself to singing classes, training a strong soprano voice for operatic roles.

She was one of the original cast of *Cats*. She joined the RSC and played the Chinese girl in *Poppy* and Tiger Lily in *Peter Pan*. Among other theatrical roles, she played Lady Percy in *Henry IV* in a season at the Oxford Playhouse.

She has sung on television, in productions of *Dido and Aeneas*; acted in action series such as 'CATS Eyes' and 'Dempsey and Makepeace', and popped up in the 'Brookside' spin-off, 'Damon and Debbie'. And in 1993 she got to dance as the Flamenco teacher in the powerful television film 'Maria's Child'.

For her role in 'The Bill', Seeta has earned an award for Best Supporting Actress from the Asian Film Academy. 'I'm glad there is always the odd racist remark – it's right, within the context of what we're doing. But it would be boring if they always made a point of the fact that I'm not white.

'I've enjoyed my time as Datta, especially an episode called "They Also Serve", which was a story about a team of us, Ackland, Quinnan, Hollis and Delia Williams among them, waiting in a transit van to see if we were needed as back-up during a demo.'

'We were encouraged to improvise around the script, and it was a terrific long scene with lots of tension. It was then that PC Young started to show an interest in Datta. I can remember thinking: What's going on? Should Datta flirt with him? Then I decided it wouldn't be in her character. When Colin Alldridge, who played Young, and I came to shoot the scene where he suddenly appears in her room, it was very creative. But there was so much to learn and think about!'

Seeta, like many of the female members of the cast, has mixed feelings about filming the rough stuff. 'Sometimes the young male actors get a little too enthusiastic. It's a bit like a football team.'

When she's not learning lines, Seeta throws herself into dance classes. 'Singing and dancing is something I do for myself. No one has to pay me for those,' she says.

DS CHRIS DEAKIN

They call it conduct unbecoming a copper. DS Chris Deakin, formerly a high-flier in the Flying Squad, calls it rotten luck. All right, having an affair with a colleague's wife was out of order, but he wasn't exactly breaking up a happy home and it didn't interfere with his work as a thief-taker, did it? That is, and always has been, damn good.

Still, this Londoner was a cop long before PACE put them all under pressure to be squeaky clean and politically correct. He took the demotion from inspector to sergeant with a shrug. He bears scars, but his skin is growing thicker all the time.

Not that coming to Sun Hill this summer was easy. The rumours arrived ahead of him. 'Bit of a stud,' the women heard in the canteen. 'Another Boyden,' was the way it sounded to the men. Then in walks this sandy-haired harmless-looking chap in his late thirties who didn't look as if he posed a threat to anyone.

Villains knew different. Deakin came into Sun Hill station after a day at the Old Bailey where he'd given evidence which had put a couple of men away for eight years apiece.

DI Johnson soon learned different. He stitched her up good and proper over Travis, who used to be Roach's snout. Meadows had put Deakin on to him

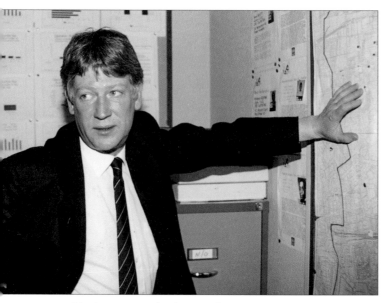

Deakin is a man who knows the territory and what goes with it

after a building society robbery. Deakin knew exactly how to handle him and protect him. But Johnson wanted to 'run' him, too. No go. Deakin saw to that.

Deakin and Johnson have clashed several times since. They were bound to: he has problems accepting women as equals let alone as superiors. She has problems with cops who do their own thing behind their boss's back.

Jim Carver seems to like his new DS, although he, too, has had his disputes with him. Deakin doesn't taunt people the way Burnside did. But more and more of his colleagues are finding that he seems to have some of that detective's style, guile and guts.

Shaun Scott

At one point fair-haired Shaun Scott thought he'd lost his chance to play the new baddie in 'The Bill'. The producers liked him but felt that rotters should really be dark-haired.

Someone must have remembered sneering sarcastic DI 'Ginger' Galloway, and luckily Shaun was asked back and hired. Then his worries began.

'When I read the scripts I saw that Deakin's image before he arrived was as some sort of sex symbol,' says the actor who says his hobby is panicking about the next job. 'That makes any actor nervous because as you walk through the door, holding your tummy in but looking your usual, ordinary, unglamorous self, everyone thinks: "That can't be him, can it?" '

Having survived that, thirty-eight-year-old Shaun thought his best policy should be 'to keep my head down and get on with it – like Deakin'.

Which is what he has done – with more and more enjoyment, he says – for the past few months.

'I decided Deakin was a man who basically doesn't give a stuff for what others think about him. He's a very self-possessed individual.

'I live close to Kensington police station and have known a sergeant there for years. He introduced me to a former Flying Squad officer, who told me some of the things that have happened to him and how people in his past often haunt his present. What he told me was amazing – so I think of Deakin as having been involved in similar capers.

'It's great fun to play the villain because society doesn't allow you to get your own back often, to stitch people up if they've done the dirty on you. But villains make it their business.'

Shaun's Irish mother was a district health officer whose work meant that the family moved a lot when he was young. So he went to a boarding school where boys left for university, to join the professions or the armed forces. Shaun wasn't too keen on any of those options but went for an interview with Surrey Police.

'I realized it wasn't for me. So to reduce the pressure I told the headmaster that I quite fancied becoming an actor. That reduced the pressure – to disbelief!'

But the headmaster turned out a 'hero'. By chance he met Sir Bernard Miles at a charity dinner and told him of Shaun's wish. Sir Bernard gave the lad a job as a stagehand at his Mermaid Theatre. He rose to become an assistant stage manager, then to take a television role in 'The Cedar Tree' as the gardener's helper and to join the National Theatre as a walk-on. At the same time he won a place at RADA.

His 'legit' career began in 1979 with a lead role in the play *Translations*. He then played Jack Fairchild (of the Union of Captwisters and Allied Trades) in the television comedy series 'Brass'; was in two major plays for the BBC before returning to the stage to appear in *The Shaughraun*, then *Heartbreak House* with Vanessa Redgrave and Paul Scofield. Then came a run in the musical *Crazy for You* as a 'demented landlord'.

He can hardly complain of a lack of variety because no sooner had that ended than, before he'd had a moment to panic, 'The Bill' was on the telephone. They knew his work because Shaun had actually taken two guest roles – one in 1992 as a slob of a landlord, one as Martella's 'bit of rough', a villain who ran a gym, a couple of years earlier.

'My only problem with Deakin has been learning to speak "Croydon" in a natural way,' he jokes. 'Every so often, I found "Kensington" was creeping in.'

PC GEORGE GARFIELD

You could call young PC George Garfield uncomplicated. Or you could be honest and call him a bit thick. Put it this way: he's unlikely to make sergeant. But, though he'd be no use helping you finish your crossword, he's a bloke you can rely on when the thumping and kicking starts. Subtlety may be lost on him, but he can do the job and he likes doing it, more and more.

Londoner George joined the Met at nineteen because it was steady employment and he'd not had much luck with other jobs he'd tried since leaving school. But he didn't much like the leafy suburb of Teddington, to which he was sent – too dull – and used up his excess energy in the boxing ring. He reached ABA quarter finals standard. He's a pretty fair snooker-player, too.

After repeated requests for a posting to a busier manor, he was transferred to Sun Hill early in 1989. He gets on with most of the people there. Stamp is a good mate. He has had run-ins with Quinnan and Loxton, both of whom can be a bit aggressive if rubbed up the wrong way. Unlike them, Garfield can control his temper. But he can bear a grudge with the best of them.

Now the Federation rep, he rates his predecessor in that union role, Reg Hollis, as 'a complete log, a waste of space'. But, like so many others, he has been taken under the wing of Bob Cryer more than once. He needed a calm father figure to advise him when everything seemed to be going wrong for him and it seemed that his second name was Gullible.

He had money troubles before the night of the party for his twenty-fifth birthday, but they got worse after it. He'd hired a room only to have Quinnan and Carver wreck it by fighting over a girl. Garfield had to pay for the repairs, which meant he had to return the flash XR3 Convertible car he'd just started buying on instalments, against the advice of his bank manager.

Lending the key of his section-house room to Loxton – who was spotted nipping up the stairs with a nurse, against the rules – was another black mark against his name. But his colleagues were on his side when Boyden let him down – nipping off to see one of his women friends and leaving him to be beaten up by the villain

Garfield with pals Loxton (left), Quinnan (right) and a suspicious-looking animal

they were supposed to be trailing. Garfield was knocked down and concussed. There were bets on if and when Garfield might get his own back. They were safe bets. Boyden learned about Garfield's right hook – the hard way.

Young women seem to be immune to the Garfield charm. There was some chance he was getting something together with a WPC whom he invited for a pizza. She never reappeared. Perhaps she's going out with Boyden.

Huw Higginson

Unlike Garfield, his character, Huw Higginson has nothing against Teddington. He has lived there since he was eight when his actor father Tim Wilton moved the family south from Stratford upon Avon where he'd been working with the RSC.

It would have been strange had Huw not become an actor – his mother Ann Curthoys used to act and is now an agent; his sister is actress Emma Higginson and, when his parents split and his mother remarried, actor Roger Walker (who was Bunny in 'Eldorado') became Huw's stepfather.

'They tried to put me off – to send me to university instead,' says thirty-year-old Huw. 'But I'd had quite a few parts as a child actor and had worked alongside Dad at the RSC, as a page, upstaging Alan Howard in mid-soliloquy, and they really couldn't put me off.

'Before I went to drama school, I took a year off and filled in with about twelve jobs. I kept getting sacked: sacked from Bentalls bookshop for stacking the books the wrong way round; sacked on the spot as a labourer for sticking a pick through a mains pipe. The only jobs I was any good at were washing up in a fish and chip shop and scaffolding – but I couldn't stand heights.'

Luckily he hasn't had to. For he was in demand for theatre and television work before getting into uniform in 1989. He had roles in series including 'Floodtide', 'How We Used to Live' and in the BBC film 'Defrosting the Fridge'. He came close to playing the boyfriend of Lisa Geoghan's character in 'Big Deal' but opted to take a stage role instead.

Huw did boxing at school but says he's nowhere near as good at it as George and is glad the only opponent he has had on screen is a punchbag. These days his sports are golf, football, cricket, fly fishing and fishing for bargains at car boot sales for the flat he shares with his girlfriend.

He doesn't think he could ever do a policeman's job. 'It's a way of thinking that most actors don't have. But when you're out on the street, wearing the uniform, the looks people give you help. Your back straightens, your shoulders go back, you feel different!'

DS ALISTAIR GREIG

DS Alistair Greig is not your average tight-lipped Scottish cop. There's a bit of the Presbyterian righteousness about him, but he has seen too much of the world in his time on the Vice Squad at West End Central before he transferred to Sun Hill nearly six years ago for him to judge his colleagues or his 'customers'. He is also bright, having done the first two years of a law degree before deciding that law enforcement at the sharp end was more to his liking.

He's ambitious and straight as a die, but clever enough to watch and wait before taking a position. So it was when he first encountered Burnside, his first boss at Sun Hill. He was appalled at the man's corner-cutting, but soon came to appreciate his skill. You don't get results like Burnside's without a bit of rule-bending.

His colleagues were impressed at his early cheekiness: he played his clarinet in the office, feet up on the desk. They laughed behind his back when Burnside had a go at it. They still make fun of his reluctance to get his hands dirty with a truculent

suspect. It's not prissiness, though; Greig simply believes he can talk most people out of anything – even thumping him with a crowbar.

As far as women are concerned – he's safe. His snobbishness would stop him having an affair with an officer of lower rank, if his courage didn't fail him first. He has had a fiancée for years.

When a woman witness flirted with him and questioned him about his romantic life he was unsettled. Lucky he can treat Suzi Croft as 'one of the boys', isn't it?

Burnside (left) and Roach are serenaded by Greig

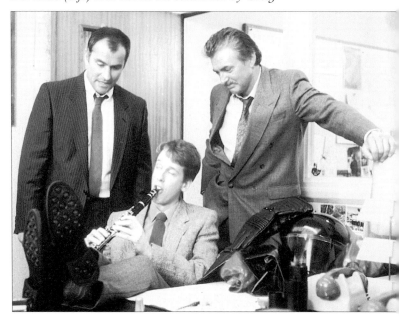

combining performing with directing the music. At Liverpool's Everyman Theatre he met Lucy, then working for Granada Television. 'It was interest across a crowded bar at first sight,' he says. 'Neither of us intended to settle down, but we were married within months.'

Andy's other television roles include an estate agent in 'Coronation Street', a diabetic choirboy in the drama 'Every Breath You Take' and a small role in 'Game, Set and Match'.

WPC DONNA HARRIS

Many's the villain who'd volunteer to have his collar felt by pretty blonde WPC Harris, one of the most pleasant, straightforward young women to work at Sun Hill. It's their loss that she works mainly in the station.

A Yorkshire lass, she left her family and friends and came to London to join the Met when she was twenty-one. She wanted to do a worthwhile job. She also wanted to make a clean break from sad memories. Her husband had been killed in a car crash there. She married again six years later, this time a man many years older who had a daughter

Meadows gives Greig a hard time

Andrew Mackintosh

One thing's certain: actor Andy Mackintosh can never complain about difficult days on 'The Bill'. At least, he can't to his wife, Lucy Abercrombie, who used to be a casting director for the series. A couple of years back the couple decided to move from North London to a cottage near Stevenage in Hertfordshire, a fifty-minute drive from the series's base.

They decided it would make no sense if their two small daughters, Melissa, aged four, and Ottilie, aged three, saw little of both their parents because they were spending so many hours travelling. So Lucy stays at home with the girls and their baby, born in June, doing the hard job. Andy has fun impersonating a detective and chatting with her former colleagues and friends.

'Actually, I wouldn't complain anyway,' says thirty-four-year-old Andy. 'I love playing Greig even though he has this short haircut and I have to remember to take my earring out before I go in front of the camera.'

Andy was born in Pennsylvania when his father was working in electronics there. When he was five, the job moved the family to Anstruther, Scotland. At school there, Andy picked up two essentials for playing DS Greig: a Scots accent and an ability to play the clarinet, to fit Greig's background as a member of the Met band. The family moved south, and Andy went to Bristol University to study English. But his love of drama and music – he 'plays everything except the bagpipes' – made him switch to drama school. He was soon working in the theatre

from his first marriage. It was the security she wanted, and in the next year she transferred to Sun Hill to become Collator, hoping the regular hours would mean she'd have more time with her family. It did, and the family has grown: she gave birth to their son, now a toddler.

Because she has a happy home life and she knows she's efficient at her job, Donna doesn't have to take flak from her male colleagues. Any 'Be a good girl and . . .' routines earn quick put-downs. Last year she became the analyst for the burglary initiative, Bumblebee. She started it up at Sun Hill, and the work entails her visiting other police stations.

Louise Harrison

Louise Harrison realized that a policewoman's lot can be a stressful one when her character Donna Harris took part in the reconstruction of events leading up to a young woman's being brutally raped and murdered. The episodes were fiction but, sadly, they mirrored fact.

For Donna 'played' the victim and was filmed walking on Wimbledon Common. Just before they were due to be screened, in the summer of 1992, a young mother with blonde hair like Louise's, was murdered on the same seemingly safe common. There was also a reconstruction in the hope of jogging the memory of witnesses.

'Donna is usually office-bound. So I tend to remember the scenes when I'm let out. And because those episodes reflected such a shocking murder they stand out for me,' says Louise. 'When we started filming it was a cold day. But the day we did the actual walk, two weeks later, it was about 86 °F and we were trying to look cool and collected. '

Louise, from Cheshire, reckons she could never have been a police officer – she has the wrong temperament. Anyway, she was determined to become an actress from when she was a teenager. It ran in the family – her father lectured in drama at Manchester University, and her sister teaches it.

Perhaps because she grew up aware that acting can mean long spells of unemployment, she took a secretarial course before going to the Welsh College of Music and Drama. 'It was to be something to fall back on, and I have fallen back on it,' she says, smiling. 'I was never the world's most brilliant secretary but I'm OK as a receptionist.'

After several stage jobs, Louise was cast as a nurse in the BBC2 serial 'A Very Peculiar Practice' and then, after many guest television roles, wound up as Dawn Prescott, one of the women to fall prey to baddie

Alan Bradley in 'Coronation Street'. Dawn later returned to have a fling with the soap's resident Lothario, Mike Baldwin.

While working on that series, Louise became friendly with actress Sally Whittaker, who plays Sally Webster, and the two are still firm friends enjoying impromptu holidays together when their equally busy schedules allow.

In her three years at Sun Hill, thirty-one-year-old Louise has never regretted putting on that unglamorous uniform. She used to worry a lot about her appearance – as a schoolgirl, she was so sensitive to remarks about her weight that she developed the eating disorder bulimia and became dangerously thin for a time, to the anguish of her parents. Now she stays slim healthily with visits to a gym and a swimming pool.

And she prefers to stick to classic styles – in clothes and in hair. 'My worst moment was when I dyed my hair pink. I tried hard to grow it out, but it all turned green. I was at a boarding school, and it didn't go down at all well.'

PC MIKE JARVIS

Tall confident Londoner PC Mike Jarvis arrived at Sun Hill from Barton Street in February 1993, after four years in the force, to find his new colleagues were wary. They were waiting to see how close to Inspector Cato, also from Barton Street, he turned out to be. They didn't have to wait long. Jarvis put as much distance between himself and his unpopular boss as he could. It became clear that he did not approve of some of the older man's methods.

It also became clear, as the months went by, that he is unimpressed by some of his new colleagues, too. He finds Loxton's approach sometimes unprofessional; he seems not to trust Boyden; but he gets on well with Quinnan and Garfield. He looks down, in both senses of the words, on some of the women. But there may be a spark of something for Polly Page. She doesn't know it, though.

Jarvis can be bad-tempered, but he's a valuable

member of the team. And good in the police rugby team, too. And long legs can be useful when the only way on to one tower-block balcony is from another tower-block balcony. With Jarvis it's 'Just step this way'.

Stephen Beckett

There he was, peaked police hat pulled down, stern-faced, square jaw jutting, long legs striding. Up the garden path went actor Stephen Beckett as PC Jarvis about to tackle a man who'd let a dangerous dog loose. Manly hand on the door knocker, rat-tat 'Aoow!' The actor caught a finger in the knocker and he couldn't help showing the crew that it didn't half hurt.

So much for macho acting, sighs Stephen. It's a good job the villain and his dog hadn't seen one of his early incarnations – as a spirit covered in blue paint and little else in *A Midsummer Night's Dream*.

Teacher's son Stephen, from Brixton, London, hadn't thought of acting as a career until he'd gone to see Derek Jacobi in *Cyrano de Bergerac* at the RSC. 'I suddenly thought: I'd love to do that,' he says. Two months later he sat his A-levels and failed them. That put paid to plans to go to university. So plan B – hatched with pal Joseph Bennett – to do something glamorous, like acting, came into play.

He applied and won a place at the Royal Academy of Dramatic Art, worked in fringe theatre and cabaret in his spare time and, after leaving RADA, joined Oldham theatre for a role in Shakespeare's *Richard II*. A small part in the film *Enchanted April* came his way. 'Lots of dancing of the Charleston wearing a tuxedo,' he recalls.

Then came the very different role in 'The Bill'. To research it he shadowed officers at Bethnal Green police station. 'Officers there told me hair-raising stories of drugs fights with machetes and guns. They seem to develop a very dark sense of humour. I'm glad I don't have to deal with that sort of aggression for real.'

Twenty-seven-year-old Stephen is, like his character, single. 'But I think of Jarvis as having a crush on Polly Page. I'm sure he's looking for love,' he jokes. 'I hope the writers allow a hint of it some time.'

So far one of his hardest tasks has been to play rugby convincingly on screen in the episode 'Pals'. He'd only ever played football at school. And he has a confession to make about the balcony heroics he performed, saving a pregnant woman in the episode 'Push': the long legs were a stuntman's.

DI SALLY JOHNSON

Bright-eyed DI Sally 'Magic' Johnson believes she is God's gift to policing and she may turn out to be just that so long as her interpretation of means-to-an-end tallies with the Met's.

She grew up in London, and it was soon clear to her West Indian family that she had brains. They were somewhat surprised when after university she chose to use them in the police force, but she rose through the ranks very quickly and now she loves going to work, loves being in control of others and, above all, loves catching thieves.

She charges along the corridors with her subordinates trying to keep up. Her easy manner wins her friends and takes the starch out of some of the senior officers. But on occasions her know-it-all air can be irritating. The word 'delegate' is not in her vocabulary – she enjoys the work on the streets and in the interview room too much for that.

She may not have shown great wisdom in the detectives she has chosen to favour – making Pearce her pet at the start was perhaps a mistake, and she has been clumsy in her treatment of Ackland, whose years of experience she undervalues.

When Lee Ruddick, a drug dealer, died following a police raid in September, Johnson was accused of manslaughter. The private prosecution rattled her, shook her faith in herself badly for the first time. Up till then she had been completely comfortable with her power. From then on she had moments of doubt.

But nothing is likely to slow her down. As for prejudice – she's heard it all before, every sexist, racist remark. If she couldn't deal with it, she wouldn't have got where she is.

Jaye Griffiths

Jaye Griffiths thinks she might have joined the police for real at one stage when she was younger.

'I like all that public-spirited stuff, being there for the good guys. But the things police officers have to do are so frightening. No wonder there's an air of bravado. How else would you cope with that amount of fear from, say, someone standing in front of you holding a knife and knowing that, if you say the wrong thing, you could be dead?'

It's one thing to act DI Johnson, 'the butchest thing this side of the Thames Barrier', and disarm huge men of their machetes without blinking, but another to do that, or have to tell a woman her child is dead, for real.

Jaye did try some real detection work earlier this year after her South London flat was burgled while she took a weekend break in Paris.

'I opened the door, and the place was just wrecked. I was hysterical,' she says.

Some of the missing items were returned quickly after Kent police arrested two men. But Jaye, angry about a missing antique pocket watch, a gift from a former boyfriend, and two clocks which belonged to her late grandmother, began searching local markets and antiques fairs. While the clocks are still 'at large', a stallholder in Greenwich market recognized Jaye's description and produced the watch, horrified to learn it had been stolen.

The daughter of a white Englishwoman and a 1950s immigrant from Barbados who went to work for British Rail, Jaye, like Sally, had a meteoric rise. The North London schoolgirl, good in school plays, worked as a dresser at the Barbican to pay her way through drama school. That cultural shock – 'I met people who ate avocados and had been abroad!' she jokes – prepared her to strike when she came on to the job market in the mid-eighties.

'It was a politically sensitive time in that at least six per cent of the workforce of publicly funded companies had to be people from ethnic minorities. The nearer to white your skin was, the easier it was. And I had long hair. And I didn't kick over the furniture; I could show "good attitude",' she laughs.

So stage work including eighteen months at the RSC, a BBC school series and a non-stop run of television parts came her way. By the start of 1994, in the league of black female faces on television only Oprah Winfrey's could have been more familiar.

Jaye smiled demurely through her Terry-Thomas teeth from the Mercury telephone advertisements. She flounced as the posh PA in 'Love Hurts'. She popped up in the series 'Anna Lee'. Before that she'd played a dopey newsreader in 'Drop the Dead Donkey', and as a right-on journalist she was between the sheets with the policeman hero in early episodes of 'Between the Lines'.

But DI Johnson is her most important part to date, she feels, because the character is a role model . 'If I don't do it right, they must sack me or it's not fair. I'm not really surprised that there are no black women DIs yet. You have to be an extraordinary person to take the flak from the public that every police officer takes. When you're black as well. . . .

'It's just a matter of time. I do believe in changing things from within. And you have to be aware of the political significance of playing a woman in a position of power on television. It's so rare.'

She'd like Johnson to steer clear of racial-issue cases for a while, then tackle some meaty ones, please. 'But people think that all black people are constantly crying "I'm oppressed, I'm oppressed!" They're not. I don't have a problem being black. It's nice.'

DC ALFRED 'TOSH' LINES

DC Tosh Lines is the heroic failure of Sun Hill. He's an instinctual copper, a decent man who understands human weakness because his home life is a happy, difficult, muddle-and-make-do existence. But no superintendent would ever dream of transferring him. He can smell a liar, and his clear-up rate is second to none. Ask any casual viewer of 'The Bill' which characters he likes, and the chances are he'll put Tosh in his list. Geoff McQueen, who created him on paper, believes he is one of his best ideas.

When Tosh arrived at Sun Hill in 1988 from a station in Essex he already had problems that weighed him down. He was in his late thirties, unlikely to be promoted because he never seemed to

would have put him at risk and then where would his children be?

At one stage, to ease his money problems, he took in a student lodger, which is against the Met rules. The young man got into trouble. Sergeant Penny, Custody Officer at the time, discovered this and, rather than turn a blind eye to it, sent a report 'upstairs' as a result of which Tosh was carpeted.

He survived, of course. He's far too good at sniffing out villains for a sniffy little man like Penny to put down.

Kevin Lloyd

Kevin Lloyd has only two complaints about 'The Bill'. He hasn't been able to have a clean shave for six years because the moustache, ordered originally so that he looked different from Burnside, has become a trademark he can't remove.

And, second, it has ruined his figure, he says. When he began in the series in 1988 he was a reasonable 12 stone. The producer said it would help if he put on a few pounds. So he forced himself to tuck in and not to refuse the chips. He found that easy, he adds with a grin. Then the writers added the details to show him constantly eating and drinking at his desk and in his car.

'I did a scene in which my car was going through a carwash and I was eating a Mars bar. We did ten

care that much about his career progress. He didn't look like a tough crime-buster. He was short, overweight – probably because he was always munching snacks on the job. And he was, frankly, scruffy. He seemed to have one suit, one shirt (which he wore from Monday to Friday), one tatty old raincoat. It all matched his car, an ancient Volvo which kept breaking down. More to the point, he had a wife, Muriel, too large a mortgage, caused by too many children – three girls and two boys – for a constable's pay.

He established his credentials as a detective with nous in his first-ever episode, 'An Old-Fashioned Term'. It featured the death of a sixteen-year-old girl which seemed like a suicide. Burnside and Carver said: 'Leave it.' Tosh felt something was wrong and eventually proved it was murder.

Viewers have seen Mrs Lines and the kids in an episode called 'Don't Like Mondays' when they were accidentally involved in a bank raid. He was once offered the chance to go to work in Northern Ireland. Burnside had put him up for it because he thought Tosh needed the money. Tosh turned it down – it

A case of Michael-extraction of Tosh, if we're not mistaken

takes, and I got through ten bars in one morning. I felt dreadful. I couldn't look at those chocolate bars for ages.' Now, he says, he hardly dare look at the bathroom scales, either. He's over 14 stone, he reckons, and he'd be more if he wasn't dashing back and forth from the 'Bill' set to his home in the Derbyshire village of Duffield several times a week.

But he's happy. In fact he so loves the role – 'it fits me to a T' – that he has always felt sorry for the other actor who was shortlisted when they were casting the part.

Part of the satisfaction comes from knowing he's getting it more or less right. So friends of his late father, Ellis Allad Lloyd, nicknamed Taff, tell him. Taff was a detective sergeant in Derby who died when his car skidded on black ice when he was rushing to what turned out to be a false alarm.

'I was twenty-one when he died, and our house had always been full of policemen. Many have kept in touch. One's a chief constable now. I've had calls from him, after an episode has gone out in which Tosh had a lot to do, saying: "That was exactly how Taff would have done it."

'They also jokily ask if Tosh could spare them half an hour because the number of cases he can clear up in that time is amazing! Of course, a real policeman would spend more than twenty minutes of a half-hour on paperwork. Tosh is much luckier.'

Kevin nearly joined the force on leaving school, but his dad thought he'd do better to become a solicitor and the young Lloyd duly signed on as an articled clerk with a local firm. He was bored.

'I joined a local amateur dramatics group, and they encouraged me to go to drama school. So I packed in the law and came to London to train with Joan Littlewood in Stratford E15.'

Littlewood's manner and temper were tougher than most police training officers. She terrified him. 'She was a most extraordinary woman, barracking her actors on their first nights.'

Luckily director Lindsay Anderson took him over. Kevin's performance as the boy in Anderson's production of Joe Orton's *What the Butler Saw* earned the young actor a 'Best Newcomer' nomination.

He went on to work at the Nottingham Playhouse and began becoming a familiar television face in 1978. His tally of roles as cops and as villains was about equal, he thinks. He recalls enjoyable stints as a villain in 'Hazell' and a police sergeant in 'Casualty'. He was also the plumber in 'Auf Wiedersehen Pet' and the ridiculous rock 'n' roller Ricky Fortune in the comedy series 'Dear John'.

He then took a West End stage role in *The Foreigner*

Kevin Lloyd with his screen wife Lesley (Duff) and three of his own children

with Nicholas Lyndhurst during which the call came from 'The Bill'. A six-month contract led to a role he has played for six years so far.

'It has changed my life,' he says with obvious sincerity.

Tosh and Kevin's lives overlap from time to time. The actor may have got to grips with his mortgage and have more than one suit, but their children have been 'shared'.

He and his wife Lesley, a former restaurateur, have seven children including a child now three, adopted during the crisis in Romania when the couple became involved with the charity TREATS, which aims to give treats to underprivileged children. Three of their seven (James, Poppy and Henry) stepped in to play three of Tosh's five children for the bank raid episode. Kevin has often been tempted to refer to Tosh's wife Muriel as Lesley, partly because she's played by actress Lesley Duff.

Kevin hopes one year to fit in a spell of theatre work, ideally playing some Shakespeare. So far he has managed only panto appearances – he'll be the villain in *Jack and the Beanstalk* for the third time at Christmas.

Meanwhile he is staying on the straight and narrow with Tosh, though keeping a straight face isn't always easy. He has been known to suffer from the 'Bill' giggles. It's catching, too.

'My line was "I had a case like that. Never forget a name. Randolph Tangles,"' recalls Kevin. 'I kept messing up the line, and we got to Take 18 and I was looking at the floor when I said it correctly. But we couldn't use it because the director laughed. We got it absolutely right on Take 20 and then the cameraman laughed. So it was Take 21 when we finally got it right – all of us! That's a record.'

PC STEVE LOXTON

Five years ago, when PC Steve Loxton came to Sun Hill from his home in Manchester, he was full of himself, confident that he could do anything the job required. At that time – when there was a recruitment drive on – to have the guts and the gift of the gab was more than enough. Loxton had more – brains, ambition and a soldier's toughness.

Many of his colleagues soon thought of him as loathesome Loxton. He seemed to have no patience with people on the streets. Whether they were villains or victims, he seemed to think they had brought their troubles on themselves. They were probably to blame. If they happened to be black, they were certainly to blame.

Loxton joined the Army when he first left school. He liked the structure, the discipline, feeling he was part of a group set apart from ordinary people, a group with special powers. But the Army was claustrophobic. He left at the end of his contract to join the police where he felt he'd have the status but also the independence. His wife preferred it, too, although Loxton doesn't talk about her. Who knows if they're still together? He's so tightly buttoned up about his private life, neither Stamp nor Quinnan nor any of the others who spend hours with him would

dare to ask.

Loxton isn't mad on macho heroic acts. When a suicidal man jumped into a river, he thought carefully about jumping in after him. He'd done that before and nearly drowned himself.

Persistent and practical, Loxton works hard and gets results; that's why even Monroe has time for him. He takes pride in being an excellent Area Car driver. He takes pride in wearing the uniform, which is always clean and neat. His aim was to become a firearms officer. But after taking the Lippett's Hill course he changed his mind. Did he discover that he didn't, after all, have the killer instinct or did he reason that with a gun he would be asking to be put in dangerous situations – and only mugs do that?

Tom Butcher

Tom Butcher is tall, skinny and nervous. His character Steve Loxton would probably think him a wimp. Where Loxton would make snap judgements about most things and see everything in black and white, Tom would hesitate and . . . hesitate.

'I like to explore grey areas, to philosophize and think about things for a few weeks. I couldn't bag anyone – they'd have left the country before I'd made up my mind,' Tom shrugs and then laughs.

But, then, thirty-one-year-old Tom never considered becoming a cop. He thought about going into the law, following in his father's footsteps. But after he took A-levels at school in the Lincolnshire market-town of Stamford he was busy hesitating about which college forms to fill in when he had one of those lightbulb moments.

'I can remember which road I was walking in, by which lamp-post,' he muses, 'when I decided. . . .' What? 'That I might as well do something I actually enjoyed.'

The answer was acting. He went to the Manchester Poly and after three years was on his way with a stage company, Think Again, to Edinburgh. Tom played Shylock in Wesker's *Merchant*. He then had a year out of work; then a stage part at Manchester's Royal Exchange; then another year or so 'off' during which time he did painting and decorating for friends and wasn't half bad at it, if he says so himself.

'I think I was taking a lot of fear into my interviews and auditions,' he says. 'Then I decided something. . . .' What? 'To make a concentrated effort.'

Several concentrated months later he wrote to 'The Bill'. He knew they wanted a copper who came from

Manchester and, though Tom has no noticeable accent, he was able to 'speak gently in Mancunian' to them. It worked. Loxton, who is ever-so-slightly ee-bah-gum, had arrived. 'I worry sometimes that the accent has slipped, but since Loxton has been down South for five years now perhaps it doesn't matter.'

When Loxton gets behind the wheel, he's behind the cameras too

Loxton wasn't Tom's first-ever copper part. That was a brief guest role in 'Coronation Street' as a bobby who called to investigate an alleged mugging at the Rover's Return. They gave him a notebook, and in his terrified hands it waggled.

'I was so scared then,' he says. 'But I was scared when I started here – like a little rabbit, shaking.' Part of the fright came from the fact that when Tom went to the wardrobe department he saw a uniform with a note pinned to it, marked 'PC Nasty'. 'I suppose it sank in then that Loxton was probably the worst kind of policeman. I don't really enjoy doing the nasty racist lines. I find it really disturbing. But I have to admit I love the fast driving. I've got used to the camera on the window. In fact, if I ever gave up being an actor, I think I'd try to become one of those people who deliver blood. You get a blue light on your vehicle,' and he laughs at the thought of derring-do.

Tom, whose hobbies are teaching himself to play the piano and composing music, has become used to people tapping him on the shoulder and saying ' 'ello, 'ello,'ello, I recognize you from the telly'. It even happened when he was contemplating the wonders of the 'Mona Lisa' at the Louvre in Paris.

He lives in multi-cultural Brixton, in South London, and was amused when a black man stopped him in a shop there and asked him, quite seriously, if he'd been the cop who'd arrested him some time back.

'Then, when I got back to my flat, there was a Panda car outside and a policeman on my doorstep. I was a bit alarmed until the man said: "My wife's crazy about you. Can she have your autograph?" Amazing, isn't it?'

PC GARY McCANN

As one of the graduate entrants to the job, PC Gary McCann is what Brownlow, his boss, describes as 'highly promising'. Certainly the young Londoner whose parents came here from the West Indies back in the 1960s has read all the books and thinks he has policing sussed. His attitudes are right for the 1990s. But, conscientious though he is, he has already found that you cannot always work by the book. On those occasions the confident style may mask knots of worry.

His colleagues find him reliable – something he wouldn't say about Pearce, a detective he'd call dodgy. Others he finds a touch old-fashioned. But for now he's prepared to be tolerant.

Clive Wedderburn

Clive Wedderburn is one of the few actors anywhere – and the only one in 'The Bill' – who thinks he could well have joined the police.

It actually occurred to him about ten years ago when he'd been kicked out of the Army after six months because they discovered he is very short-sighted.

'I'd scraped through the eye test at the start, but they realized I needed specs all the time. These days I could have it corrected with laser treatment. Then I was shattered. I just remember travelling home on the bus, tears streaming down my face,' the tall twenty-seven-year-old says.

'I think I had a baptism of fire when I first started here two years ago. Everything moved so fast. I felt it was a heavy responsibility not to let the other actors down. I was waking up at four in the morning, worrying. But since then I've seen seasoned actors who come in for one episode quake with nerves. So I don't feel so bad. I suppose I'm just a perfectionist.'

Clive's mum, an auxiliary nurse, is delighted at her boy's success. And Clive hopes he is doing his bit to show young black kids that the police force may be a job for them.

'I think you can improve things as a police officer. Just acting as one has taught me a lot about dealing with strangers. You have to see everyone as an individual, not one of "them".'

Black coppers Clive has talked to for his research have all stressed that they'd like the humour of police work brought out in the show. So he was chuffed to work on the 'Cutting Edge' story in which McCann and Page had to bring three severed fingers into custody. 'They ended up in Brownlow's fridge,' he chuckles.

Clive says he has now stopped following women. 'You never know where they'll lead you,' he says. And he hasn't yet had that laser treatment on his eyes. He 'fools' the Sun Hill brass by wearing contact lenses.

On the beat – without specs

WPC CATHY MARSHALL

Crisp WPC Cathy Marshall is one of the brightest women at Sun Hill. At times she seems also one of the bossiest – but that's just because she's neat, prepared, raring to go and can't understand those who aren't. She has passed her sergeant's exams and has often been an 'acting' sergeant. When there are visiting officers around to order about, Cathy has fun.

She arrived five years ago to work as the Collator (in what's now called the LIO) to look after all the files and records. She thought it was time for a more peaceful life, with only her brain getting tired by the end of the shift. After all, she'd been pounding the pavements for several years and she'd seen her share of excitement. She came with a brand-new commendation for single-handedly arresting an armed robber, and her colleagues knew that she was more than a filing clerk.

What we also learned later was that she had been married for ten years to a CID officer and he'd beaten her up. (There's a high rate of domestic violence among serving police officers, especially those doing stressful work.) Cathy confessed this to Viv Martella in an episode called 'Kidding', and in another, 'Forget Me Not'. At one point, he returned to see Cathy to try to persuade her that they could patch up their differences. He soon showed his true colours, and she sent him packing.

For this reason probably, her attitude to her colleagues is a bit cynical, but she has never lost her sense of humour. She soon tired of sorting the files, regular hours or no regular hours. A spell in the Domestic Violence Unit – during which time she helped the abused wife of her own doctor, a man she had consulted when she'd been abused in this way herself – didn't really suit her, either.

She asked to return to the beat, and Inspector Monroe reluctantly agreed. He couldn't stop her. Cathy Marshall likes it out there.

Lynne Miller

Lynne Miller laughs to confess that she wouldn't have minded being a screen battered wife a bit longer. 'Jack Ellis, who played my violent husband, was very amusing and very yummy,' she says. 'But don't tell my real husband!'

The petite London-born actress loves her role, especially as it gives her the chance to do things she could never do for real, such as winning in a knife fight or wielding a huge truncheon. Then there was the matter of dropping a set of bookshelves on a woman who'd been pursuing her with a grievance. 'That was great fun,' she says.

She even enjoys the long, cold night shoots – when there's an unintentional funny side to them. 'I remember filming part of an episode under some railway arches. The director wanted to start the shot with a train passing over the bridge. Everything was lit. He'd checked in the BR timetable, and we all stood around waiting. The train arrived exactly to time but then stopped midway on the bridge. The driver leaned out and said: "I can't go on because of that ——ing light!"

'Needless to say, the director had to change the shot.'

Lynne, who's in her early forties, was stagestruck early. Her father was manager of a number of London theatres, so she had no problem sneaking into the stalls as a child. She studied English and drama at Hull University and was soon earning her Equity card as an acting assistant stage manager. She was soon in demand for television roles. 'I looked very young then and I was offered lots of sixteen-year-old-waif parts,' she says.

Little Cathy can tackle a tall customer

She appeared opposite Michael Kitchen in a 'Love Story' play, played a governess in 'Poor Girl' in the 'Haunted' series. Her role of Nicola Davies in two Steven Poliakoff plays, *Hitting Town* and *City Sugar* won her a Most Promising Actress award in 1975. She followed that with a season with the Old Vic which included a tour of Australia with productions of *Trelawny of the Wells* and *The Merchant of Venice*.

Married to photographer Nobby Clark, Lynne took eighteen months off to bring up daughter Jessica, now seven, and a life of television crime was the last thing on her mind when a call came to see the people at 'The Bill' early in 1989.

'It has turned out to be a great job for a mum,' she says. 'You work very hard a lot of the time but you also have time off, and Trudie Goodwin and I have been able to help each other with child-minding from time to time.'

She could never, ever do a police officer's job for real, she says. 'It's a job that requires you to see things that I don't really want to see.

'But I'm very glad they're there.'

DCI JACK MEADOWS

There's still a faint suspicion that DCI Jack Meadows may have been lucky to get the top CID job at Sun Hill when DCI Kim Reid was promoted and left. It was the job that Burnside wanted and was asked to do on a temporary basis. Till Meadows came.

Meadows had been a superintendent for AMIP and had worked on a number of cases with Sun Hill people over a period of about five years. His future looked bright until his 'bagman' Lovell was sacked for corrupt dealings. Did Meadows know? Was he involved in the corruption? Apparently the answer to both was 'no', but he was demoted for lack of supervision. He was then transferred to Sun Hill and had to take on the understandably resentful Roach and Burnside.

There was friction but not, as it turned out, a confrontation. Meadows insisted the men in CID tighten their ties, smarten themselves and their office. He insisted they behave in a professional manner. So a mutual respect grew between beady Burnside and the brusque and businesslike Meadows. It made sense.

All the detectives knew that Meadows was a seasoned officer; he'd seen his share of gruesome murders and caught his share of black-hearted criminals. He is too intelligent to allow what happened with Lovell to make him bitter, although he can become angry when he thinks of it.

His intelligence is clear when he deals with suspects. Stick a suspected child-molester on the other side of a table from him and Meadows will coax a confession. His cunning was revealed in the 'Cry Baby' story where he interviewed a man who had killed his stepchild. He told him a tale, pretended that he knew from experience how easy it is to lose your temper with a noisy kid, got the man to confess.

He's still not entirely sure of Johnson. He's not anti-women, but he gives her as hard a time as he'd give any man. Woe betide anyone, male or female, who does not deliver the goods. But, if he thinks that an officer has done well, Meadows doesn't fail to say so.

Remarried to a woman several years younger than he is, he now has a son and a daughter.

Simon Rouse

Like several of the male stars of 'The Bill', Simon Rouse often receives photographs of women in a state of undress and letters which discuss what the writers and he could do together – and they're not talking about playing pontoon.

Unlike the others, Simon's solution is simple – he passes the letters to his mother.

'She calls herself the secretary of my fan club and answers all my "Bill" letters for me,' he says, grinning, 'She's very broad-minded, very intelligent and well read.'

Simon is naturally pleased that viewers like the programme and his performance in it. But the difference between the highly professional, disciplined Meadows and himself is vast, he says. It's so vast, it makes him laugh. And that's the trouble.

Burnside maps it out for Meadows

He's the worst 'corpser' in Sun Hill.

Take a comment he had to make about forged banknotes in one episode. 'Feel this; it's a real one' was the line; but Bradford-born Simon, who's forty-two, started sniggering, and the rest of the crew joined in.

'Usually I start laughing at the absurdity of someone like me pretending to be this authoritarian character when I am completely the opposite,' he says.

'I had to turn to some beast and say, "Do you make a habit of battering frail old-age pensioners?" and I suddenly had this surreal vision of them being lined up. When Chris Ellison [Burnside] was around, the laughter fits could go on and on.'

Simon's father was an Inspector of Education and his three sisters are teachers, but he knew he had to be an actor from the age of thirteen and thought of nothing else. He won a scholarship to Rose Bruford's Drama School. Halfway through his course he took the lead role in the film *The Ragman's Daughter*.

When he left he had roles in almost every type of drama from the classics to 'Coronation Street', in which he played a husband who beat up Mike Baldwin in revenge for dating his wife. He was in *The Master Builder* with Miranda Richardson, in *Sheppy* with Bob Hoskins, and a favourite part was Yizzle's mate in the comedy 'Bread', usually intent on putting the frighteners on Joey Boswell. (Yizzle himself was played by Charles Lawson, currently to be seen as Jim McDonald in 'Coronation Street'.)

'I usually played villains or lunatics – another reason why the fact I'm playing Meadows tickles me," he adds.

Married to former actress Annie Holloway with whom he has a son, Toby, at university, and a daughter, Leah, aged fifteen, he says he discovered sport at the age of thirty and it has changed his life.

'As a young actor I was pretty wild, chasing girls, getting drunk, smoking and generally being self-destructive. Then, after a heavy night on the Guinness, I looked in the mirror and saw a wreck.'

He began a fitness regime of running and squash, and developed a passion for cricket. He has organized his own team, Actors Anonymous, with its own badges and colours and Australian-style hats, for ten years. 'I wanted to call it the Old Faggots but I had no support.'

The family now lives in Richmond, Surrey in a house that backs on to a tributary of the Thames. A member of the Labour Party, he tries to fit in some voluntary work with the Low-Pay Unit when his schedule at 'The Bill' allows him the time.

His indulgence is a petrol-guzzling white Jaguar Sovereign car. He feels he ought perhaps to change it for something more modest. But not yet.

'I don't smoke. I hardly drink. I enjoy the occasional glass of champagne and beer after cricket,' he pleads.

Meadows would approve.

INSP. ANDREW MONROE

Granite-faced Inspector Andrew Monroe looks as though he rates riding a bike with a loose mudguard as a capital offence. His frown is said to put the fear of God into Brownlow. So the effect he can have on a new WPC may only be imagined. He's a stickler for the rules, an authoritarian who does not believe there is a light or funny side to law enforcement. That's probably because there was nothing amusing about Monroe's early life as a Derbyshire miner. His struggle to improve himself and make a secure future for his wife and his daughters, now in their late teens, has not been a piece of cake, either. But he developed a flawless grasp of police procedure, and with his beacon-bright honesty and politeness moved easily up the ranks. His colleagues may make fun of his seriousness, but none has ever complained of bias.

In 'Workers in Uniform', Monroe showed that he

Monroe casts a serious eye over evidence with Reid (Carolyn Pickles) and Roach

would dress down whoever seemed to be in the wrong. In this case it was PC Turnham, who seemed to have scraped one of the Panda cars while out on patrol. In fact Quinnan had borrowed the car without entering the fact in the log; but Turnham didn't want to land him in trouble.

On occasions a depth of sympathy and understanding is apparent in his stern features, although little may be said. 'Broken', in which a former miner died, and another episode, in which a woman helped her terminally sick husband to die, were episodes where Monroe was seen to have been quietly moved.

His solid good sense is a perfect foil for Hollis's quibbling and Boyden's weaknesses.

Colin Tarrant

If Colin Tarrant can spot a chance to take the weight off his feet when playing Andrew Monroe, he'll take it.

'It's not idleness – it's just that they like me to wear stepped-up shoes because I'm too short, and my feet get terribly sore,' says the forty-two-year-old actor.

In every other way the former teacher from Shirebrook, Derbyshire, who's five feet eight and a half inches tall – 'I insist on the half,' he jokes – measures up to the part.

'I have the right accent and I come from a mining area, so I try to remember Monroe's background. I think he's quite difficult to write for because he has no great sense of humour and he's usually driving a desk.

'When I came for my interview here about five years ago, they thought I had the right stern face but they were worried about people like Stamp and Jarvis, who are giants, towering over me. So, although I'm not too short to be a copper in fact, they gave me a bit of help with lifts in the shoes.'

Colin, who smiles so readily Monroe would find him suspicious, wanted to be a footballer as a boy. He wished, in some ways, that his grocer father had encouraged him when his pal Michael Parks went on to play for Huddersfield Town.

'Our village produced Ray Wilson, and we went to see his 1966 World Cup Winner's Medal in the local working men's club. I was about fourteen, and it was the age to dream.'

A little later the man who was to play his boss, actor Peter Ellis, gave him something else to dream about: the theatre. 'This chap turned up with a bunch of hairdressers and coalminers at our youth club and performed extracts from plays. It was a great revelation to me. I contacted Peter at the Stainsby Arts Centre afterwards, and he sent me a copy of Pinter's *The Dumb Waiter*. I learned one of the parts off by heart. I was definitely hooked.'

Fast forward a few years, and Colin went to Exeter University to study English and drama; earned his Equity card at the nearby Northcott Theatre; fitted in a teacher training course and for many years led a 'double life', in school by day and on stage, when roles came up, by night. He toured with the Stoke-on-Trent company Shared Experience, and was two years at the Royal Shakespeare Company.

When in 1988 he landed the role of the father in 'The Rainbow' with Imogen Stubbs, he was rumbled by his East End comprehensive-school pupils. 'They said: "What you doing, sir? You were on telly last night, and now you're teaching 4N?" '

As much as he enjoyed teaching, he was relieved to land the full-time role of Monroe in 'The Bill', which meant he would not have to face thirty or more young critics the next morning.

'I miss them even though they gave me a hard time,' he says.

Colin's own son, Juma, who's seven, has the occasional comment to make on his performance. But the fact that Juma is of mixed blood (his mother's family came from the West Indies) makes Colin shudder sometimes at the insensitivity his character Monroe displays towards black people.

'He refers to Asians as "them", but it's not a conscious racism. I think he's typical of his age and background,' he says.

The actor is now separated from Juma's mother. 'But I like to think I'll settle and raise more children some day,' he says.

DS JO MORGAN

By the way she frowns and charges off on a limb, you sometimes think of DS Jo Morgan as a female version of Burnside. She can be a reliable member of a team. But so certain is she of her own judgements that she lands herself in hot water with DI Johnson and her other bosses, not to mention colleagues like Alan Woods, from time to time. With victims and witnesses she can be brusque and sharp. Sympathy is a waste of time in her book – she wants results and she often gets them. When she doesn't, it doesn't cut her up. Her sense of humour saves her, and her wit keeps her stock high with the others.

She comes from Rochdale, and the accent's still strong although she came to Sun Hill from another tough London district, Hoxton CID, where she earned promotion to sergeant.

Don't expect her to talk about her marriage. Things didn't work out. Perhaps her ambition got in the way. She's divorced now and not looking for someone new. Don't expect her to bleat about being a woman in a man's world. To her these are irrelevant. Her job is cracking the next case. The job is her life.

Mary Jo Randle

Dark-haired, quick-smiling Mary Jo Randle holds her hands up to 'fraud'. Her character was meant, in a sense, to replace Viv Martella, the caring cop who was shot out of the show in 1993. But Jo Morgan didn't turn out anything like Viv.

'It was me, really. I didn't want Jo to be wet. I wanted her to be tough and even brutal at times,' she confesses. 'I'm interested in what happens to people's personalities when they achieve power and status. Whenever it has happened briefly to me, it has brought out the worst in me. I rise to all the wrong baits and disgrace myself.'

Teacher's daughter Mary, who comes from Rochdale, too, jokes that her doughty detective sergeant would never have been as indecisive as she was earlier on: secretly yearning to act but feeling she 'ought' to do something more worthy, such as training as a nurse.

'I think I've wanted to be an actress since I was thirteen. I went to Birmingham University to do drama, but I had a social-conscience attack and changed courses in the first week to Social Administration. For four years I didn't even go to see a play. I think I knew that, if I did, I'd want to switch back.'

Mary went to work for a pregnancy advisory service, then a housing project. 'I was one of a group of hippies who took holidays in the Third World and thought they ought to "help".'

Influenced by friends, her 'sacrifice' was to have been nursing: she applied and won a place to train at St Thomas's Hospital. 'But then I had this silly little image of having an actress as my patient. I'd give her an injection so she could pop off and appear on stage in some wonderful role and I'd be left holding the kidney bowl! I realized that all I really wanted from nursing was the nobility of the calling. So I quickly applied to go to RADA and was accepted. I was twenty-four and I loved it. I could cope with the monstrous comic-strip life of actors then. At eighteen I would have shrivelled up and hidden in the toilet!'

After the course Mary, now forty, was busy in the theatre at Stoke on Trent; then spent a year at the Royal Shakespeare Company; wrote a one-woman show which she took to Edinburgh and worked in most of the repertory companies before parts in television began coming her way. A plum one of those was a lead in the BBC's 'Olly's Prison' trilogy by Edward Bond. She appeared as a malingerer in 'Casualty', had a role in 'Between the Lines' and was a policewoman in 'Inspector Morse'. Ask Mary what that detective was like, and her eyes glaze over.

'She was very well dressed!' she says. 'I bought two of the Jaeger suits she wore from the company when we'd finished and I thought they'd be the mainstay of my winter wardrobe for about ten years. Then I left all my clothes in the flat of a friend who was moving to Holland. They were packed off and then lost!'

Even though DS Morgan is no designer clothes' horse, the character appealed to Mary when a job in 'The Bill' came up in January 1993. 'I was as high as a kite. At the same time I'd been offered a gutsy long-running part in "Brookside" – like two buses coming at once! But I chose Jo because every week it's a different story, working with different artists.'

Mary, who lives with her theatre director partner in Leicestershire, adds that she likes her fast action scenes. But adds 'wetly': 'I'm always covered in bruises afterwards, though. Even knocking on a door leaves my fists black and blue!' You somehow know that the skin on DS Morgan's fists is thicker.

Polly Page and a lucky lost dog

WPC POLLY PAGE

Coppers don't come more caring or more conscientious than Polly Page. The tall twenty-two-year-old from Bermondsey wants to clean up this town – her town. Not for her a placement in a posher suburb. She's just concerned to do the job and support her Sun Hill mates.

Bright and brave, her keenness means that she sometimes takes risks, dives in and gets herself hurt. But she's not gung-ho like some of the blokes, and when Cato once suggested that she was trying to prove that she could be tough like them she snapped back. There had been staff cut-backs, she pointed out. It was nothing to do with her being female.

Soft-hearted – perhaps too soft-hearted – Polly wants to be a good cop, wants to be sure that experienced men like Stamp don't think, when paired with her, that they're being burdened.

In the two years she has been at Sun Hill, she need never have worried. When Polly's on a case, it's the guilty who should worry.

She lives at home with her parents and her younger brother. Make-up? Dresses? Boyfriends? What does this cockney kid care about besides her job? Nuffink.

Lisa Geoghan

There's an out-take of film in a safe place at 'The Bill' in which Lisa Geoghan as Polly Page walks to the canteen. Her uniform is fine, down to her stockings. But, caught by the camera, though edited out for viewers, is a shot of a pair of golden slippers in place of the regulation lace-ups.

This exotic footwear – all that could be found in a hurry by the wardrobe department – was needed for a sprained ankle and a swollen foot. Lisa had been filming a struggle with an angry man in 'No Job for a Lady', screened in May. She was supposed to get hurt – that's why she had a faked bloody nose and a bruised eye. The ankle was a 'bonus'. But, despite the pain, the show had to go on.

'The trouble was that I was whizzed off to see a doctor but I couldn't get him to look at my leg,' Lisa recalls. 'He was staring at my face, calling for a nurse to come and clean me up. Of course, I'd forgotten that I had a large lump of congealed blood and stuff hanging from my nose. I'd been wearing that for days on the shoot. I said, "Oh, don't worry about that; it's only make-up," which made him look even more baffled. He must have thought: Strange make-up she likes to wear!'

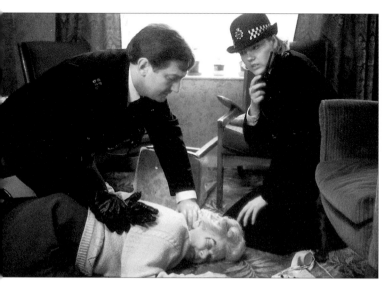

Page calls for help when a woman is injured

Lisa isn't complaining about the side-effects of Sun Hill life. It just makes her glad she's only acting it, she says.

'I could never be a policewoman in a million, zillion years. I'd just be crying and running away from every violent situation. It's all I can do to carry that heavy walkie-talkie and the handcuffs that weigh a ton. I was knackered every night when I got home when I first began.'

Lisa is like Polly in that they're both cheerful cockneys, both live in Bermondsey and neither wants to move or become a housewife. Twenty-seven-year-old Lisa lives with her long-term boyfriend, postman Michael Power. But they have no immediate plans to marry or have children. 'We're happy as we are, and I feel really lucky.'

Like Polly she's certain she's in the right job. 'Acting is the one "through" thing in my life. When I was at school I went to Anna Scher's drama classes, and she taught us that if we became actors we should expect to be out of work a lot of the time. But, even if I was out of work for the rest of my life, I'd still think of myself as an actress.'

She enrolled at a college to study drama, only to be offered a part as the girlfriend in 'Tucker's Luck', the children's series which spun off from 'Grange Hill' and in which Todd Carty starred. 'I'd been in love with Todd on the screen for years, so I said "yes". I finished that job on a Friday and began in the BBC series "Big Deal" on the following Monday. That lasted three years, so I never got to go to college.'

Parts in 'Rockcliffe's Babies', 'Saracen' and several stage productions followed. Then for four series of the sitcom 'Desmond's' Lisa played a friend of the family.

She was thrilled when the role in 'The Bill' came up. But the early days were tinged with sadness. In fact she even missed her first day.

'My dad suffered a heart attack and died just before I started. His funeral was held on the first day. It was a terrible shock for the family because he was only sixty-one. But at least all my worrying about being the new girl and getting things right went out of the window. Suddenly it wasn't a priority. I just knew I had to go on with my life, go to work and do my best.'

DS DANNY PEARCE

Essex man DS Danny Pearce looks ready for the Costa Del Crime. Blame the flash suits, gold watch and dark Mediterranean looks. Pearce looks like a villain and he can think like one, too – which has made him very useful in Sun Hill CID since he arrived in 1993. It may be why DI Johnson took a shine to him.

Mind you, he didn't half try to impress her with his 'contacts', his pals from the world of sport. He was making it plain that he has no problem working for a woman. He has no problem with any of the police practices, come to that. A cop for the 1990s, that's him. Or, rather, that's what he has chosen as his image. Scratch the surface, and there's a regular, ambitious, capable cop, one who is not averse to landing a colleague in trouble if that way he himself escapes. That's what he did to Loxton, when his snout's information led Johnson to head a drugs bust in completely the wrong place. He can be snide about his colleagues, too – and it's a fair bet that he has skeletons in his cupboard at that nick in Romford where he last worked. When Jarvis and McCann were having trouble making an arrest stick, he told them about his former sergeant whom he watched blatantly twisting the facts to secure a similar arrest. Pearce may have inherited Roach's desk, but he's a newer, slicker model.

Pearce and his similarly smart young colleague Skase make a pair. Handle with care.

Martin Marquez

As the slick new detective sergeant at Sun Hill, actor Martin Marquez has dealt with a number of drug dealers, thieves and villains, but he looks forward to working on an episode about a more mundane sort of criminal: a drunk driver.

The twenty-nine-year-old actor believes people should be shown the dangers to others. He strongly feels this because a drunk driver killed his best friend, Mark. 'Mark and I had been friends at school in Colchester. He broke my nose in a pretend fight when we were twelve. Then when he was cycling to Paris he was knocked down by a driver the police believed had been drinking. Mark was left in a ditch with a broken neck and died a few hours later. He was nineteen.'

Martin's father, Juan Carlos, comes from Almeria in Spain where he ran a spit-roast chicken shop. When he met Martin's English mother there, the couple married and made Coventry their home. Young Martin left school to help in the family fish and chip business, and for a time ran his own shop. 'But when I was about twenty-one I realized it wasn't for me. I was hating the work because some friends had got me interested in Youth Theatre and all I could think of was becoming an actor.'

So, the dramatic possibilities of battered cod and chips being limited, Martin sold his business back to his dad and went, via drama school, into the theatre. He played Macduff in *Macbeth* in the West Country with the Orchard Theatre Company. He was in *Romeo and Juliet* in Nottingham and in *Biloxi Blues*, a Neil Simon play, in Manchester. He also appeared as a Jewish refugee in an episode of 'In Suspicious Circumstances'.

It was then that Martin was called to Sun Hill. 'I've learned so much about television from it, and about the police. I went to Tottenham Court Road police station when they were running a workshop for police interrogation and pretended to be a suspect. It was very strange.'

Even stranger was his experience in a Coventry garage last year where he'd gone for petrol. 'There was a policeman there just staring at me. Of course I felt guilty straight away, but I couldn't work out what I'd done. Then it dawned on me that the policeman was a pal I'd had at primary school who'd recognized me from "The Bill".'

Martin still enjoys cooking for himself and friends, but despite frequent visits to relatives in Spain his paella isn't perfect. 'I'm never happy with it,' he sighs.

PC DAVE QUINNAN

When PC Dave Quinnan arrived at Sun Hill five years ago, he thought he had the place sussed out pretty quick. A bit fly, a bit of a manipulator, was our Dave.

Unlike most of the others, he'd been around. He trained as an electrician and he'd worked on the oil rigs up in Aberdeen until the oil boom ended and he came back south to find a new life. Police work appealed – not because he wanted to help the victims of crime. He simply feels that someone has to keep order and nick wrong 'uns and it might as well be him. The pay's not bad and, unlike the oil business, thieving isn't likely to go into a decline.

Early in his career at Sun Hill he caught a child-abductor and got a commendation. Then he did a bit of electrical work for money – strictly against the rules – and, when the chap he did it for turned up, he worried he'd be found out.

These days he's more careful and more thoughtful; he's not so ready to judge a book by its cover. He helps old ladies cross the road, and he goes back and checks on them, too. But don't expect deep caring from Quinnan – he might just wind you up to laugh in your face.

His best mate is Tony Stamp with whom he's been on dozens of escapades. They've helped each other out of dozens of holes. Loxton is another pal. In the early days Bob Cryer would always support Quinnan when the young man's sometimes unconventional methods got him into trouble with Monroe.

He enjoys some variety in his work. He's now in the Bumblebee squad, so he manages to work in plain clothes quite often. He might like to transfer to CID – but not yet.

Quinnan comes from a large South London family. His mother appeared in one episode, and it seems he's her favourite. There's a girlfriend in the background, too, although Quinnan doesn't introduce her to his pals. They've been going out for years, and she wants them to marry, but Quinnan won't commit himself. Who knows, he reasons, there may be a better 'catch' out there for him?

Andrew Paul

Actor Andrew Paul sweated as he read the script. He got up to something like page 54 of the story in which Quinnan had to confess to Monroe that he'd been doing extra work and he worried. He needed to see if his character would get dismissed from the force and the actor would be out of a job. Then – phew!

'I was so pleased that Monroe decided to turn a blind eye. I'd really miss Quinnan. I'd always thought "The Bill" was a super show and, frankly, it's so hard to stay in this acting business. When the opportunity comes up for employment for more than three months at a time, it's great,' he says.

Andrew should know. He has been making a living as an actor since he was fourteen. The East End lad had attended weekly classes at the Anna Scher school with other London kids including Pauline Quirke, Linda Robson (best-known as television's 'Birds of a Feather') and Nula Conwell, who was Sun Hill's Viv Martella.

He'd appeared in a play in the Thames series 'Shades of Greene'. At sixteen he played the mixed-up son of Tom Bell in the ground-breaking Thames drama 'Out'. He appeared in the film *Scum* and was in demand generally throughout his teens in what he calls 'yob' roles. Then came a lean time, so he was delighted when, after appearing in a small guest role in 'The Bill', he was offered the part of Dave Quinnan.

'I was making a living as an actor early, so compared with some of the people who join this cast it wasn't so daunting for me. I knew a bit about how television was made. At the same time, I knew how difficult the business can be. So being typecast is the last of my worries.'

Married to Laura, the girl he met on his eighteenth birthday and with whom he fell instantly in love, he has two sons: Ben, five, and Freddie, three. Andrew revels in family life, the fortunes of Arsenal football team and, when he has the energy, running marathons.

Normally one of the cheeriest members of the cast, Andrew got down in the dumps playing Quinnan once.

'I was working on a cracking episode called "We Could Be Heroes". It was a night shoot with rain machines. I had a cold. It was three in the morning. I knew I had to run ten miles to train for a marathon before I was due on set the next day and I felt more miserable than you could believe.'

He doubts that he could ever have joined the force for real. 'I don't think I would like the formal discipline of it,' he says. And there was his 'brush with the law' at the age of nine. 'My mate and I were trying to get two-pence pieces out of a phone box. We got a telling-off from a copper, and it frightened the life out of me.'

Quinnan gets it in the face

DC ROD SKASE

More than a bit cocky, that's DC Rod Skase, one of the new boys of Sun Hill. It's his second posting within the Met. It won't be his last. This one's ambitious. He already considers that he's effectively in charge of CID; Jack Meadows is his equal. The only difference in Skase's eyes is that he's younger, stronger, and devastatingly attractive to women. How could they resist this perfect package – the swagger, the smart suits, the slicked-back hair? He showed in an episode with colleague Suzi Croft, 'Honour and Obey', that in his mind women are predictable and weak. Oddly, she cracked the case despite his lack of support.

From a middle-class family in Kent, Skase is in fact intelligent. That stops him from being so insolent with his superiors that he'd be thrown out. And he is quick-thinking. But his inexperience tends to lead him up blind alleys. That's why his success rate so far has been negligible and he is often made to look a fool.

He came into the force because he wants to be a hero. He has a strong personal hatred of petty villains, especially drug-dealers. He has seen his own brother fall victim to drugs.

In 'Snow Blind' he took a young woman dealer into the station, cut corners and had her strip-searched. She was concealing nothing, as it turned out. A more important dealer had set her up. The wrath of Meadows was incurred; and DS Pearce, who'd been running a complex operation, left him to face the music alone.

Only Woods seems to trust the Skase style. His other colleagues are increasingly wary. As well they should be.

Iain Fletcher

Iain Fletcher may play a hard man; but the actor hasn't been in a fight since he was twelve, and it took only a curse from a drunk to turn him to jelly. 'I was scared stiff. I couldn't carry on with the scene. I wanted to run away,' he admits.

It happened when the 'Bill' team was filming a scene in a pub one afternoon. The director had decided to use the real drinkers rather than hire extras, and one of them took exception to the handsome twenty-six-year-old in a smart suit who had to dash through the public bar in pursuit of a suspect.

'There was a wall of guys at the bar who'd clearly been drinking all day; and there were two or three who, I could tell, hated me. I remember walking out to try the shot again and behind me I heard this voice saying: "The next time you ——ing come in, I'm gonna kick yer ——ing head in!"

'I had to call to the woman first assistant to deal with them before we could proceed. It made me realize that there are people who resent actors, who they think are paid far too much, playing policemen.

'A couple of days later, when a car drew up as I was walking in the street, and a man wound down the window and said, "You're a real bastard, aren't you?" I was terrified. It was only when he grinned and said, "Keep it up!" that I relaxed.'

Iain, from Littlehampton, reckons the odd insult is a price worth paying for the break 'The Bill' has given him. After leaving school, he started to study engineering to please his family. It was soon clear that his heart wasn't in it, and he switched to a theatre arts course.

Moving to London, he spent two years working in 'front-of-house' jobs in West End theatres, doing everything from stocking the bars to posting up the review notices. He also managed to watch almost every play in town free.

Sure by then that acting was for him, he trained at the Drama Centre and then found himself out of work for fifteen months.

'I'd been called to audition for a number of parts as villains in "The Bill" but never got the job. But they kept me in mind when the role of Skase came up. I did a screen test here with Mark Wingett last autumn and I landed the role even though I was extremely nervous. Thank goodness it wasn't in a pub surrounded by drunks.'

PC TONY STAMP

If it's a choice between a call on an armed raid or on a domestic dispute, no one need think long or hard about which PC Tony Stamp would answer. He'd go for the action, the tough stuff, the chance of glory. No one would call Stamp the Mr Sensitive of Sun Hill: he often lacks tact, puts his foot in it, and can lose his rag with people who are not looking for trouble at all.

Protecting and nursemaiding the community was not what he joined all those years ago to do. Stamp wants to nab 'chummy', make arrests and be patted on the back by his mates. The male ones, that is. Not the women. He has little time for them. He could deal with a harridan charging at him with a pick-axe, but the distraught mother of a missing child finds him floundering. Perhaps he is frightened of other people's emotions in case they unleash some of his own. Then where would he be? Big, physical Stamp shown to be human and frightened sometimes? That's an appalling thought to him.

Stamp was born and brought up in Slough but chose to join the Met rather than Thames Valley, hoping for more excitement in the city. He likes sport – karate, rugby, the rougher the better. His girlfriend of long standing has given up trying to change him or trying to make him name the day for their wedding. She just hopes he won't eat too many doughnuts or bags of chips on the beat. And that it'll be old ladies rather than villains with shooters who require his attention.

None of his mates in the nick underestimates him. He can be cunning. When Garfield was beaten up because of Boyden's lack of support, Stamp appeared to be the one cop not straining to thump the sarge. Uncharacteristically, he was the voice of reason. Then it transpired that he was devising a plan to get Boyden transferred.

It suits him fine staying a constable. He'd have to mind his p's and q's, play management games and probably never use the gun he is allowed, as a pink card holder, to use if he were trying to go up the ladder. As he would say: 'Stuff that!'

Graham Cole

Graham Cole was busy slapping plaster of Paris on the fractured leg of a patient at the hospital in Harlow, Essex, where he had worked for four years. Then a secretary in the orthopaedic department said to him: 'Are you going to do this for the rest of your life?' He knew then that he wouldn't: that he really wanted to do what he did as an 'extra' for patients and colleagues – entertain. 'I used to write hospital revues, do impersonations of doctors on the phone and muck about generally,' says the forty-two-year-old North Londoner.

'At twenty-one, I thought I was the right age to try something new.' His method was to become a holiday camp 'redcoat' while applying for jobs advertised in *The Stage*. He moved into the chorus lines of various summer shows and worked as a singer and a comedian's 'feed'. Those jobs led to panto parts and, gradually, more and more straight roles on stage. On television he played many characters for Kelly Monteith and Kenny Everett, and was thrilled to be able to play a Ciberman and 'other monsters' for 'Dr

Stamp has a special touch with women

Who'. Sadly he was too big – he's six feet three inches – to play a Dalek.

He came to 'The Bill' first as a cop in the background, useful for fight scenes. He was then hired to appear in some of the dummy runs made before the half-hourly episodes began to be made, and was surprised and delighted to be made a Sun Hill regular.

Married to Cherry, the lovely fair-haired girl who won the beauty contest at the first holiday camp he worked at, with a son Matthew, aged ten, and a daughter Laura, aged nine, Graham is frequently mistaken for a real copper.

'Mind you, that happened before I joined the show,' he says. 'I was at the Hilton Hotel once, and a chap pointed to his vehicle through a window and said: "On your rounds, keep a look out on my van, mate." '

Happily no one has ever challenged him to see if he's as hard as Stamp – which he claims he most definitely is not. One of the show's stars who enjoys socializing and doing charity work with police friends, Graham's also a keen Lord's Taverners cricketer. He also jogs a few times a week near his home in Bromley, Kent – a good way to learn lines, he finds. He'd like to play rugby, too, like Stamp, but the producers have imposed a ban. 'I've had my nose rearranged several times on the rugby field,' he says, 'so there's a risk of Stamp turning up covered in bandages and bruises, which wouldn't be funny.'

Short of Steven Spielberg calling him to Hollywood for a role, Graham has no plan to surrender his badge. 'I've disagreed only once with the writers – when they tried to get Stamp to the altar. I argued that I'd be playing myself,' he says.

'I like playing him driving, even though it can be a strain, fitting all of me in the seat with the camera at my elbow, taking the weight on to my left buttock. And I like playing him in the off-the-wall episodes, like the one with three old ladies.'

That he likes the bloke is clear: 'If my house was burgled or my car wrecked, I'd like a copper like him on the case. At least I'd feel he'd try to get something done.'

SGT. RAY STEELE

It's nearly two years since Sergeant Ray Steele transferred to Sun Hill from Barton Street, that notorious neighbouring nick. He already knew most of the officers at Sun Hill, and they knew him, although they weren't sure if he was in Inspector

Steele can be a man of iron, as Clayton (Mark Anthony Newman) found in 'The Road Not Taken'

Cato's pocket.

He soon proved that he wasn't. In fact he has had more run-ins with that tough nut than anyone else. In 'No Job for a Lady' he quoted Cato in the minutes of a meeting to say that officers who complain of being assaulted on the streets are wimps. Cato was incensed and told Steele: 'You're dead.'

Old for his years, Steele's an unsmiling man – grumpy even. He looks after his troops, sometimes at the expense of the higher ranks. He's the Federation rep for the sergeants, and he takes his responsibilities seriously.

Like most of the coppers he talks only rarely of his life at home. But Steele has a partner. She was pregnant but miscarried, and he took it hard. Perhaps that's the cause of his grumpiness.

Episodes such as 'Mix and Match', in which he went in 'civvies' to sort out a spate of thefts, showed his skill as a policeman. And in 'Desperate Measures', about an illegal immigrant who has vital information about drug dealers, he showed a human sympathetic side.

But his most dramatic scenes came this summer when, in 'Death in Custody', an old lag died in a cell. A cloud of suspicion hung over Steele. Had his temper snapped? It turned out that it hadn't – the man died from a heart attack and there was no foul play – but the days to the inquest were long and hard for the sergeant.

Robert Perkins

Actor Robert Perkins has never complained about getting into police uniform. Compared with the black stockings, suspenders and stiletto heels he wore for the role he had immediately before he began in 'The Bill', in *The Rocky Horror Show*, a copper's shirt, tie and boots are casual comfort.

Ideally, though, he would have liked Sun Hill to be the home of a mounted division of the police. For every morning early he is on horseback near his home in Surrey. As they exercise in the countryside, Burma, a nine-year-old black mare of 16.3 hands, is more important to him then, he admits, than the London crimewave.

Far younger, at twenty-seven, and more dashing

than his solid sergeant, Robert grew up in Somerset where his father was a teacher and his mother a nurse. A schoolboy sports star, he ran the 1500 metres and played rugby at county level. He also enjoyed appearing in school plays. He managed to find a university course at St Mary's Twickenham which combined studying both drama and sport, then went on to the Webber Douglas drama school to polish his act.

A stage tour with Dora Bryan was soon followed by roles on television. Series he worked on included 'The Paradise Club', 'Shrinks', 'Inspector Alleyn' and 'EastEnders' (he played a social worker who tackled dole-fiddler Arthur Fowler) .

In the mean time Robert decided to give up weekend sessions as a full back on the rugby field. It proved too expensive. 'I was up for an aftershave ad,' he recalls, 'but I couldn't go to the interview because my face was covered in cuts and bruises from the game.'

He trained as a stunt rider instead in his spare time, and was encouraged to enter competitions for eventing and dressage.

Within a few weeks of appearing as Steele, Robert was receiving fan mail. Most of it 'sweet', some of it downright raunchy.

Despite the flattering attention, there are no females in his life at the moment, apart from Burma. 'Women have to take very much second place to her,' he jokes.

Steele backs Garfield on the street

DC ALAN WOODS

Few people ruffle DC Alan Woods. The detective from Glasgow has seen most things in over twenty years in the force, and nothing puts him off his stroke. Or nothing did, until DI Johnson arrived and got right up his nose. To him she spelled trouble: a cop who would stop at nothing to get her own way. Jo Morgan isn't his favourite DS, either. The dogged determination she displays is not his style, and when she said she would cover for him once, and didn't, he told her exactly how he felt: insulted.

Unlike them, Woods has nothing to prove. He has an umblemished reputation for honesty and stability. He is married for the second time, to an English woman, although he keeps his family, like his feelings on most things, close to his chest.

So long as Johnson doesn't stop him from zooming around in the Astra, bashing down doors and frogmarching suspects to the cells, he'll be content.

Tom Cotcher

When Glasgow teenager Tom Cotcher told his parents that he fancied becoming an actor when he left school, they took what he now jokes were 'the appropriate steps'.

They sent him to the shipyards to be an apprentice draughtsman. 'I only lasted about a year because I kept drawing cartoons over the plans,' he says.

Luckily, by then Cotcher senior, a former

policeman, had grown used to the idea of his lad wearing tights and spouting Shakespeare, and Tom began another 'apprenticeship' at the Royal Scottish Academy of Dramatic Art.

Neither knew it then, but Tom's dad had already helped him prepare for the role of DC Woods he was to take up in 1992. He passed on his police driving skills by teaching the boy to drive at the age of twelve on a private estate.

'The "Bill" people arranged for me to go round the racetrack at Goodwood because Woods does a lot of driving. But I think I was pretty good already. I certainly enjoy it when I'm flinging the wee Astra around. I like all the belting around, charging through traffic, running up escalators and down the Underground. I hope it reminds people of the chases in the film *The French Connection*.'

Not that it's always quite as exciting to do as it looks, says the Brighton-based actor. 'When I've left home at dawn and I'm on set at eight for a fight scene, coming face-to-face with some eight-feet-tall stuntman who wants to make it look good and convincing, I've been known to groan.

'And I've had my share of slip-ups. I tripped and fell the length of a hallway when Sun Hill CID was on an important raid, and I seem to be one of those Equity members who can be relied upon to get his coat belt caught in a door!'

But there was nothing dramatic about the back injury he suffered this year – as far as he was concerned. For the 'corpse' in the episode, 'Dear John', it was another matter. Tom went home to rest the pulled muscles while the complicated jigsaw of fitting the actors to that week's three episodes had to be hastily reworked. When a new day was fixed, all the guest artists could be rebooked except one: he who had been a dead ringer for another man except that he was dead. That actor was busy somewhere else. They thought about making a dummy corpse, but in the end *Spotlight*'s pages were studied and a new look-alike live actor was happily hired to play dead.

Tom tried to take advantage of extra time with his wife, the actress Cookie Weymouth, and their two boys, Edward, aged six (whose godfather is Tom's pal, near neighbour and former co-star Chris Ellison), and Andrew, who's twelve. He also made time for his writing, which has already led to a couple of children's books which Chris illustrated. 'I'm hoping to turn *The Adventures of Andrew and Otto* into an animated series,' he says.

Tom met Cookie outside the gents' at Dundee Rep. Their respective friends had warned them about each other. 'I was told this English girl with a plummy voice was coming up and I was to keep my hands off her. She was told roughly the same. Three weeks later I asked her to marry me and she said "yes",' he says.

That was fourteen years ago. By then Tom had become resigned to the fact that he'd probably have to live in England to find the variety of work he wanted. In Scotland at that time there was stage work, which he enjoyed, but fewer chances of television roles.

Plenty of those had come in, though. He played a policeman in the series 'Turtle's Progress', appeared in 'Flickers' and 'On the Line' (on which he met Chris). In 'Making News' he played the hardworking news editor, and after a number of plays and guest television roles he decided he'd like to tackle a long-running part. He dropped a line to 'The Bill' (as one of the producers had suggested) saying he was available and within a few weeks he was following orders from Burnside – alias Chris.

He likes Woods but jokes that he himself must be the opposite of a police high-flier. 'I was a detective sergeant in "Turtle's Progress" at twenty-eight, and at forty-three I'm a detective constable!'

They have to look like careful drivers minding our mean streets. In fact, the actors in 'The Bill' who get behind the wheel are regularly minding the back seat drivers – the camera and sound crew, sometimes the director too, crouched in the rear. Or there's a lens at their shoulder, making them sit on one buttock only. No wonder they frequently wear a frown.

All Right on the Night

Despite the detective work and diplomacy that Micky Moynihan and his location managers put into finding the right, safe places in which to film the 'Bill' stories, problems do arise.

When a crew filmed scenes in Wandsworth prison last year, sign language had to be arranged in advance to signify 'Action!'. This was the result of an earlier experience of filming inside a busy jail. On that occasion, when the first assistant called 'Action!' the prisoners shouted out, 'Action Stations rah-rah rah!' and other unprintable commands which ruined every 'take' - much to their amusement.

Because Sun Hill is a fictional area in the run-down East End of London, for the sake of authenticity crews often film on shabby housing estates which are hardly showpieces for their local councils. Almost always local people welcome a crew from 'The Bill'. But children have been known to regard the trucks full of expensive equipment as adventure playgrounds. The cast have to be ready to sign autographs by the dozen. Items have been known to fall from balconies, too. An occasional tomato is annoying. The lavatory bowl dropped on to the catering truck was more dangerous - but happily no one was injured.

In the early days of 'The Bill' a woman resident of an estate in Kensington decided to protest at what she considered to be the stereotyped depiction of council estates as hotbeds of crime. While a crew was trying to film Brownlow planting a tree, she planted herself in the background with an ironing-board, iron and basket of laundry. It held up the schedule - but at least she explained her point of view. Residents have been known to express themselves more unreasonably. Small donations, such as a video for the community centre, have been known to help.

Sometimes 'accidents' aren't accidents - they're merely surprises to the actors. In a scene for a 1990 episode Ben Roberts and Peter Ellis as Conway and Brownlow were deep in conversation as they picked their way through scaffolding at the station. The conversation came to a halt when a sack of rubble, bricks, cement and bits of wood came hurtling off the roof, narrowly missing them. In fact the 'landing' had been calculated precisely. The director had decided not to warn them so as to be able to catch their genuine reactions.

Of course the actors have caused occasional 'accidents' themselves - though Mark Wingett would probably not refer to the birth of his daughter Jamilla in exactly that way. When the message came through that his partner Sharon was in hospital, Mark had to call a halt to playing Carver.

It called for the 'Bill' superfixer, Nigel Wilson, to

By the bunker - 'The Bill' cast and crews don't expect the exotic

Pearce goes to prison - but real inmates can make a racket

consult his oracle-like Cards on the Walls. These are the columns of red, blue, green and beige papers pinned in rows on the walls of his room, each relating to a scene to be worked on by the unit of that colour and listing the regular characters who'll be needed, day by day up to six weeks in advance. Anyone and everyone consults them during the day to see who's where. The thirty-two regular actors who may be working on scenes for up to four episodes in one day frequently need to. Nigel, who was a stage manager of such series as 'Rumpole' before he was recruited for the first run of 'The Bill', got cracking.

'It's never a problem to tinker with the smaller parts to balance out the work. I'm always doing trade-offs. When Andy Mackintosh who plays Greig suddenly came down with chickenpox, we had to insert lines such as "Where's Alistair?" "He's in the loo." Then his lines were redistributed throughout the CID. We had a similar problem when Tom Cotcher pulled a muscle in his back and had to hobble home.

'But when the episode's a virtual two-hander, and it's a last-minute thing, it's a headache. But we did it for Mark and his baby. We swapped Woods for Carver because Tom Cotcher, who plays Woods, could be freed at those times.'

Although many of the show's regular actors are released for weeks at a time to recharge their batteries by appearing in stage-plays or Christmas pantomimes, there's a rule that stars should not appear in advertisements. This, however, cannot stop advertisements made before the actors joined. So the producers have had to accept that Jaye Griffiths' face is seen on television, in newspapers and on hoardings extolling the benefits of a telephone company.

Often the non-human actors cause unforeseen problems. One story called for scenes in a disused church where a corpse, festooned with flies, is found. Micky's spies located a derelict church in Teddington,

Reg Hollis spots something fishy in the bath - a Koi carp

full of pigeons but not flies. An animal agency was able to supply them. But they were accustomed to the hothouse in which they had been bred. They were 'hired' on the basis of a fee which escalated if fewer than the number counted out were counted in. The pigeons were chased out, the unhygienic droppings removed by the skipload, and the actor playing the corpse duly installed. Then, as the camera turned, the flies entered on cue. Unfortunately for the budget, it was so cold that they were soon dropping . . . like flies.

Dogs have given 'The Bill' grief from time to time, too. When a script calls for a fierce Alsatian the dog sent by animal agencies is almost invariably the sort to lick to death the actor playing the criminal. Although working police dogs and their handlers are hired when necessary, getting a dog to pee on cue, as the script says, has also proved impossible.

Then there was the fish which got on the gills of the Blue Unit's production manager, Brian Heard. The script for 'Giveaway' called for a theft of a valuable Koi carp (one of those fish which resemble giant goldfish) from a school pond and for it to be found in a bath in a council flat.

'We contacted all the Koi carp societies, and they were all loath to loan us one because these things are worth around two thousand pounds. In the end we hired a brute called Kong, but only on condition that the water in the pond and in the bath would be analysed in case there was anything which might harm it. We duly changed all the water in the pond and made sure the temperature was exactly right, and then the thing swam under a leaf and wouldn't move. We didn't dare coax it with a stick. We just had to wait. If it had died, we'd have had to pay a fortune.'

Often the screening of an episode has to be changed at the last moment because of current events. An episode this year about the work of a group of neo-Nazis had to wait until local council elections had taken place. The filming of a reconstruction of a young woman's last walk on Wimbledon Common before she was murdered had also to be changed because of a similar case which was happening at the time.

However careful the writers and producers are, there are always critics. Because the programme tries in small ways to avoid suggesting that the police are perfect, a scene was written in which Quinnan chucked a half-eaten ice-cream in the street. 'Litter lout!' screamed a legion of letter-writers. An episode featuring a rabbit in someone's garden provoked a letter from a member of the Society for the Prevention of Cruelty to Rabbits protesting that the hutch was too small for the creature. Producer Pat Sandys wrote back: 'This is an acting rabbit that enjoys great luxury.'

Pat took satisfaction also in replying to a solicitor who wrote complaining that the programme had made a mistake in law. 'Haven't you got anyone to advise you on these legal niceties?' he asked loftily. Pat replied: 'Yes. A judge.'

If the Sun Hill officers aren't always portrayed as supercops, those making the episodes are sometimes super neighbours. On one occasion when filming on a housing estate they helped to spot a flasher and were able to alert the police. And when preparing to shoot a scene in Beddington, near Croydon, this year they suddenly heard a massive crash. Stuntmen raced to the scene a few streets away to find that a Ford Transit van had collided with a lorry. A seventy-four-year-old woman was trapped in the remains of the van. They managed to free the poor woman, call for help, give her emergency first-aid and comfort her until an air ambulance arrived to take her to hospital. Meanwhile the members of the gang diverted traffic and kept the road clear until the real Bill arrived.

Aren't British police show crews wonderful?

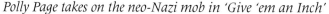

Polly Page takes on the neo-Nazi mob in 'Give 'em an Inch'

Teach Yourself BillSpeak

AC
Assistant Commissioner

ACTIVE
an official term of praise for an enthusiastic detective

ADVICE
a disciplinary tongue-lashing

AFO
Authorized Firearms Officer

AGGRAVATION
harassment imposed either by the police or by villains on each other

ALCO
anything to do with the breath-test procedure

ALADDIN'S CAVE
the home or store of a successful thief

AMIP
Area Major Incident Pool

APA
Annual Personal Appraisal

APPO
Area Press and Publicity Officer

ARB
Accident Report Book

AREA CARS
the white, obvious police cars which patrol each subdivision and respond to 999 calls

ARV
Armed Response Vehicle

BANGED TO RIGHTS
no possible error

BANGED UP
incarcerated

BEAK
judge

BEAT
an area patrolled by a uniformed officer

BIG HOUSE, THE
refers to Crown Courts

BIRD
time in prison

BLACK RAT
traffic patrol officer

BLAG
rob

BLAGGER
robber

BLAGGING
robbery

BLOCK, THE
an embargo on information imposed from above

BLOW-OUT
a case, theory, accusation, or observation falls down and breaks apart

BODY
an arrested person

BOTTLE
nerve, courage

BRAMSHILL
Bramshill House, Hartley Whitney, Hampshire: police college

BRAINS DEPARTMENT
CID (as they are referred to by uniform)

BREAKER
person who breaks into a house or shop

BRIEF
solicitor

BROWNIE POINTS
recognition or recommendation for oneself

BUBBLE
disclose damaging evidence

BUTTON MOB
uniform officers (as referred to by CID officers)

CAD
Computer Aided Despatch

CHIEF SUPER
Chief Superintendent

CHUMMY
a criminal

CID
Criminal Investigations Department ('C' Division)

CIVVIES
the general public; or street clothes. See also Joe Public.

CLEAR-UP
the identification, capture and prosecution of perpetrators

CLO
Community Liaison Officer

CLOCK
to look at quickly and unobtrusively

CMO
Chief Medical Officer

CONS
previous convictions. See also Form.

COPPER
the word police officers use to describe themselves

CORRES
correspondence/paperwork

COUGH
confess

CPO
Crime Prevention Officer

CPS
Crown Prosecution Service

CRO
Criminal Records Office

CSG
Crime Support Group

CSU
Crime Support Unit

CUFF
to handcuff

A 'body' (Tim McInnerny) is 'nicked'

CUFFS
handcuffs

DABS
fingerprints

DAC
Deputy Assistant Commissioner

DC
Detective Constable

DCI
Detective Chief Inspector

DCO
Divisional Community Officer (Inspector)

DCS
Detective Chief Superintendent

DI
Detective Inspector

DIGS
place of abode

DIPPERS
pickpockets

DODDLE, A
easy

DONE FOR
to be convicted of an offence

DOWN TO
a person's responsibility (e.g.
'It's down to him')

DREAM FACTORY
Scotland Yard

DRUM
a house or home

DS
Detective Sergeant

ESSO
'Every Saturday and Sunday Off' (applied to non-shift workers)

FACTORY, THE
the police station

FATAC
Fatal Accident

FENCE
receiver of stolen goods who then disposes of them

FILTH
police

FIRM
team of villains working on a particular job

FITTED UP
concocted evidence against (e.g. 'He fitted me up'). See also Stitched Up.

FME
Force Medical Examiner

FORM
previous convictions. See also Cons.

FRAME
the general scene; the area of suspicion

GAME, THE
prostitution

GESTAPO
internal investigations; MS15

GOBSMACKED
taken aback; surprised

GOING UP THE ROAD
refers to Crown Courts

GOVERNOR
Guv; a superior in the police; a term that expresses respect without servility. Also used face-to-face as 'sir'.

GP
General Purpose (used for unmarked vehicle)

GRASS
inform on someone

GRIEF
what a police officer's life is full of, for themselves and for other people

GROUND
a police officer's area of operation. See also Patch and Manor.

GRUB
food

GUTTED
devasted

GUTTY
tedious, difficult to bear

HANDLER
one who handles stolen goods

HAVE IT ON YOUR TOES or DANCERS
run away

HAVE OVER
trick or deceive

HEADBANGERS
TSG; Territorial Support Group

HENDON
Peel Centre, Police Training

HO
Home Office

HOMEBEAT
Police officers patrol the area around their station, working what hours they consider appropriate in order to cover the whole twenty-four hours.

HOUSE-TO-HOUSE
questioning occupants of homes in order to find witnesses or information relating to a crime

IC 1-6
identity codes (nationality)

IFFY
(adjective) suspect; not quite right

INDIA 99
radio call-sign, helicopter support

INFORMANT
a person who gives information about a job: either a member of the public who dials 999 or a snout

IR
Information Room

Now that's what they call an RTA

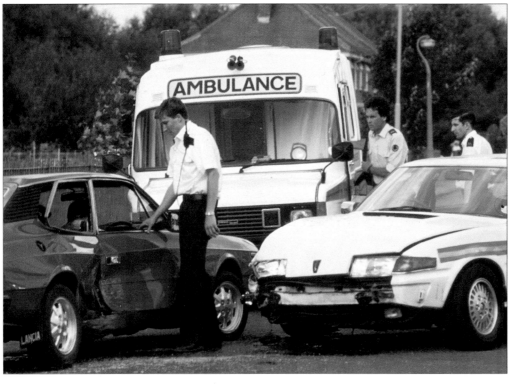

IRB
Incident Room Book (also used for arrests)

JOB, A
a piece of police work

JOB, THE
being in the police force

JOE PUBLIC
the public. See also Civvies.

KIP
sleep

LAW, THE
police

LEGGED IT
ran away

LIO
Local Intelligence Officer

LIPPY
inclined to talk back

LOOPY
insane

M2MP
full call sign for main set channel for Information Room

MANOR
a police officer's area of operations. See also Ground and Patch.

MEET, A
rendezvous with a snout

MET, The
Metropolitan Police

MIDDLE-OF-THE-YARDER
confidential conversation

MOTOR
a car

MS15
Internal Investigations, referred to as 'Gestapo'

MSS
Message Switching System

MUMPING
accepting cheap or free goods or services from tradespersons

NAUGHTY
violent

NCPA
No Cause for Police Action

NDIU
National Drugs Intelligence

Mary Jo makes contact on a PR

Unit

NFA
No Further Action

NIB
National Identification Bureau

NICK
(verb) arrest or apprehend

NICK
(noun) police station

NONDESCRIPT
observation vehicle (or 'nondy')

NOSH
food. See also Grub.

NSY
New Scotland Yard

NUTTER
crazy

OAP

Old Age Pensioner

OB
Occurrence Book

OBBO
observation, or observation post

OLD BILL
thieves' slang for police

OP
Observation Point

OPPO
mate (someone you're paired with for specialist tasks)

OPS
operations

OSCAR
call sign for Traffic Control on main set

OTS
'over the side': to be about

one's affairs, usually of a sexual nature, during time on duty

PACE
Police and Criminal Evidence Act

PANDA
a police car driven not by a specialist but by an ordinary uniformed police officer and employed not on traffic or other specialized duties but on ordinary patrol beat work

PARS
particulars of an occurrence

PATCH
a police officer's area of operations. See also Ground and Manor.

PINK CARD
(or Red Card), police firearms permit

PLODS, PLODDERS
uniformed police

PLONKS
women police officers

PLOT UP
to become familiar with a criminal's habits preparatory to arresting him

PNC
Police National Computer

POLAC
Police Accident

POISON
an unflattering but accurate account of a convicted person's life and character given by the police in court before sentence is passed

PONCE or PIMP
a man who runs a prostitute; also an all-purpose police insult

PORRIDGE
a prison sentence

PR
Personal Radio ('Batphone' or 'talking brick')

PRAT
idiot

PROCESS

Who's tax disc is out of date then? . . . thinks Jarvis on a 'process'

anything to do with reporting motorists

PULL
stop a vehicle or bring in a suspect

PUPPY-WALKING
escorting a probationary constable on the beat for the first time

RADIO RENTAL
mental

RCS
Regional Crime Squad

RECEIVING
receiving stolen goods

RED CARD
(or Pink Card) police firearms permit

REFS
refreshments

RELIEF
a selection of uniformed officers under the command of a section sergeant, who do

shifts together. 'The Bill' is mostly concerned with 'A' Relief.

RINGER
a car thief who welds together parts of similar stolen cars or motorcycles to make it difficult to detect such vehicles

RINGERS
such vehicles or motorcycles

ROLLICKING
a dressing-down; being told off

ROZZER
police officer

R/T
Radio Telephone, used in Area Cars and specialized vehicles other than Pandas

RTA
Road Traffic Accident

RUBBER HEEL
internal police investigation

(in contrast to a noisy steel-tipped heel of the traditional police boot)

RUBBISH
police jobs that do not tax the abilities

RUCK
a fight, a scuffle

RUN-IN
yard where stolen goods/vehicles are housed

SARGE or SKIP
sergeant (not 'skipper')

SERGEANT'S ROLES
CAD, Custody, Section

SCS
Serious Crime Squad

SCREW
(noun) prison warder

SCREW
(verb) break into houses

SETAC
Specially Equipped Traffic Accident Car. A police vehicle equipped with jacks, road signs, etc., in order to deal with serious traffic

accidents.

SHELL-LIKE
ear

SHOP, TO
for a criminal to give information to the police about another criminal

SHOUT
a call on the radio; a job

SHOOTER
gun

SHUNT
car crash

SKIPPER
sergeant, 'Second-Hand Skipper', Skip

SLAGS
the aimless riff-raff of society; drunks, tramps; general insult

SNOUT
paid police informant

SOCO
Scene of Crimes Officer (pronounced 'Socco')

SO5
index for missing persons

McCann is the real McCoy - a 'rozzer' with a big hat

('Mispers'); juveniles

SO13

Anti-Terrorist Squad, Scotland Yard

SPECIAL

Special Constable, part-time volunteer police officer

SPOOK SQUAD

Special Branch

SPROG

police constable on temporary secondment to CID

SQUAT

the abode of a squatter

SQUATTER

person who settles or occupies a building without right or permission

STIR

prison sentence

STITCHED UP

concocted evidence against (e.g. 'He stitched me up'). See also Fitted Up

STORNO

PR handset (brand name)

STRAIGHT UP

fair dinkum

SUPER

Superintendent

SUPERSTARS

uniformed branch's term for CID officers

SUS

suspicious behaviour or act

SUSSED OUT

to have a hiding-place or disguise penetrated

TEA LEAF

thief

TIC

taken into consideration

TOM

prostitute; or jewellery (as in cockney rhyming slang: tomfoolery)

TSG

Territorial Support Group

TUG

(as in 'Give him a tug') invite suspect to station for a chat

TURN

a police shift. Early turn: 6am to 2pm. Late turn: 2pm to 10pm. Night turn: 10pm to 6am

UBS

Unit Beat System

UPSTAIRS

the management side of policing

VSU

Victim Support Unit

VILLAIN

a respectable criminal; a worthy opponent; one who generally plays the police-criminal game as the police understand it

WARRANT

document signed by a magistrate in order for police to search premises

WARRANT CARD

police identification card

WELL TASTY

highly professional (uncaught)

WELL AT IT

criminally active

WIND UP

play a practical joke on someone, or give false evidence

WOODENTOPS

CID's term for uniformed officers

WORK

a police officer's arrests and reports for prosecution

WDC

Woman Detective Constable

WPC

Woman Police Constable

YARD, THE

Scotland Yard

Dashwood studies the 'tom'

Closed Files:
Past Stars of Sun Hill

DI FRANK BURNSIDE

You could see DI Frank Burnside as a rough diamond; but a lot of people would tell you he's not a diamond – never has been. He's a chunk of cubic zirconium.

There was always a bit of a mystery about DI Burnside. Everyone knew he bent the rules – broke them if he thought no one was looking. Everyone knew he was a bully who shouted at his staff as loudly as he did at the villains.

But was he actually a good guy or a bad guy at Sun Hill? Right up to the night he left, in September 1993, no one could really answer that question.

Burnside first appeared at Sun Hill in the early days as a visiting detective sergeant from another nick with a reputation as grubby as Brand X in a soap powder ad. Bob Cryer just didn't want him around. 'How that man got past Operation Countryman, I'll never know,' the veteran Desk Sergeant muttered. Operation Countryman was a covert long-term investigation to trap bent London coppers. But, despite whispers about this one's methods throughout the Met, Burnside might actually have been working with Operation Countryman.

We just don't know. No one at Sun Hill ever really knew where they were with Frank. Sometimes he was loyal to his staff to the point of putting himself in trouble.

When Tosh Lines was hauled up for having a lodger in his house without official permission, Burnside lied that he had given Tosh permission verbally. Brownlow knew he was lying, of course, but let it go. But, when DS Ted Roach was getting good results from a snout called Sinbad, Burnside deliberately double-crossed the informer because it

suited him. He gained Brownie points from the treachery because he was aiming to get into Special Branch.

Mind you, the blood was never good between Roach and Burnside. When DI Galloway left Sun Hill, Burnside was brought in as his replacement. Roach had the job on an acting basis – thought he was going to get it permanently.

So the pair were always having a go at each other, Roach sneering at Burnside's corner-cutting, the DI turning the Burnside burn – a glare that could melt steel at ten paces – on his detective sergeant and giving him the worst jobs he could find. Beaten up by a bent security guard he had nicked six years before, Burnside got a tasty revenge. He made the guard look like a police informer, then stood back to watch him worked over by fellow-villains. But, then, no one could ever accuse Frank Burnside of being less than a superb thief-taker.

He thinks the way a villain thinks. He's energetic, fast-thinking, imaginative, physically brave. He carries a pink card, which means he's licensed to carry firearms, even if Armed Response Units make the card almost redundant these days. Divorced Frank is a bit of a letch. He left the Chief Super's party with Viv Martella; he had a go at June Ackland; he was never above getting a phone number from a barmaid or a receptionist when on an investigation. When Ted Roach was having an affair with Inspector Christine Frazer, Burnside counselled her to give him the Big E, because she could do better. Plainly the better she could do was Frank Burnside. A lot of women are attracted to his uncompromising hard-man looks and attitudes.

Burnside could be sidetracked easily into pursuing personal feuds and vendettas. Remembering that a solicitor called Pembridge had managed to keep a dangerous villain called Barry Dwyer at liberty by legal chicanery, Frank decided on a plan to entrap the lawyer. Brownlow found out, stopped his game and warned him severely.

With a writ on his hands from a doctor, Burnside had a go at blackmail. If the writ was dropped, there would be no report to the General Medical Council.

The man had a human side. We saw it when his god-daughter died of a drugs overdose. Her parents were abroad, and Frank was her legal guardian. But he hadn't even seen the girl for three months, and his guilt showed itself – even if he did try to pin the blame on her boyfriend. There were attempts to tame Frank by bringing in detective chief inspectors above him: first Gordon Wray, then that tough Kim Reid. They kept Burnside under control to some extent, but he got away with a lot they didn't know about. In the end the maverick but effective detective left Sun Hill. He'd been transferred to special duties. Ulster? Special Branch? Anti-Terrorist Squad? He simply wasn't there, and when his mates went round to his flat it was exactly as you'd expect: like a not very nice hotel room that had just been vacated. It gave nothing away.

So was Frank Burnside a good baddie or a bad goodie? I still don't know, having watched the man

Burnside gets tough

operate for five years. But I do know he was the most powerful personality ever to shake up Sun Hill nick.

If ever Burnside returns with the power of a DCI, there'll be a good deal of panic in Sun Hill's criminal community. And quite a lot of quaking in size-twelve police boots.

Christopher Ellison

Early in 1993, Chris Ellison felt stressed and tired. He was suffering from eczema on the hands. His treatment was to say 'no' to a new contract to continue playing Frank Burnside. 'I felt as if I was on a conveyor belt after the show went three times a week. It wasn't a challenge for me any more. Burnside was a great character, an unmitigated sod, but I felt something was missing: he had become filmic shorthand,' he said.

But the man who always said he sees acting as a business and not an art was practical to the end. 'I would have stayed another six months if the money had been right. They tried to persuade me, but not with money, and there's a price to everything,' he chuckles.

Now forty-seven, Chris, who played Frank Burnside for five years, came into acting almost by accident. He was born in Fulham, joined the Merchant Navy as a lad, worked on a ranch in Canada, sold encyclopedias and finally ended up at art college in Camberwell determined to be a sculptor. He has also had stints as a graphic designer and mini-cab driver, and done demolition work. He helped knock down Nine Elms gasworks in South London.

But the acting bug bit him, and instead of going to drama school he took the traditional route of working for fourpence a week as an assistant stage manager in rep. After years in various reps he joined the Royal Shakespeare Company. Twenty years ago he started to play small-time villains in films and on television. Soon he was a wanted man for tough-nut parts, but 'The Bill' gave him his first chance to go straight, to work on the right side of the law for a change.

Nothing like the abrasive aggressive guys he played, the laid-back actor lives in a biggish house in Hove, and his hobbies as such include buying 'too many' clothes, sleeping in the daytime if he gets the chance and 'drinking with disreputable friends'.

He used to paint in watercolours, has illustrated children's books his friend and former co-star Tom Cotcher wrote, and enjoys watching boxing among many sports.

With his wife Anita – married fifteen years, he proposed to her three days after they met – Chris has two children, Louis and Francesca. And, yes, the girl was named after Frank Burnside.

When he felt the time had come to move on to something new he and writer Don Webb devised the character of Ellington, a sports agent. He has made a pilot film and hopes a series will follow. He also filmed a BBC drama, 'Two Golden Balls', in which he played a pornographer. But soon after leaving Sun Hill he was proving that there was life in the old dog yet. He was the voice of one: the dog in the comedy series 'Conjugal Rites'.

DC MIKE DASHWOOD

DC Mike Dashwood was probably the best-looking policeman ever posted to Sun Hill. When you add to that the fact that he had a private income, went off for country weekends with socially prominent people and wore much more expensive clothes than anyone else at the nick, you can see why he was regarded with suspicion and some jealousy.

Some people thought he was just a poser, some felt he saw himself as Miami Bill, the Don Johnson of East London. There was even a certain suppressed glee when Mike screwed up on a case, which he

occasionally did.

When he was accused of taking money from a snout, there were plenty at Sun Hill who were happy to believe he'd done it – even after the charge was withdrawn and Mike's innocence established. His rich family saw Mike as the black sheep, because he'd joined the Met instead of becoming a City high-flier. But Mike probably thought he was destined to be Commissioner one of these days, and when he finally left Sun Hill to join Scotland Yard's Fine Art Squad there was a general feeling that his style and his contacts were doing their job and moving him up the ladder.

But this was unfair to Mike Dashwood. Lack of experience did cause him to make mistakes in early cases, but he was willing to learn and became an efficient detective. And Sun Hill respected the guy more after he stood up well after being held at gunpoint by an escaped convict. And the lads had to accept that not too many of them would have behaved as coolly as Mike when he found himself alone in a house with a full-grown black panther.

So when he left Sun Hill he had a lot more respect than when he arrived. All the same, they are watching his career carefully. If he comes back one day as a DCI, there will be mixed feelings.

Jon Iles

Jon Iles, who played Mike Dashwood, had something in common with the detective. He admits he likes clothes, does glance in the odd mirror. And like Mike he is ambitious. 'I want to be a big star,' he says simply.

He was born in May 1954 into an RAF family, in Ripon, Yorkshire. He spent most of his childhood in the West Country, and decided at sixteen that he was going to be an actor. Drama school in Sidcup, Kent, was followed by a job taking theatre into schools. He learned his craft well, but there followed a tough time – little work, a grotty flat, sometimes the dole. But then he started getting work in television commercials, and they kept him going.

After that there were small parts in sitcoms – 'Never the Twain', 'To the Manor Born', 'Fresh Fields'. He especially enjoyed working with the late comedian Dick Emery.

Mike Dashwood was Jon's first major role on television. 'The Bill' was looking for a smoothie copper for a couple of episodes. Jon's photograph was rated 'good-looking and interesting', and he soon showed he could play the part well. Mike Dashwood became established as a regular character, and Jon

got a taste of the fame he fancied. A lot of fan mail arrived from young girls, some of it quite raunchy. Proposals of marriage came in from more mature women. But Jon saw something of the disadvantages of fame, too. Fans approaching him in supermarkets when all he wanted to do was buy a jar of coffee, for instance. Or people turning up on his South London doorstep first thing in the morning, demanding autographs.

He is, he claims, naturally shy. He used to be a skinny six-foot beanpole, but weight training put muscles on the frame. Ambitions? Not the Royal Shakespeare, but he would like to play the lead in a big romantic movie and he probably will one day. He also fancies more television comedy and maybe fronting a quiz show.

PC FRANCIS (TAFFY) EDWARDS

PC Taffy Edwards had an exciting career at Sun Hill. He was a bit shocked in his early days on the beat when he and Jim Carver arrested a car thief and saw him set free because he was a useful police informant. Taffy got well drunk at his stag party and

Colin Blumenau rode off as Taffy Edwards

ended up stripped naked and left in the street by his mates. He got over that, though his Welsh bride wasn't impressed. Another incident he'll never forget was when he and June Ackland investigated a shed in which chickens had been kept in disgusting conditions. The owner turned up with a shotgun and held the pair of them prisoner. Sergeant Peters arrived, but the gunman handcuffed him and Taffy together. June finally resolved the situation by letting out some chickens and creating a diversion. Almost as dangerous for Edwards was the time a Falklands veteran threatened to bomb a busy shopping centre unless his dead comrades were shipped home to England. With PC Ramsey he found a rocket-launcher set up in a gents' toilet. It was safely defused. Finally Taffy decided to leave London and go back to Wales – something his wife really wanted to do.

Colin Blumenau

Colin Blumenau, who played Taffy Edwards, has been mainly writing and directing since he left the programme. He is now artistic director of the Brewhouse Theatre, Taunton.

Sam Miller felt he had taken Sgt Maitland as far as the character would go and now directs episodes

SGT. JOHN MAITLAND

Sergeant John Maitland arrived at Sun Hill under a bit of a cloud. At his previous North London station this young sergeant had shopped two traffic cops for drinking on duty. No one could argue that he didn't do the right thing by the book, but the incident left a nasty taste. Sun Hill looked at him more kindly when Ted Roach was attacked by a gang of thugs. Maitland waded in to help, and from then on was respected as a sergeant who led from the front. He was also seen as a career officer with ambition. John was good at dealing with the public, not always a diplomat when telling older and more experienced officers what to do.

Sam Miller

Sam Miller, who played Maitland, is a Suffolk man, born in the village of Saxmundham in 1962. After leaving school he was in a New Wave band called The Push, which did well in East Anglia. The group gradually evolved into an avant-garde cabaret act, and Sam found he liked this side of the business. So he signed up at a London drama school and gradually began to get good-class theatre work. He joined 'The Bill' in 1991, and is now a director on the series and on other projects. John rides a mountain bike, likes restoring old cars and plays golf.

WDC VIV MARTELLA

When WDC Viv Martella's body was carried off on a stretcher, covered with a black sheet, in March 1993, Sun Hill lost one of its liveliest characters. Viv was shot dead in the line of duty.

We never hated Burnside as much as when he turned to her shocked colleagues and said: 'Don't you go all frosty on me – we've already lost one silly bitch!'

For the station her death was a tragedy. For PC Tony Stamp, himself wounded in the same incident, it was a trauma so deep it took him months to get over it. Sun Hill conducted its own bitter inquest into how Viv, a girl everyone loved, was allowed to approach a car unarmed when it was strongly suspected that the thieves inside had guns.

She was the third Sun Hill officer to be killed on duty and the first woman. (In July 1989, PC Pete Ramsey was shot during a bank siege; and, in May 1990, PC Ken Melvin died in a bomb blast.) Viv had joined the station nine years before as a uniformed

officer, an attractive dark-haired, dark-eyed girl with an Italian grandfather, a sharp cockney mouth and a determination not to get swamped in a male-dominated world.

She never did. She shrugged off the chauvinism she found round every corner, she resisted all prying male attempts to find out about her love-life. She found a way of turning down the chat-ups with a smile and a witty word that didn't leave the up-chatters feeling too knocked-back. ('Not while there's a phone-book!' she told Roach when he suggested a date.)

There were plenty of chatters. Burnside had a go, so did staid Sergeant Penny, so did Reg Hollis if you'll believe it, and so did Lennie Powell, a villain-turned-grass Viv had to guard in a safe house one night. Viv always had a civvy boyfriend on the go – nothing too heavy – but she was determined that she wouldn't get involved with anyone in the Job. The only time she came close was when charming DS Hooper

arrived at Sun Hill. Viv fancied him and was stunned when he turned out to be a divorced wife-beater, once married to another woman officer.

What did happen was that DC Tosh Lines became a close friend. She felt she could talk to Tosh unofficially, and more than once he cried on her shoulder – or came as close as Tosh could ever get to crying.

The CID took to using Viv Martella every time they needed a woman to work undercover, and after a time her title changed from WPC to WDC. It didn't start too well, her career as a detective. She'd bought herself a stunning new suit – hardly plain clothes – and she was sent out on her first job to pick up a prostitute needed as a witness. The girl gave Viv the slip a couple of times and was only finally caught after an exhausting chase, during which Viv fell over and tore her new outfit.

She arrived back at Sun Hill triumphant but dishevelled, and reacted angrily when the male CID establishment laughed at her scarecrow appearance – and told her the girl she'd brought in was no longer needed. But they praised her, too. She'd become, said Burnside, 'one of the boys'.

When she joined up Viv Martella saw the Job as just a job. She wasn't ambitious, she didn't have a burning social conscience, she just thought it would be an interesting life. But as she got involved in police work Viv began to care more and more about the victims and sometimes about the villains, too. Her generous heart was easily touched by a hard-luck story, and other officers sometimes accused her of being too soft on criminals.

At the same time her quick temper with a wife-beater or a child-molester or a rapist sometimes made her blow an interview because she couldn't keep her cool. But that was Viv, a girl who cared and who couldn't always stop it showing.

A girl, too, who was always willing to have a go. When Sun Hill was challenged to a football match with a local youth team, Viv went in goal. She let in five, and Sun Hill lost, of course. She didn't care. She'd done her best. She had a go once too often on that day in March 1993 when she approached the gunman's car.

They'll never forget Viv Martella at Sun Hill.

Nula Conwell

The main reason Viv Martella never had an affair with a serving policeman was this: Nula Conwell, who played lovable Viv, was determined that she shouldn't.

PC KEN MELVIN

Action Woman – even with a handbag

Nula did a couple of early 'Bill' episodes almost as a walk-on, just a WPC who had dark hair in contrast to Trudie (WPC June Ackland) Goodwin's fair cop mop. When she was asked to sign up as a Sun Hill regular Nula handed in her notice as the barmaid in 'Only Fools and Horses' and climbed into Viv's sensible lace-ups.

From the start she had her own ideas about how Martella's character should develop. To have the girl involved romantically with a Sun Hill male, she believed, was 'too obvious'. The 'Bill' brass listened, saw the sense of her viewpoint, and left her uninvolved. Nula also felt that Martella shouldn't cry in public, however much she wept into her pillow with sadness and frustration. Again the no-crying rule was accepted. It gave Viv a special vulnerability. You knew she wanted to weep many times and you admired her for keeping a dry eye.

Nula Conwell was born in Highbury, North London, second of four daughters of Irish parents. She was educated in Islington, where she signed up with Anna Scher's Children's Theatre. (So did Andrew Paul, who plays PC Dave Quinnan.) She had no plans to become a professional actress, just drifted into it. She played small parts on television, with the usual pay-the-rent jobs in between – catering, hairdressing, more unusually public relations, arranging photo-sessions and auditioning models.

But a part in the film *The Elephant Man* convinced her she had an acting future, and she's been very busy ever since. Nula is married to record company executive Martin Frederick.

PC Ken Melvin was a bit of a surprise to Sun Hill. They had found him a likeable enough bloke, but when he revealed he was a Born Again Christian they looked at him in a slightly different way. There's not too much religious chat at the nick. Handsome, fair-haired Ken was killed while parking a booby-trapped car in Sun Hill yard. A bomb went off, and he had no chance. It was a great blow to many female fans of the series. Damage caused by the explosion pushed ahead the planned rebuilding and refurbishment of the station.

This dramatic episode came about when Mark Powley, the young actor who played Melvin, decided to leave and pursue his career outside 'The Bill'.

Mark Powley

Mark Powley is now working in the theatre. He has appeared in 'May to December' and 'Moon and Son' on television.

The late and much missed PC Ken Melvin

SGT. TOM PENNY

Sergeant Tom Penny was a quiet sort of bloke who had more going on under the surface than most people realized. He upset a few people when he tried to impose a ban on smoking at Sun Hill, and Bob Cryer realized he was under some strain when his wife turned up and asked for help: Tom was beating her. At the end of 1988, Penny was shot in the stomach after investigating a complaint about a crazy woman who kept cats.

He survived, but when he returned to work he was constantly swallowing painkillers washed down with alcohol to deaden the pain of the wound. He confessed to Cryer that he did have a drink problem, and Cryer tried to help. But when Penny was working in an overheated room, being irritated by a chattering electrician, he spilled his coffee over the computer, put it out of action and blew his top. It became clear that Tom needed more convalescence. He was the hero of the Canley Fields child-murders investigation, bringing the killer in and slowly working through the confession. But the details played on his mind. He attended the party for Cryer's twenty years' service, but was stopped, breathalysed and found to be over the legal limit as he left. It was a frame-up, but he was out of the force.

Roger Leach

Roger Leach, who played Tom Penny, now occasionally writes scripts for the series. He has also been busy touring in *The Rocky Horror Show* and is involved with a theatre group in the West Country.

SGT. ALEC PETERS

Sergeant Alec Peters was an old-fashioned copper with a touch of Dixon of Dock Green about him. He was one of the original three sergeants at Sun Hill, a friend of Bob Cryer, though in some ways Alec saw Bob as a rival. The two men were both up for the post of Duty Sergeant. Peters turned it down; Cryer accepted it. Alec was genial and friendly, though not above a little petty jealousy. He was stabbed in the stomach by a kid on drugs while out on a housing-estate raid. He recovered eventually but was never mentally or physically the same, needing to resort to pills and the occasional strong drink on duty. He was eventually moved 'upstairs' to a desk job when Larry Dann left the series.

Larry Dann

Larry Dann spoke the first words on screen of 'The Bill' proper when Peters handed over the relief to Cryer. He has had a long and successful career, entering showbiz in 1946 at the age of five in a Stewart Grainger movie. At eleven he opted for an acting career and went to a stage school. He worked in the great days of the industry in more than a hundred films, including four Carry Ons. In 1959,

Alec Peters, stabbed by a drug-crazed kid

when he was eighteen, Larry went into very early 'Coronation Street' (when it was called 'Florizel Street'), as Elsie Tanner's son Dennis. Married to costume designer Liz, Larry works in many fields – film, stage, television, directing as well as acting. He has appeared this year in the West End in *The Invisible Man*. He writes television scripts with his friend Roger Leach, who played Sergeant Penny.

PC PETE RAMSEY

PC Pete Ramsey didn't last too long at Sun Hill. It's not surprising really. Pete arrived at the nick in a Porsche, having filled up at a petrol station and driven off without paying. Unluckily for him, the owner was a friend of Bob Cryer, so he didn't get away with it. Pete had a reputation for cheating at cards and shocked PC Melvin by driving their patrol car at some children 'for a bit of sport'. Then he threw his truncheon at a tin can on a wall and broke a window. Later he had a run-in with PC Tony Smith about which of them made a racist remark to a schoolgirl. Pete Ramsey ended up by being kneed in the groin. It couldn't have happened to a nicer man.

Nick Reding

Nick Reding, who played Rotten Ramsey, went on to star in 'Angels in America' at the Royal National Theatre before playing smooth businessman Dave Griddings in ITV's 'Frank Stubbs Promotes'.

Pete Ramsey, Porsche driver

Kim Reid, now flying high off screen

DCI KIM REID

DCI Kim Reid was the most powerful woman officer ever to work at Sun Hill, both in rank and in personality. She moved in when DCI Wray was transferred because of his affair with June Ackland. CID were not expecting a woman boss and were none too pleased when she turned up. In fact she arrived in style, with a sandwich in one hand and a prisoner in the other. The lads soon began to appreciate her sharpness, toughness and humour. When she left – with an inappropriate silver tankard as a parting gift – it was clear that she was going to become a very high flier indeed.

Carolyn Pickles

Carolyn Pickles, who played Kim Reid, thinks her background may have suggested her for the part. She is the daughter of retired judge James Pickles, and when she became Kim he sent her a detailed job description of a DCI and a list of qualities she should display! Carolyn also got to know a real female DCI based in West London and partly based the character on her. Born in Halifax, Carolyn is married to an artist, and they have two daughters. She read Drama at Manchester University, had an early small part as a tart in 'Coronation Street' and is well known for playing the Folies Bergères dance-troupe leader in 'Bluebell', her work in 'We'll Meet Again' and as the awful vicar's wife, Simone, in 'May to December'.

DS TED ROACH

When DS Ted Roach walked out of Sun Hill in May 1993 it was entirely in character. Police had been called to a pub where two men were fighting over a woman. One of them turned out to be Ted Roach, an Irish detective who drank a lot of Scotch in times of stress and who did not always behave sensibly when it came to girls he fancied.

Burnside saw at once that the incident could be the last straw for Ted, whose work and disciplinary record had been sliding downhill for some time. Burnside did everything he could to save Ted's job and finally negotiated a position where Roach could stay on if he apologized to Inspector Monroe. After all, he had been at Sun Hill for nine years.

Roach finally agreed to make the apology, went down to Monroe's office, but changed his mind at the last moment and walked out of the job.

That was typical of the man. A mixture of bitterness and bravado often made him act disastrously. Ted was always his own worst enemy – though there was a time when Burnside might have added: 'Not while I'm alive.'

But the two men had reconciled their differences, had reached a kind of edgy truce. What Ted Roach could never become reconciled to was the fact that he was never going to be more than a detective sergeant. He'd been boarded for promotion several times but was always passed over. It was common knowledge throughout Sun Hill that Brownlow would never promote Roach because he could never feel the man was entirely trustworthy.

But there was no doubt that Ted was a good copper, old-fashioned, perhaps, when it came to bypassing the odd rule – though he constantly accused Burnside of doing the same thing – but determined, tough, physically brave, imaginative. 'A good catcher of villains,' was how his old boss DI Galloway described him, and Ted was just that.

Bitterness spoiled some of his best work, though. He called DC Mike Dashwood 'a grammar-school

ponce', which revealed a lot about Ted. He thought he was being overtaken by people with more education and smoother manners, and that often made him difficult to work with.

He lost his temper easily, sometimes became inappropriately violent, hit the Scotch at the wrong times. (Once he drove off drunk from a party, landed his car in someone's front garden and tried to get himself off the hook by promising to get the householder into the Specials.) He was always changing girlfriends, was Ted, always having a go at attractive women he met through his work. ('Have you never slept with a bird you've nicked?' he asked another copper.)

Ted saw himself as an expert on women. He was fond of making pronouncements like 'Girls who wear red shoes don't wear knickers,' but the truth was he didn't understand them.

His affair with Christine Frazer began badly when

he chatted her up without realizing she was an inspector posted to Sun Hill. She became attracted to his sexy wildness, his passion, and soon the nick was ablaze with gossip.

Then, they also talked about Ted when he had a transvestite snout called Roxanne. They were always talking about him. And they'll continue to talk about Ted Roach for a long time at Sun Hill, as a good policeman who talked quite a bit himself. In fact he talked himself out of the Job.

Tony Scannell

Tony Scannell was lucky to be able to join 'The Bill' – or any other television programme – in 1985. He had been selected to play Ted Roach but was badly beaten up just two weeks before he was due to start.

Tony was on his way home one night when he saw an old woman being mugged. 'Two big guys were pushing and shoving her, trying to rip away her handbag,' Tony recalls. 'She was screaming and shouting, and I ran towards the commotion.

'I thought the guys would run; instead they beat

the hell out of me. As I hit the ground they booted me in the head and body, and left me for dead.'

The woman being mugged disappeared, and the hooligans got clean away. Nobody helped Tony until police picked him up staggering around the streets six hours later. He was dripping with blood, his clothes were torn, yet people just walked past, says Tony. 'An injured dog would have been treated better.'

Taken to hospital, he was in such a state of shock that he tried to fight off the doctors, thinking he was being attacked again. His head had swelled up like a balloon, and his handsome face was very badly battered.

The scriptwriters saved the day. Ted Roach, the changed script revealed, had been beaten up in a pub when he'd gone in to sort out some drunks.

Oddly, the real wounds helped to set Ted Roach's character; for, like Tony, Ted was always ready to have a go. Some viewers weren't too pleased, though. They complained that the make-up people had gone over the top and that Roach's genuinely battered face was just unbelievable!

Ted Roach looking the worse for wear

Tony, who played Ted Roach for nine years, was temporarily out of the acting business when he was recruited for 'The Bill'. He was working for a salvage company in Northern Ireland when he was auditioned in 1984.

Originally Roach was meant to be a cockney, but Tony was so right for the part that Ted became an Irishman. Tony, who was born in Kinsale, County Cork, in 1945, the son of a professional footballer who played for the Republic of Ireland, had no idea of taking up acting when he left school. He joined the RAF after stints as a deckchair attendant, bingo caller and salesman. Posted to Cyprus, he became interested in British Forces radio and worked as a disc jockey in his spare time. By the time he left the RAF in 1970, Tony had decided to take up the theatrical life.

He went to drama school, worked with Joan Littlewood's Theatre Workshop in Stratford East, moved into rep ('seven plays in seven weeks'), progressed to playing lead parts, appeared on television and made the odd film.

But it was a fringe theatre play at the King's Head pub in Islington that turned him into Ted Roach. Casting Director Pat O'Connell saw him there and remembered the actor when Roach was being cast.

Tony took to Ted like an Irish duck to Liffey water. He understood the passion of the man, the contradictions in his character, saw Roach as a man flawed but not basically bad. The result was a string of powerful performances that made the DS, originally intended to be in 'The Bill' only occasionally, one of the best-known fictional cops in the country.

Tony Scannell has done well since leaving the programme. 'Frugality has never been one of my assets,' he says and he admits to a temptation to spend money too freely. 'I've always believed in living within my means – even if I have to borrow to do it!'

Luckily, his first year post-Roach, spent mostly in theatre work, was his most successful financially. Tony lives in a 200-year-old converted mill-house in East Malling, Kent, where there is always a room ready for his son Sean, aged twenty. Tony was divorced in 1974, and Sean lives most of the time with his mother.

PC Ron Smollett in his working clothes

PC RON SMOLLETT

PC Ron Smollett was Sun Hill's Collator – he followed Reg Hollis and Cathy Marshall – before he went out to be cop-on-the-spot on a tough estate. As Collator – called Local Intelligence Officer these days – Ron was reckoned to have a memory like an elephant. He had done twenty years in the Traffic Division before coming to Sun Hill, and this gave him a certain lack of respect for his bosses. But they knew Ron was a good and conscientious cop, and most of the time let him go his own way.

Nick Stringer

Nick Stringer had been in 'The Bill' before he became Ron Smollett. In an early episode he'd played a Fagin-like fence! Nick was born in Torquay in 1948, grew up in Bristol and worked in a bank as a youngster. But showbiz called, and he left to work backstage at two Birmingham theatres. Then, at twenty-two, he got himself into the Guildhall School of Music and Drama in London, and later worked in the Liverpool Everyman Theatre. Nick has suffered for his art: he had to shave off his moustache to play Ron Smollett so as not to resemble Tosh, and in the film *The Long Good Friday* he played one of the gangsters hung upside down on meat-hooks in an abattoir by evil Bob Hoskins. Like most of the hanging actors Nick passed out a couple of times. Once Bob was so worried about him that he took his weight on his back!

PC BARRY STRINGER

PC Barry Stringer was involved in one of Sun Hill's most incident-filled days. A kid on drugs stabbed Sergeant Alec Peters as Stringer was driving back to Sun Hill to get a faulty radio fixed. The boy ran into Barry's car, was injured but ran on. Barry – knowing nothing of the stabbing – jumped out to help the injured youth, but the boy kept going and finally ran into a disused power station. More than 150 feet above the ground, the two men struggled, with a snarling guard dog below them. Barry fell off a ledge but managed to save himself by grabbing some netting. Trying to dislodge him, the drug addict fell to his own death. Barry Stringer was a Midlands-born copper who brought a different accent to Sun Hill and a different approach from some of his mates – liberal-minded, non-racist, non-sexist.

Jonathan Dow

Jonathan Dow, who played Stringer, was born in Redditch, Worcestershire, in 1965 into a family of doctors. After a public-school education he broke with family tradition and chose the theatre rather than medicine. He went to the Guildhall School of Music and Drama but left before completing his course to act as Head Boy in Alan Bennett's school play *Forty Years On*. He worked in rep and on the London stage, and began to get television parts. As Penelope Keith's secretary in 'No Job for a Lady', Jonathan was well noticed, and the 'Bill' job

Stringer hangs on: his attacker was not so lucky

Sensitive PC Phil Young took his own life

followed. Jonathan lives with his actress wife Anna Healy in South London. Currently he is playing a womanizing anaesthetist in the BBC's 'Cardiac Arrest'.

PC PHIL YOUNG

PC Phil Young never really fitted in at Sun Hill. He was too sensitive for the rough and tumble of station life, and couldn't really join in the comic badinage that helps keep coppers going in tough times. When he arrived at the station he was Sun Hill's youngest constable, and lack of experience didn't help in his work there. Phil began to crack up when he found the body of a fifteen-year-old who had killed himself. He reached out for help from WPC Norika Datta, but when she refused to go out with him he attacked her. Later he found another suicide, and that was the end for Phil. He took his own life, feeding exhaust fumes into his car.

Colin Alldridge

Colin Alldridge, who played the tragic young copper, was born in Bournemouth in 1965. At sixteen he worked in *Toad of Toad Hall* for a community theatre and was hooked. After that it was professional training and then a cabaret act with another actor, Rob Faulkener. Work in musical theatre followed, small television roles, commercials and pop videos, and then as the baby-faced rookie in 'The Bill'. Colin was glad Young died. 'Young didn't know that policemen aren't supposed to have feelings or to show them. In the end he was seriously ill. I'd have hated it if he'd gone off to get a pencil and no one had mentioned him again.'

Since leaving at the end of 1991, Colin has sung with a band called Stand and attended dance courses. He has also filmed a role as the climber Joe Simpson in the drama-documentary 'Hanging by a Thread', part of ITV's 'Dead Men's Tales' series, and has toured in *The Rocky Horror Show*.

VILLAINS AND SNOUTS

Sun Hill can probably boast some of the most colourful villains in the history of petty crime. Roger Lloyd Pack, best-known as Trigger in 'Only Fools and Horses', shut himself in the cold store with Hollis and a shop assistant played by Kathy Burke, now famous as Waynetta Slob in 'The Harry Enfield Television Programme'. Danny Webb played a villain who won a fortune in damages only to lose it to a couple of tarts he and his partner had picked up to help them celebrate. Oscar nominee Pete Postlethwaite was another baddie who almost beat the boys from 'The Bill'.

Sun Hill's snouts have been memorable, too. Michael Robbins played a cringing informer who helped Dashwood. Cindy O'Callaghan played a villain's ex-wife, turned informer by Roach. She gave him more than information. Roach didn't know it, but she was giving the same good time to sexpot Sergeant Boyden. Neither kept his side of his private bargain with her, and in the end she went to the front desk and neatly 'shopped' the pair of them.

One glamorous informant who would never have complained about Roach was Roxanne, who loved him truly. But Roach, who wasn't generally that fussy about the pedigree of his women friends, wasn't interested. Even he spotted that Roxanne wasn't all woman. She was a transvestite played by Paul O'Grady, who is now the successful drag artist behind the monstrous Lily Savage.

Paul recalls that he was excited to receive a call from 'The Bill', his first television appearance. 'But I thought they wanted me to play a copper, so I had my hair cut very short and spoke in my lowest voice. When I found out they wanted me to play this tranny, I was outraged. But they agreed to let me play her as a proper gangster's moll, to give her some substance, meat and potatoes, and in the end I enjoyed it. But after the episodes were screened I was persecuted! I was offered transvestite roles everywhere. Personally I think I'm hopeless as a transvestite. You'd need to be Helen Keller not to notice that I'm a bloke.'

Roger Lloyd Pack took to villainy before comedy

Roxanne was played by Paul O'Grady, now better known as Lily Savage

Casebook

PILOT EPISODE: ONE HOUR

WOODENTOP
Shown: 16.8.83
Writer: Geoff McQueen
Director: Peter Cregeen
June Ackland puppy-walks probationary PC Jimmy Carver, and they find the decomposing body of an old lady. Later Carver's first day almost becomes his last when he clips a young tearaway round the ear.

SERIES 1: ONE-HOUR EPISODES

FUNNY OLD BUSINESS – COPS AND ROBBERS
Shown: 16.10.84
Writer: Geoff McQueen
Director: Peter Cregeen
Carver and Edwards arrest a suspect car thief, and Galloway arrests double-glazing fitters for burglary.

A FRIEND IN NEED
Shown: 23.10.84
Writer: Barry Appleton
Director: Peter Cregeen
There is a series of bomb hoaxes in Sun Hill; while a drunk, who is arrested by Carver, drops his wallet in the gutter and accuses Carver of stealing it.

CLUTCHING AT STRAWS
Shown: 30.10.84
Writer: Geoff McQueen
Director: Christopher Hodson
A gang leave their victim glued to a wall in a block of flats, and his brother takes revenge. Carver investigates a child-molester.

LONG ODDS
Shown: 6.11.84
Writer: Geoff McQueen
Director: John Michael Phillips
Litten recognizes the picture of a man wanted for armed robbery but, instead of telling Cryer, he goes straight to Galloway – and is reprimanded by both men. Acting on Litten's information, Roach and Dashwood follows suspects to a post office, arriving just as the men are robbing it. Meanwhile Edwards pursues a mugger into a dangerous building, the floor collapses, and Edwards lies buried until help arrives.

IT'S NOT SUCH A BAD JOB AFTER ALL
Shown: 13.11.84
Writer: Barry Appleton
Director: John Woods
Bad-tempered DS Galloway's treatment of June Ackland almost makes her resign. The discovery of a teenage suicide leads to the seedy world of pornographic videos.

THE DRUGS RAID
Shown: 20.11.84
Writer: Barry Appleton
Director: John Woods
During a drugs raid Galloway's informant, Tombo Robertson, is fatally stabbed, and the gang's leader makes his getaway in a car with Diplomatic Corps plates. Back at the station Galloway is infuriated by the obstructive intervention of the Home Office.

A DANGEROUS BREED
Shown: 27.11.84
Writer: Barry Appleton
Director: Christopher Hodson
Litten receives false information concerning a burglary. His informant is after the reward, and sets up two boys.

ROUGH IN THE AFTERNOON
Shown: 4.12.84
Writer: John Kershaw
Director: Christopher Hodson
A car is retrieved from the police pound by a man who is not the owner; while Ackland deals with a domestic dispute.

BURNING THE BOOKS
Shown: 8.1.85
Writer: Barry Appleton
Director: Peter Cregeen
The theft of a briefcase from a car by a young thug leads Sun Hill CID into the investigation of a pornography racket.

DEATH OF A CRACKSMAN
Shown: 15.1.85
Writer: Barry Appleton
Director: Christopher Hodson
Mullins, a safebreaker, is reported as having escaped from prison; but in fact he prefers prison to life on the outside, and is trying to get himself rearrested. However, he is killed by thugs.

THE SWEET SMELL OF FAILURE
Shown: 22.1.85
Writer: Barry Appleton
Director: John Michael Phillips
Ackland investigates fake perfume; information from an old couple caught stealing from private houses leads to the discovery of the perfume factory.

Episode 12 not completed owing to industrial action

SERIES 2: ONE-HOUR EPISODES

SNOUTS AND RED HERRINGS
Shown: 11.11.85
Writer: Geoff McQueen
Director: Peter Cregeen
Electrical work at Sun Hill causes inconvenience for all; and there is tension between Roach and Galloway. A driving licence fiddle is uncovered.

SUSPECTS
Shown: 18.11.85
Writer: Barry Appleton
Director: Michael Ferguson
Following a wages robbery at a clothing factory, the wages clerk is suspected; but he has angina and he dies. Investigating thefts at a cigarette factory, Martella arrests a woman who has been pregnant for thirteen months, hiding the cigarettes in the 'bulge'

LOST
Shown: 25.11.85
Writer: Ginnie Hole
Director: Christopher Hodson
An eight-year-old girl goes missing, allegedly abducted. A full-scale search is put in motion; but the girl is found safe and well, and returned to her parents.

HOMEBEAT
Shown: 2.12.85
Writer: Christopher Russell
Director: John Michael Phillips
Burglary and racial hatred on the Dairy Street Estate. A Neighbourhood Watch meeting is broken up by leftist agitators.

HOSTAGE
Shown: 9.12.85
Writer: Barry Appleton
Director: Michael Ferguson
Smith and Dashwood are in pursuit of Archer in connection with the armed robbery of a milkman. Archer takes a woman hostage in a block of flats. Cryer has almost talked Archer into surrender when Galloway and others crash in and Archer is shot.

THIS LITTLE PIG
Shown: 23.12.85
Writer: Christopher Russell
Director: John Woods
Edwards and Carver return a lost pig. Con-men are burgling houses by delivering a wardrobe (with one of the men hidden inside).

RINGER
Shown 6.1.86
Writer: Barry Appleton
Director: John Woods
A Porsche involved in a serious road accident in which six people die turns out to be made from three different vehicles. The trail leads to a scrapyard. Burnside from the Robbery Squad is already there, posing as a buyer.

PUBLIC AND CONFIDENTIAL
Shown: 13.1.86
Writer: Lionel Goldstein
Director: Christopher Hodson
A man is on a roof hurling slates down; Edwards eventually talks him down. A Polish seaman arrives at Sun Hill and requests asylum. Penny's wife informs Cryer that Penny is beating her up.

LOAN SHARK
Shown: 20.1.86
Writer: Tim Aspinall
Director: John Michael Phillips
A roadsweeper who

witnessed the fly-tipping of rubble in the street is injured. A woman caught shoplifting is in debt to a loan shark.

WITH FRIENDS LIKE THAT . . .?
Shown: 27.1.86
Writer: Barry Appleton
Director: Christopher Hodson
Two girls come in: Debbie, who alleges that she has been assaulted and raped by her boyfriend, Chris; accompanied by her friend Sandra. However, it emerges that Chris is actually Sandra's boyfriend, not Debbie's, and that Sandra set the whole thing up.

WHOSE SIDE ARE YOU ON?
Shown: 3.2.86
Writer: Jim Hill
Director: Peter Cregeen
Community fortnight. Five-a-side football, with Martella in goal. Carver sprains his ankle while chasing muggers and has to miss the match.

THE CHIEF SUPERINTENDENT'S PARTY
Shown: 10.2.86
Writer: Barry Appleton
Director: Peter Cregeen
Retirement party for the Chief Super's clerk. Burnside is there, but is not popular with anybody. Scotch stolen from a bonded warehouse turns up behind the bar – brought by one of the Chief Super's guests from the golf club. Roach drives home drunk and ends up in someone's front garden. (Hollis grasses on him in the hope of promotion.)

SERIES 3: ONE-HOUR EPISODES

THE NEW ORDER OF THINGS
Shown: 21.9.87
Writer: Geoff McQueen
Director: Michael Ferguson
Operation Watchman: Roach and Carver on observation at a building site. JCB reported missing. The security guard is the villain. Martella talks down a would-be suicide who has AIDS; the woman jumps to her death from the hospital fire-escape. Hollis faces an armed man alone and

disarms him.

SOME YOU WIN, SOME YOU LOSE
Shown: 28.9.87
Writer: Barry Appleton
Director: Peter Cregeen
A drugs raid on a community centre sparks off a riot. The pusher escapes. When members of the public come to identify stolen silver and antiques a snuffbox goes missing; a little old lady is the culprit and is in collusion with the thief.

BROWNIE POINTS
Shown: 5.10.87
Writer: Christopher Russell
Director: Mary McMurray
Sun Hill prepares for an inspection. The Brownies visit the station. Investigating a noise complaint, Shaw and Martella discover what appears to be child-beating. A vanload of prostitutes rounded up by the Tom Squad is kept waiting outside until the inspection is over.

MISSING PRESUMED DEAD
Shown: 12.10.87
Writer: Barry Appleton
Director: Michael Ferguson
Galloway investigates a gangland murder. Cryer knocks down an old lady, and she dies. Roach is stabbed in the bottom by louts in a pub. He attacks them with a crowbar.

DOMESTICS
Shown: 19.10.87
Writer: Edwin Pearce
Director: Peter Cregeen
Dashwood tries to put pressure on a black suspect, and Martella reports him; local opposition to a women's refuge causes problems for Sun Hill; and at a party to celebrate his forthcoming marriage Edwards finds himself stripped naked and locked out.

WHAT ARE LITTLE BOYS MADE OF?
Shown: 26.10.87
Writer: Christopher Russell
Director: Peter Duguid
A headmaster refuses to co-operate with an anti-drugs campaign; the Chief Super's car is advertised for sale in the local paper; Roach and Penny clash over the release of a prisoner; and Hollis wants officers vaccinated

against AIDS.

BLIND ALLEYS, CLOGGED ROADS
Shown: 2.11.87
Writer: Lionel Goldstein
Director: Graham Theakston
Galloway gets a parking ticket, bumps a taxi and arrests the driver. Taxi drivers stage a protest by clogging the roads around Sun Hill, but Galloway refuses to drop the case. Ackland and Martella send up Hollis by demanding a crèche. While on patrol with Carver near Tower Hill, Martella is stabbed by a mugger.

DOUBLE TROUBLE
Shown: 9.11.87
Writer: Barry Appleton
Director: Michael Ferguson
The early relief is interviewed by the Complaints Investigation Bureau following an allegation that an on-the-spot fine was pocketed by two bent PCs. During the investigation a motorist calls with a similar complaint, and Roach and Carver bring in two bogus officers.

SUN HILL KARMA
Shown: 16.11.87
Writer: Christopher Russell
Director: Mary McMurray
Penny practises his lotus position; there are racial attacks on Asian families; Martella applies to join the Bermuda police force; Ackland and Martella arrest a man in a bearskin causing an obstruction; a woman threatens suicide at a multi-storey carpark, Martella is unable to stop her and is left feeling that she is not up to the job; and at the end of a hard day Cryer tries to lotus position, too.

SKIPPER
Shown: 23.11.87
Writer: Christopher Russell
Director: Richard Bramall
There is a hold-up at a petrol station, and the cashier says that the man was naked. Later Carver arrests a naked man at a similar hold-up. Cryer breaks into a flat and finds an old man in bed with his dead wife; and Kite thinks he is on to illegal dumping of toxic waste – but he has been set up. Ackland's father dies.

OVERNIGHT STAY
Shown: 30.11.87
Writer: Barry Appleton
Director: Graham Theakston
Attempted jury-nobbling. Sun Hill has to provide protection. Smith brings in a drunk with a blow-up doll. Ackland, upset by the death of her father, gets drunk at a hotel bar; and Cryer and Penny put her in the hotel sauna to sober up. In the morning Ackland spots a suspicious customer booking into the hotel: they find an IRA cell buying arms, and arrest three men.

NOT WITHOUT CAUSE
Shown: 7.12.87
Writer: Barry Appleton
Director: Peter Cregeen
There is contaminated chocolate at a local supermarket; the public is warned by loudspeaker-van. Investigating a crazy woman and her cats, Penny is shot in the stomach and trapped in the flat out of reach of his radio. There is alarm at Sun Hill as they realize Penny is missing. He is found and taken to hospital.

SERIES 4: HALF-HOUR EPISODES

LIGHT DUTIES
Shown: 19.7.88
Writer: Geoff McQueen
Director: Derek Lister
A body is fished from the Thames; an old man collapses in the street; Penny returns, still affected by his gunshot wound; and a new inspector arrives.

THE THREE WISE MONKEYS
Shown: 21.7.88
Writer: Geoff McQueen
Director: Bill Brayne
Smith and Ackland are involved in a shoot-out. Back at Sun Hill, Penny suffers at second hand and turns to the bottle.

GOOD WILL VISIT
Shown: 26.7.88
Writer: Barry Appleton
Director: Bill Brayne
When twenty sailors are arrested, the Royal Navy is not amused; neither is Chief Inspector Conway. Penny is more concerned with who has left a Porsche in the Chief Super's parking-bay.

HOME SWEET HOME
Shown: 28.7.88
Writer: Nicholas McInerny
Director: Gareth Davies
Cryer and his colleagues get a less than friendly welcome from some squatters; and Haynes and Smith are involved with the problems of a homeless family

ALL IN GOOD FAITH
Shown: 2.8.88
Writer: Barry Appleton
Director: Gareth Davies
An arms amnesty offers Roach a chance to shine as acting DI, and a bogus gasman gets more than he bargained for.

JUST CALL ME GUV'NOR
Shown: 4.8.88
Writer: Geoff McQueen
Director: Brian Parker
An early-morning raid uncovers more than football hooligans, and the new guv'nor makes his presence felt.

CAUGHT RED HANDED
Shown: 9.8.88
Writer: Barry Appleton
Director: Derek Lister
Larceny, a stabbing and illegal drug-taking are all on the cards at Sun Hill today.

HOMES AND GARDENS
Shown: 11.8.88
Writer: Christopher Russell
Director: Derek Lister
Micky Cozens has the body of a heavyweight boxer and the mind of a seven-year-old child. Out on the streets he becomes a problem for Inspector Frazer, and a real danger for Smith.

COUNTRY COUSIN
Shown: 16.8.88
Writer: Barry Appleton
Director: Sharon Miller
A detective from Derbyshire is in Sun Hill to arrest an arsonist; Haynes and Edwards have to deal with a bus crash; and Penny visits a consultant.

ALARMS AND EMBARRASSMENTS
Shown: 18.8.88
Writer: Christopher Russell
Director: Sharon Miller
Frazer is heading for a confrontation with Roach over an identity parade, but a chance encounter with a tramp gives her an even bigger headache.

CASEBOOK

●●●●●●●●●●●●●●●●●●●●●●●●●●●●●●●●

STEALING CARS AND NURSERY RHYMES
Shown: 23.8.88
Writer: Julian Jones
Director: Paul Harrison
Smith befriends Jimmy from the local youth club, and a mongrel dog befriends Ramsey.

HOLD FIRE
Shown: 25.8.88
Writer: Barry Appleton
Director: Paul Harrison
Smith and Melvin are hospitalized; Roach goes for a firearms refresher course; and Carver and Martella get involved with a skinhead.

BAD FAITH
Shown: 30.8.88
Writer: Julian Jones
Director: Frank Smith
On the Poletry Lane Estate, where residents ask for a police escort to get safely home with their shopping, two small children and a teenage artist engage the attention of the Sun Hill police.

REQUIEM
Shown: 1.9.88
Writer: Peter J. Hammond
Director: Sharon Miller
A man working to modernize the family flat finds more than he bargained for when he decides that the lounge needs a fireplace.

TRESPASSES
Shown: 6.9.88
Writer: Christopher Russell
Director: Brian Parker
A spate of thefts from churches becomes an embarrassment for Hollis; while Ramsey is more concerned by what people leave in their dustbins

SAVE THE LAST DANCE FOR ME
Shown: 8.9.88
Writer: Barry Appleton
Director: Brian Farnham
Lying in wait for an armed-and-dangerous escaped prisoner leads Ackland and Dashwood into an unusual and unexpectedly dangerous situation.

RUNAROUND
Shown: 13.9.88
Writer: Al Hunter
Director: Derek Lister
Martella deals with a corpse and a family of excitable Italians; while a drunken bus-driver leaves a trail of destruction for Haynes and Ackland to clear up.

THE TRAP
Shown: 15.9.88
Writer: Jonathan Rich
Director: Brian Farnham
Burnside sets a trap for an old antagonist, and overheating in the CAD room contributes to a crisis for Penny.

COMMUNITY RELATIONS
Shown: 20.9.88
Writer: Christopher Russell
Director: Frank Smith
With Melvin and Ramsey out on observation, and Conway politicking at the Town Hall, all is quiet. Or is it?

A DOG'S LIFE
Shown: 22.9.88
Writer: Graeme Curry
Director: Brian Parker
An investigation of fly-tipping leads to Haynes being attacked with a machete. Edwards tries to interest his colleagues in a greyhound syndicate.

TROUBLE AND STRIFE
Shown: 27.9.88
Writer: Julian Jones
Director: Brian Parker
Haynes and Ramsey are called to a 'domestic', and all hell breaks loose.

RUNNING LATE
Shown: 29.9.88
Writer: John Milne
Director: Sharon Miller
An armed robbery on a security van, and Brind finds herself in trouble with Burnside.

THEY SAY WE'RE ROUGH
Shown: 4.10.88
Writer: Douglas Watkinson
Director: Frank Smith
Hollis copes with two angry motorists and with a traffic warden who has more than his best interests at heart; and stolen army surplus brings the military police to Sun Hill.

BLUE FOR A BOY
Shown: 6.10.88
Writer: John Foster
Director: Paul Harrison
A domestic argument provokes a clash between Burnside and Frazer – and a crisis for Sun Hill.

CHASING THE DRAGON
Shown: 11.10.88
Writer: Brendan J. Cassin
Director: Frank Smith
In the course of closing down a drugs ring, Haynes

and Ramsey are involved in a car crash that seriously injures a child.

THE COOP
Shown: 13.10.88
Writer: Garry Lyons
Director: Graham Theakston
Edwards waxes lyrical to Ackland about his country childhood. In Sun Hill the air doesn't smell so sweet.

THE QUICK AND THE DEAD
Shown: 18.10.88
Writer: Christopher Russell
Director: Philip Casson
The physical training officer visits Sun Hill; and a corpse goes missing at the local undertaker's.

WITNESS
Shown: 20.10.88
Writer: Christopher Russell
Director: Graham Theakston
'Look, when it comes to feeling collars, I'm there, right? None better. But this is just another Mickey Mouse job, innit? – housemaid to a plonker?'

HERE WE GO LOOPY LOU
Shown: 25.10.88
Writer: Julian Jones
Director: Brian Farnham
Cryer, Edwards and Brind investigate reports of a man wearing a flowing white robe – and become involved in a dangerous game of hide and seek.

STOP AND SEARCH
Shown: 27.10.88
Writer: Geoff McQueen
Director: Terry Marcel
Special constables Ronnie Defoe and Mary Kilnair are learning the ropes at Sun Hill.

SPOOK STUFF
Shown: 1.11.88
Writer: Geoff McQueen
Director: Terry Marcel
Roach gets lucky when he meets an informer at the dog track; but, with Burnside to work with, luck isn't all that Roach needs.

EVACUATION
Shown: 3.11.88
Writer: Edwin Pearce
Director: Terry Green
Smith makes a discovery that disrupts life at Sun Hill, and that could have fatal consequences.

PERSONAL IMPORTS
Shown: 8.11.88
Writer: Kevin Clarke

Director: Brian Farnham
Drugs are stolen from a chemist's shop; Carver conducts a surveillance; Martella and Roach look into a case of truancy.

PAPER CHASE
Shown: 10.11.88
Writer: Barry Appleton
Director: Niall Leonard
A schoolgirl has been kidnapped, a ransom of half a million pounds has been demanded, and for Sun Hill CID the chase is on.

INTRUDER
Shown: 15.11.88
Writer: Roger Parkes
Director: Graham Theakston
A single unarmed policeman bravely tackles a man with a knife, but what really happened? Haynes, Cryer and Frazer have different views.

CONFLICT
Shown: 17.11.88
Writer: Al Hunter
Director: Graham Theakston
An observation on a suspect develops into an ugly domestic incident, and provokes a clash between Burnside and Cryer.

DUPLICATES
Shown: 22.11.88
Writer: Simon Moss
Director: Niall Leonard
Brind re-enacts the last movements of a missing girl.

SNOUT
Shown: 24.11.88
Writer: Arthur McKenzie
Director: Paul Harrison
There are days when working with Burnside is something you wouldn't wish on your worst enemy.

OLD HABITS
Shown: 29.11.88
Writer: Nicholas McInerny
Director: Barry Davis
The death of an elderly lady following a break-in causes disquiet among the older residents of Sun Hill; but one of them, Maurice Harvey, is not all he seems.

THE SILENT GUN
Shown: 1.12.88
Writer: Christopher Russell
Director: Terry Marcel
A gunman locks himself in an upper-storey room and provokes a full-scale alert for Sun Hill.

AN OLD-FASHIONED TERM
Shown: 6.12.88
Writer: Geoff McQueen
Director: Philip Casson
Tosh Lines has not progressed above the rank of DC for twelve years, but Carver discovers that there's more to Tosh than meets the eye.

GETTING STRESSED
Shown: 8.12.88
Writer: Christopher Russell
Director: Philip Casson
Hollis is anxious to talk to everyone about their stress problems; but with an assault, a rape and a drunk in charge of a baby Inspector Frazer has enough on her plate.

TIGERS
Shown: 13.12.88
Writer: Edwin Pearce
Director: Terry Marcel
An unexpected and very unwelcome gift is waiting for Carver when he turns up at Sun Hill.

GUESSING GAME
Shown: 15.12.88
Writer: Peter J. Hammond
Director: Jan Sargent
A man called Kessel is found dead in his flat, but what might be the secret that he's taken to the grave?

THE ASSASSINS
Shown: 20.12.88
Writer: Douglas Watkinson
Director: Terry Daw
A bunch of upper-class hooligans wreck a restaurant, while Mr Cooper is worrying about another kind of damage.

OUTMODED
Shown: 22.12.88
Writer: Barry Appleton
Director: Terry Green
Sun Hill is being subjected to a series of bogus calls; Ackland has to deal with a woman who won't venture out of her flat; and a car is hauled out of the river.

DIGGING UP THE PAST
Shown: 27.12.88
Writer: Barry Appleton
Director: Barry Davis
Building workers unearth a skeleton; Ramsey and Edwards investigate a ticket forger; and Cryer comes to terms with the fact that his son has been charged with a serious offence.

TAKEN INTO CONSIDERATION
Shown: 29.12.88
Writer: Lawrence Gray
Director: Christopher Hodson
Does Dashwood know that the last man who dealt with Kevin is in a psychiatric ward?

GETTING IT RIGHT
Shown: 3.1.89
Writer: Barry Appleton
Director: Terry Daw
An early-morning raid does not turn out as expected; and Cryer's son is in court.

A REFLECTION OF GLORY
Shown: 5.1.89
Writer: Brendan J. Cassin
Director: Christopher Hodson
Haynes and Ramsey go to pick up a shoplifter, Melvin and Ackland go to somebody's rescue, and everybody gets more than they bargained for.

ONE TO ONE
Shown: 10.1.89
Writer: Christopher Russell
Director: Jan Sargent

THE MUGGING AND THE GYPSIES
Shown: 12.1.89
Writer: David Halliwell
Director: Barry Davis
Edwards, Smith and Ackland find more resistance than they had bargained for when they enforce a Place of Safety Order at a gypsy encampment.

THE CHAIN OF COMMAND
Shown: 17.1.89
Writer: Christopher Short
Director: Robert Tronson
CID are called in to close down a pirate radio station, and Cryer makes some surprising discoveries when he rounds up a group of winos.

LIFE AND DEATH
Shown: 19.1.89
Writer: Kieran Prendiville
Director: Robert Tronson
Telling a woman that her husband has been killed is never easy, but has Melvin told the right woman?

HOTHEAD
Shown: 24.1.89
Writer: Edwin Pearce
Director: Philip Casson
The custody area is overcrowded, local councillors are due to pay a visit, and Cryer has

toothache. An accusation of assault is the last thing he needs.

STEAMERS
Shown: 26.1.89
Writer: Gerry Huxham
Director: Terry Green

DUTY ELSEWHERE
Shown: 31.1.89
Writer: Brendan J. Cassin
Director: Jeremy Summers
Haynes goes undercover, and faces danger above and beyond the call of duty.

SATURDAY BLUES
Shown: 2.2.89
Writer: David Squire
Director: Jeremy Summers
A young woman is seriously ill after a suspected drugs overdose. Burnside takes the case too seriously for his own good.

NFA
Shown: 7.2.89
Writer: Arthur McKenzie
Director: Keith Washington
Ramsey thinks of Foxy as the dregs. Lines believes he's a man worth saving. The difference of opinion sets them on a collision course.

THE PRICE YOU PAY
Shown: 9.2.89
Writer: Kieran Prendiville
Director: Keith Washington
A friend of Martella is assaulted, and she is accused of becoming too personally involved in the case.

THE KEY OF THE DOOR
Shown: 14.2.89
Dashwood discovers the seamy side of the property business, and Cryer tries to persuade a woman to testify against her own son.

COCK UP
Shown: 16.2.89
Writer: Tony Grounds
Director: Brian Farnham
Cryer receives a tip-off about a drugs-dealer – and plunges Sun Hill into a major operation.

REPERCUSSIONS
Shown: 21.2.89
Writer: Tony Grounds
Director: Brian Farnham

A DEATH IN THE FAMILY
Shown: 23.2.89
Writer: John Foster
Director: Christopher Hodson
A cot death has to be investigated. Sun Hill

officers have done it before, but it's something they will never get used to.

IN THE FRAME
Shown: 28.2.89
Writer: Barry Appleton
Director: Barry Davis
'Yorkie' Smith is working undercover in an operation against football hooligans; but it's only a matter of time before his cover is blown.

A GOOD RESULT
Shown: 2.3.89
Writer: Christopher Russell
Director: Jeremy Summers
Burnside gets involved in Operation Backwoods, Cryer insists that an American move his illegally parked car, and both of them are in trouble.

CONSCIENCE
Shown: 7.3.89
Writer: Barry Appleton
Director: Jeremy Summers
Roach crosses the path of an ex-commander and is forced to rake through the ashes of his past.

SUNDAY SUNDAY
Shown: 9.3.89
Writers: P. Fletcher and R. Le Parmentier
Director: Terry Marcel
Racial violence leaves Edwards injured; and Ackland's involvement in a case of euthanasia brings painful memories of her own recent bereavement.

CLIMATE
Shown: 14.3.89
Writer: Peter J. Hammond
Director: Brian Parker
It's one of those days when nothing is right and everyone's in the wrong.

BAD COMPANY
Shown: 16.3.89
Writer: Brendan J. Cassin
Director: Terry Marcel
Bail-jumper Hacket knows only too well what he is running from; but Melvin has no idea what he's walking into.

SUSPICIOUS MINDS
Shown: 21.3.89
Writer: Kieran Prendiville
Director: Terry Green
Sun Hill officers join forces with Scotland Yard for a series of raids, but it is an uneasy alliance.

INTUITION
Shown: 23.3.89
Writer: Jonathan Rich

Director: Brian Parker
No one has ever been able to convict villain Frankie Barron. Roach and Lines have just one night to succeed where all others have failed.

LOSS
Shown: 28.3.89
Writer: Peter J. Hammond
Director: Brian Farnham
Smith and Martella are put on special assignment; but the discoveries they make are none too popular.

PROCEDURE
Shown: 30.3.89
Writer: John Milne
Director: Terry Green
A normal morning of paperwork and routine, but for Sergeant Peters the day takes an unexpected and unpleasant turn.

LUCK OF THE DRAW
Shown: 4.4.89
Writer: Patrick Harkins
Director: Keith Washington
A protection racket in a brewery puts Roach at risk; while Cryer deals with a crooked debt-collector.

NO STRINGS
Shown: 6.4.89
Writer: Kevin Clarke
Director: Brian Farnham
Roach's informant Roxanne puts him on the trail of credit-card thieves.

FOOL'S GOLD
Shown: 11.4.89
Writer: David Squire
Director: Keith Washington
When a prisoner turns informer, Burnside has a lot to gain – and plenty more to lose.

THE VISIT
Shown: 13.4.89
Writer: Barry Appleton
Director: Alan Wareing
A shooting has South African connections; and a drug addict has a knife at Ackland's throat.

ONE FOR THE LADIES
Shown: 18.4.89
Writer: Brendan J. Cassin
Director: Terry Green
An apparently ordinary man is found dead in a hotel; but Tosh Lines finds out that he was not what he seemed.

NO SHELTER
Shown: 20.4.89
Writer: Julian Jones
Director: Terry Marcel
An attempted break-in on a trading estate and a rowdy

all-night party leave Martella the worse for wear.

OUT TO LUNCH
Shown: 25.4.89
Writer: Julian Jones
Director: Brian Parker
A wife on the warpath leads to a chase round a hospital. Burnside is bewildered, but Brind saves the day.

FREE WHEEL
Shown: 27.4.89
Writer: Peter J. Hammond
Director: Alan Wareing
An odd couple, a mystery envelope and an unusual hotel receptionist play unexpected roles in a watching-and-waiting game.

ONLY A BIT OF THIEVING
Shown: 2.5.89
Writer: Chris Barlas
Director: Brian Parker
Melvin is on secondment to CID. The night he works with Ted Roach is one he will never forget.

COMMUNICATIONS
Shown: 4.5.89
Writer: Jonathan Rich
Director: Alan Wareing
Conway behaves uncharacteristically and gets some surprises – especially about Edwards and Ackland.

SILVER LINING
Shown: 9.5.89
Writer: Colin Griffin
Director: Mike Dormer
A white Rolls-Royce proves to be full of surprises for Melvin and Haynes.

SUFFOCATION JOB
Shown: 11.5.89
Writer: Peter J. Hammond
Director: Brian Farnham
A woman who dare not go out becomes a headache for Ackland; and Melvin is looking for a burglar who keeps opening windows.

MICKEY WOULD HAVE WANTED IT
Shown: 16.5.89
Writer: Kieran Prendiville
Director: Brian Farnham
Burnside has a guarded respect for villains of the old school like Mickey Lovett; but he feels very differently about Mickey's sons, Michael and Mark.

BLOOD TIES
Shown: 18.5.89
Writer: Chris Barlas
Director: Mike Dormer

A 'domestic' on the posh side of Sun Hill is the last thing Stamp needs, especially with Brind for company.

YOU'LL BE BACK
Shown: 23.5.89
Writer: Shirley Cooklin
Director: Richard Standeven
A scuffle in a market leads to a disagreement between Cryer and Frazer. Brind finds out the truth behind a respectable marriage.

FORT APACHE – SUN HILL
Shown: 25.5.89
Writer: Barry Appleton
Director: Antonia Bird
An unexpected official inspection does nothing to lift spirits at Sun Hill – already overflowing with unwelcome guests.

WASTE
Shown: 30.5.89
Writer: Al Hunter
Director: Richard Standeven
A contractor tips waste illegally. The results are disastrous, even for Burnside.

THE STRONG SURVIVE
Shown: 1.6.89
Writer: Brendan J. Cassin
Director: Sharon Miller
Drugs and violence often go together, but no one expects a group of mourners to behave like hooligans

LOVING CARE
Shown: 6.6.89
Writer: Al Hunter
Director: Michael Owen Morris
Carver investigates a burglary and finds the burglar unconscious in the victim's back garden.

BACK ON THE STREETS
Shown: 8.6.89
Writer: Simon Moss
Director: Alan Wareing
Hollis surprises everyone at Sun Hill.

FATAC
Shown: 13.6.89
Writer: Julian Jones
Director: John Bruce

SOMEWHERE BY CHANCE
Shown: 15.6.89
Writer: Barry Appleton
Director: Terry Marcel
A bomb scare sets Sun Hill on its toes. Brind has a scare of a different kind when she answers a call to a luxury flat.

A QUIET LIFE
Shown: 20.6.89
Writer: Simon Moss
Director: Sharon Miller
Has Cathy Marshall settled for a quiet life as Collator? Meanwhile a man in a blue sweater is making problems for Dashwood.

TOM TIDDLER'S GROUND
Shown: 22.6.89
Writer: Peter J. Hammond
Director: John Bruce
Patrolling Sun Hill's local park is a routine exercise for Ackland and Martella. Why should Burnside be so interested in what they're doing?

MAKE MY DAY
Shown: 27.6.89
Writer: Barry Appleton
Director: Michael Ferguson
A new copper's first day is almost his last as old villains rake over the past.

PROVOCATION
Shown: 29.6.89
Writer: Edwin Pearce
Director: Michael Ferguson
Interviewing a juvenile in the presence of a parent is a job that Dashwood finds particularly difficult.

OVERSPEND
Shown: 4.7.89
Writer: Christopher Russell
Director: Terry Marcel
Brownlow has called for an economy drive at Sun Hill, and everyone is feeling the pinch.

BETWEEN FRIENDS
Shown: 6.7.89
Writer: Barry Appleton
Director: Barry Davis
A young burglar shops his victim, while Brownlow almost makes the gaffe of his life.

TRAFFIC
Shown: 11.7.89
Writer: Christopher Russell
Director: Bill Brayne
A hit-and-run accident has unexpected complications. Cryer returns the worse for wear from walking the beat with Turnham.

THE SACRED SEAL
Shown: 13.7.89
Writer: Brendan J. Cassin
Director: Michael Owen Morris
Vital evidence is withheld, but Carver and Burnside can do nothing about it.

SUBSEQUENT VISITS
Shown: 18.7.89
Writer: Arthur McKenzie
Director: Bill Brayne
Tosh Lines has some loose ends to tidy up before taking his annual leave, but everything he does seems to create more problems.

USER FRIENDLY
Shown: 20.7.89
Writer: Barry Appleton
Director: Graham Theakston

DON'T LIKE MONDAYS
Shown: 25.7.89
Writer: Barry Appleton
Director: Antonia Bird
Tosh Lines's wife goes to see the bank manager – with tragic consequences for Sun Hill.

PICKUP
Shown: 27.7.89
Writer: John Milne
Director: Michael Owen Morris
Cryer and Frazer have to keep Sun Hill going, but Haynes and Lines find it hard to come to terms with recent events.

KIDDING
Shown: 1.8.89
Writer: Jonathan Rich
Director: Michael Ferguson
Stamp and Turnham are called to a shopping centre where three youths are picking pockets. Turnham loses one of them. Stamp captures the other two, but is forced to clip one of them round the ear. This causes problems back at Sun Hill.

BLACK SPOT
Shown: 3.8.89
Writer: Arthur McKenzie
Director: Michael Owen Morris
Lines pursues a personal vendetta against Box, who batters his own wife, threatens Lines's wife, and is a suspect in a violent robbery. One-armed bandits at a club are raided. Carver catches one villain; the other, before escaping, bites Roach's arm. The toothmarks provide evidence to catch Box.

TAKEN FOR A RIDE
Shown: 8.8.89
Writer: Barry Appleton
Director: Terry Marcel
Roach's promotion board at Scotland Yard. Anticipating rejection, Roach walks out before his hearing is over. Meanwhile Burnside's surveillance of a large lorry he believes is about to be hijacked goes badly, and the

lorry is lost.

TIME OUT
Shown: 10.8.89
Writer: Barry Appleton
Director: Terry Marcel
A suspect under surveillance is kidnapped under CID's nose. Later a security van is held up outside a supermarket, and groceries are spilt all over the pavement. CID are not convinced by the 'kidnapping', and their doubts are confirmed when traces of the groceries are found on their suspect's shoes.

LEAVING
Shown: 15.8.89
Writer: Christopher Russell
Director: Terry Marcel
On his last day at Sun Hill, Smith arrests a teenager for possession of drugs. Mentally handicapped Mr Kellow throws furniture out of his window in the middle of the night. Smith's colleagues 'steal' his Panda, and Brind presents herself as a Kissagram.

STREET GAMES AND BOARD GAMES
Shown: 17.8.89
Writer: J. C. Wilsher
Director: Barry Davis
After a drugs raid, local feelings are running high. Meanwhile Brownlow learns the theory of riot control at a conference.

PRESSURE
Shown: 22.8.89
Writer: Kevin Clarke
Director: Barry Davis
Frazer suggests to Haynes that he should become a sergeant. A wealthy black 'businessman' tries to bribe Haynes. Edwards's wife goes to the station and causes a scene about the delay in his request for transfer.

A LITTLE KNOWLEDGE
Shown: 24.8.89
Writer: Christopher Russell
Director: James Cellan Jones
Takeaway-pizza boys are being mugged. Garfield goes undercover to investigate. Lines goes undercover as a minicab driver to expose an illegal gambling club; but Greig raids the wrong premises!

PATHWAYS
Shown: 29.8.89
Writer: Peter J. Hammond
Director: Michael Ferguson

While dealing with a fatal traffic accident near some allotments, Peters and Brind turn their attention to the allotments themselves and discover that they are being used for purposes other than gardening.

SEEN TO BE DONE
Shown: 31.8.89
Writer: Jonathan Rich
Director: James Cellan Jones
Penny, Melvin, Able and Turnham are put through an MS15 interrogation when a drunk, detained earlier, is found dead in the front interview room.

TULIP
Shown: 5.9.89
Writer: Barry Appleton
Director: Keith Washington
Roach and Dashwood arrest Bartlett for GBH; but he is stabbed while in their custody by a prostitute, Tulip. Bartlett, a client of Tulip, confesses to his need for sexual stimulation through violence and that he caused Tulip to lose her baby.

NOTHING BUT THE TRUTH
Shown: 7.9.89
Writer: Arthur McKenzie
Director: Keith Washington
Burnside is unimpressed by Carver's recent record; but in court, giving evidence against Thompson, Carver's performance is more successful than Burnside's.

IT'S NOT MAJORCA
Shown: 12.9.89
Writer: Julian Jones
Director: Niall Leonard
During chaotic scenes in a crowded custody area, Brind is attacked and Peters, in trying to rescue her, knocks over Mrs Gunn, a lay visitor, who breaks her leg.

MENDING FENCES (Part 2 of IT'S NOT MAJORCA)
Shown: 14.9.89
Writer: Julian Jones
Director: Niall Leonard
Stamp, Melvin and Hollis patrol a school fête and encounter a group of disruptive youths. Peters visits Mrs Gunn to apologize for her fall.

EXIT LINES
Shown: 19.9.89
Writer: Brian Finch
Director: Derek Lister
Garfield befriends an old woman who claims

someone has stolen her birdseed and window-box bulbs; CID investigate a con-man claiming to sell racing pigeons; Cryer helps Mr Preston to find his missing daughter; and the new WPC Norika Datta has a busy day.

THAT OLD MALARKEY
Shown: 21.9.89
Writer: Julian Jones
Director: Barry Davis
A woman complains of harassment by a neighbour. Stamp investigates and discovers that the woman is not as sane or as attractive as he initially thought.

GREIG VERSUS TAYLOR
Shown: 26.9.89
Writer: Christopher Russell
Director: Clive Fleury
When Greig arrests Eric Taylor on suspicion of armed robbery the evidence is circumstantial, but through a carefully planned interrogation Greig gets a confession.

TOTTERING
Shown: 28.9.89
Writer: Simon Moss
Director: Chris Lovett
Ackland and Martella deal with a group of children who have Superglued a lavatory door, trapping an old lady; while Melvin and Able return a totter's horse and cart to the owner's yard. Penny tries to discover if a man found knocked unconscious is that owner.

I COUNTED THEM ALL OUT
Shown: 3.10.89
Writer: Kieran Prendiville
Director: Paul Harrison
Sun Hill officers help to foil a supermarket wages robbery. Elation is short-lived when they discover that a bag containing £10,000 has gone missing.

ZIG ZAG
Shown: 5.10.89
Writer: Peter J. Hammond
Director: Chris Lovett
Dashwood and Lines investigate the disappearance of private detective Harry J. Wallace, who has information about villains illegally importing girls for prostitution. The detectives are unaware that Wallace is following them; and Wallace is unaware that he is being followed by the villains.

A MATTER OF TRUST
Shown: 10.10.89
Writer: Kieran Prendiville
Director: Derek Lister
Burnside receives information from villain's wife Maggie Moran about a security van robbery, but she withholds the time and place of the raid until he locks up her husband so that he can't take part in it.

TOURIST TRAP
Shown: 12.10.89
Writers: Linda Dearsley and Steve Wade
Director: Diana Patrick
Dashwood and Ackland join a party of tourists on a walking tour of undiscovered London while Greig and Carver stake out the hotel and catch a thief who is working with the tour guide.

THE ONE THAT GOT AWAY
Shown: 17.10.89
Writer: Jonathan Rich
Director: David Attwood
Brownlow finds himself alone dealing with a criminal who turns out to be part of a gang that Roach is investigating. There is conflict between the two officers.

FOUND OFFENDING
Shown: 19.10.89
Writer: John Kershaw
Director: Eva Kolouchova
Stamp takes a teenage beggar to the station to find out why she left home. She won't talk to Stamp, but Datta gets her to admit that the baby she is expecting is her father's.

ALL PART OF THE JOB
Shown: 24.10.89
Writer: Colin Griffin
Director: Bren Simson
Inspector McCann is impressed with Brind's handling of a pub incident and invites her for a drink. Clarke, from Special Branch, informs Conway and Burnside that he plans to arrest Grimes when he returns from abroad for his involvement in prostitution and murder. Grimes is processed at Sun Hill and is shot as Clarke drives him out of the station.

IN THE COLD
Shown: 26.10.89
Writer: J. C. Wilsher
Director: Graham Theakston
A security man finds a middle-aged woman's scantily clad body on waste ground in a railway yard. Sun Hill treats it as a 'death in suspicious circumstances' until the pathologist diagnoses the possible cause of death as hypothermia.

JUST A LITTLE RUNAROUND
Shown: 31.10.89
Writer: Richard Ireson
Director: Eva Kolouchova

A FAIR APPRAISAL
Shown: 2.11.89
Writer: Garry Lyons
Director: Nick Laughland
Called to a warehouse where an alarm is ringing, Edwards misses the fact that there has been a burglary. This reflects badly on him during his annual appraisal.

VISITORS
Shown: 7.11.89
Writer: Kevin Clarke
Director: Clive Fleury
Sun Hill holds its annual Open Day – and someone steals the snooker cup. One visitor gives Brind and Marshall a hard time. Lines is distressed over the death of his mother, which causes him further financial difficulties. Lines and Ackland investigate a dating agency which is a cover for prostitution.

PRIVATE WARS
Shown: 9.11.89
Writer: Guy Meredith
Director: Nicholas Prosser
After having been beaten up by a security guard called Simpson whom he had put in jail several years earlier, Burnside discreetly arranges for Simpson to get his comeuppance.

FEASTING WITH PANTHERS
Shown: 14.11.89
Writer: J. C. Wilsher
Director: Simon Cellan Jones
When a homosexual head teacher is burgled by his lover, who then threatens to blackmail him, Dashwood is disgusted when Burnside does a deal with the lover in exchange for information about armed robbers. Penny accepts a free cigar from a newsagent, and this causes problems.

BY THE BOOK
Shown: 16.11.89
Writer: John Milne
Director: Jeremy Silberston
Dashwood becomes over-involved with Lisa, a young drug addict living in Cardboard City. Later she is attacked – not by her down-and-out boyfriend, as Burnside suspects, but by three affluent drunk young men. Frazer sets up an exercise to improve the statement-taking technique of Able and Garfield.

BEER AND BICYCLES
Shown: 21.11.89
Writer: Christopher Russell
Director: Nick Laughland
Edwards visits a welfare officer for counselling. Conway lectures staff on their public image and searches the station for cans of lager. Able patrols on a bicycle and finds a car involved in a wages snatch. Stamp objects to having a police dog and his handler travelling in his Area Car.

GRACE OF GOD
Shown: 23.11.89
Writers: P. Fletcher and R. Le Parmentier
Director: David Hayman
Charles, a reclusive ex-soldier, has returned to his former home in a terrace earmarked for development. Cryer knows about it but has turned a blind eye, and Charles's elderly parents are not interested. A group of children are making trouble for Charles, and he kidnaps one of them but is forced to let him go.

JUST ANOTHER DAY
Shown: 28.11.89
Writer: Jesse Carr-Martindale
Director: Nicholas Prosser
Burnside puts pressure on Benjamin, a well-known drug-dealer, to become a snout. A pregnant woman is bitten by the family Rottweiler; Brind helps her to have her baby; and Peters gets the dog put down. Melvin and Turnham encounter an angry female cyclist alleging indecent assault by a passing motorist.

GONE FISHING
Shown: 30.11.89
Writer: Jonathan Rich
Director: Nick Laughland
Mrs Fitzgerald is in a coma following a road accident. Carver thinks she is the victim of a hit-and-run. Roach believes that Mr Fitzgerald ran over his wife and treats the case as attempted murder. Mrs Fitzgerald regains consciousness and denies that her husband ran her over; but Roach suspects that she's concealing the truth for personal reasons.

EARLY BIRD
Shown: 5.12.89
Writer: Tom Needham
Director: Eva Kolouchova
Lines and Carver pick up a sockless cat burglar. They are unable to tie him into a recent safe-cracking, but his wife inadvertently supplies their evidence when she recognizes his socks in the interview room. Mrs Usher, a runaway from an old people's home, dies in the Sun Hill canteen.

JUST FOR THE CRACK
Shown: 7.12.89
Writer: Steve Trafford
Director: Jeremy Silberston
Most of the shift become involved in trying to crack a stolen-motorbike ring. Ackland and Melvin deliver two CPS letters. One recipient is furious that the case has been dropped, assaults Melvin and is arrested.

WOMAN IN BROWN
Shown: 12.12.89
Writer: Alan Clewes
Director: Eva Kolouchova
Ackland and Melvin investigate the kidnapping of a baby girl. Ackland believes the kidnapper is Janet Watson. The baby's father, being interviewed at Sun Hill with his wife, sees Janet's address on the custody sheet; and he attempts to break into Janet's house while Ackland is inside trying to get her to give up the baby.

SPEAKING FREELY
Shown: 14.12.89
Writer: Garry Lyons
Director: David Attwood
Conway gives Frazer a bad annual appraisal. Frazer tells Brownlow that she thinks Conway has been unfair and airs her views about the prejudice women encounter in seeking promotion. Brownlow endorses Conway's appraisal and refuses her promotion.

THE RETURN OF THE PRODIGAL
Shown: 19.12.89
Writer: Barry Appleton
Director: Keith Washington
Henry Gill, long wanted for fraud, gives himself up

while abroad. He is brought back by Roach, and is met at Sun Hill by his family and by his solicitor, Melford. Melford states that Gill is terminally ill. As the Gill family are leaving with Gill's suitcases, sniffer dogs brought to Sun Hill on a different investigation detect large quantities of drugs hidden in them.

CHINESE WHISPERS
Shown: 21.12.89
Writer: Christopher Russell
Director: Julian Amyes
On his first day at Sun Hill, Quinnan impresses Stamp with his detection of a stolen diamond's hiding-place in a jewellery theft, flirts with all the WPCs and invites the entire shift for a drink. The appearance of a surveyor at Sun Hill raises speculations about the station's future.

POWERS OF EXCLUSION
Shown: 26.12.89
Writer: J. C. Wilsher
Director: Julian Amyes
A black minister and well-known community worker, Rev. Ogun, is arrested by Garfield and Turnham for possession of an offensive weapon. Burnside suspects him of involvement in drugs and stolen goods. He enlists Frazer's help in delaying bail for the minister until he has questioned his terrified associates; but his plan is blown when Ogun's solicitor forces Cryer to release him on a technicality.

SATURDAY NIGHT FEVER
Shown: 28.12.89
Writer: Edwin Pearce
Director: Bren Simson
When Leon Cornelius's body turns up stabbed through the heart, Burnside and Carver bring in a string of suspects – including Joshua Rodrigues. Peters is doing his best to deal with the regular Saturday-night chaos when Hermione, a young black girl, is brought in for allegedly assaulting her mother. Just as Burnside is about to charge Rodrigues with Cornelius's murder, Brind discovers that Hermione knifed him after he had attacked her.

BY THE SKIN OF OUR TEETH
Shown: 2.1.90
Writer: Arthur McKenzie

Director: Bren Simson
Able is still serving his probationary term at Sun Hill, but his superiors aren't all convinced he can cope

OFFICERS AND GENTLEMEN
Shown: 4.1.90
Writer: Steve Trafford
Director: Diana Patrick
Turnham arrests a man using a stolen credit card; the man admits that he obtained it in a burglary he committed. Carver sent down another man three weeks ago for the same burglary. Conway and Carver have an embarrassing situation on their hands. Frazer asks Brownlow for a reference; she has applied for transfer to Bramshill.

CARRY YOUR BAGS, SIR?
Shown: 9.1.90
Writer: John Milne
Director: Simon Cellan Jones
Burnside and Cryer are detailed to help Krantz, a German police officer, to track down stolen German diesel engines. Burnside is delighted to find that Krantz is a tall, blonde, attractive WPC.

I THOUGHT YOU'D GONE
Shown: 11.1.90
Writer: J. C. Wilsher
Director: Nick Laughland
Brownlow gives a farewell party for Frazer. Her replacement, Inspector Monroe, meets with Penny's approval, Peters's horror and Cryer's 'no comment'. Edwards's colleagues gather in the pub to say goodbye, but he slips away quietly.

CAD
Shown: 16.1.90
Writer: J. C. Wilsher
Director: Christopher Hodson
The CAD room loses radio contact with Martella when she enters a dead area under some flats. A search is started. Hollis is wandering round the station trying to persuade people to give blood.

A DAY LOST
Shown: 18.1.90
Writer: Les Pollard
Director: Philip Casson
Sun Hill officers are mobilized to search for a missing boy. In the end Carver finds the boy by accident.

A CLEAN DIVISION
Shown: 23.1.90
Writer: Julian Jones
Director: Derek Lister
Brownlow insists that Burnside attend a seminar at Stafford Row on Inter-Station Communication and Co-operation. While he is at Stafford Row, Carver is brought in on a charge of obstruction and intent to drive while under the influence of alcohol. Carver is cleared, not with the help of Inter-Station Co-operation, but by a negative breath-test.

ROGER AND OUT
Shown: 25.1.90
Writer: John Kershaw
Director: David Giles
Roger, a student lodging with Lines, is picked up drunk. As Lines has not obtained permission for a lodger, he is in breach of regulations. Penny puts in a report, which forces Brownlow to act. Lines's dismissal looks imminent until Burnside states that he personally advised Lines not to seek permission, Faced with the prospect of losing two CID men, Brownlow decides to let the matter rest.

ADDRESSES
Shown: 30.1.90
Writer: Peter J. Hammond
Director: Chris Lovett
Cryer and Martella, patrolling in a Panda at night, deal with Sharon Sharp, a disturbed woman 'visiting friends' from her therapy group who would rather forget they ever knew her.

MICHAEL RUNS THE FAMILY NOW
Shown: 1.2.90
Writer: Kieran Prendiville
Director: John Michael Phillips
Burnside is set up by his snout Danny to investigate Michael Lovett. Lovett is having an affair with Danny's wife, and Danny wants him put away. A pupil from Stamp's self-defence class is brought in after breaking a man's arm.

AGAINST THE ODDS
Shown: 6.2.90
Writer: Arthur McKenzie
Director: Keith Washington
In Burnside's absence, Dashwood investigates stolen property on the Mangan case – a robbery that had previously been

screened out. He questions Harry Purvis, the man suspected of the robbery, and eventually identifies Purvis's watch as Mangan's, and gets his man.

BLOODSUCKER
Shown: 8.2.90
Writer: Steve Trafford
Director: Christopher Hodson
Investigating a loan-shark operation, Lines and Roach are led to a pawnbroker wanted by Brownlow but they are unable to nail him. Brownlow has initiated a charity collection to which the pawnbroker contributes generously. Quinnan is trying to sell calculators which turn out to be faulty.

WORKERS IN UNIFORM
Shown: 13.2.90
Writer: J. C. Wilsher
Director: Colm Villa
Quinnan borrows Turnham's Panda car without booking it out. While in his possession the car is dented. He does not tell Turnham, who gets into trouble with Monroe over it.

SOMETHING TO HIDE
Shown: 15.2.90
Writer: Tom Needham
Director: John Michael Phillips
Lines investigates the mysterious theft of an emerald, and Turnham and Datta are called out to a 'domestic' involving ferrets.

THE OLD MEN'S RUN
Shown: 20.2.90
Writer: John Milne
Director: David Hayman
Cryer trains for a quarter-marathon and pulls a muscle chasing some muggers; and a shortage of sergeants means that Marshall has to 'act up' for the day.

LEGACIES
Shown: 22.2.90
Writer: Peter Gibbs
Director: Christopher Hodson
Lines involves himself with Tina Benskin, the burglar's daughter, hoping to rescue her from a life of crime; while Hollis deals with an amnesiac.

YESTERDAY, TODAY, TOMORROW
Shown: 27.2.90
Writer: Geoff McQueen
Director: Colm Villa
Brownlow faces personal and professional problems when Susan Petersfield, daughter of Commander

Petersfield, is arrested for dealing in drugs after Burnside's raid on an acid house party.

SOMETHING SPECIAL
Shown: 1.3.90
Writer: Guy Meredith
Director: David Giles
DS Martins, recruiting for a six-month special operation, visits Burnside. Roach and Greig deduce that the operation is in Northern Ireland and compete fiercely; but Burnside puts the job Lines's way, believing he could use the extra money. But Lines has second thoughts, and Martins leaves empty-handed.

ENEMIES
Shown: 6.3.90
Writer: Philip Martin
Director: Alan Wareing
Sonora, a modern Asian girl from Bombay, visits her parents in England and is outraged at their reactionary attitudes. When her father strikes her for disobeying him, she wants to bring an assault charge against him.

SAFE PLACE
Shown: 8.3.90
Writer: Peter J. Hammond
Director: Tom Cotter
Martella works undercover in a psychiatric hospital to investigate Mr Brand, a bank employee who had a nervous breakdown following a robbery at the bank. Roach suspects that Brand was involved with the raiders and that his breakdown is a front. Martella believes that he is not so much the perpetrator of crime as a natural victim attracting it.

BURNSIDE KNEW MY FATHER
Shown: 13.3.90
Writer: Lennie James
Director: Tom Cotter
Dom Reeves comes into Sun Hill claiming that his father intends to kill his mother, who is seriously ill. Burnside visits the Reeveses, who are old friends, and tells Papa Reeves that if he goes ahead with his plan he will be arrested.

WATCHING
Shown: 15.3.90
Writer: Peter Gibbs
Director: Chris Lovett
Quinnan and Garfield are called to investigate an intruder at a school. He

turns out to be a self-styled vigilante who is patrolling the premises. Martella and Stamp investigate fly-tipping.

UNIVERSITY CHALLENGE
Shown: 20.3.90
Writer: Simon Moss
Director: Derek Lister
During a robbery Burnside sees a man he recognizes as Joey Buchan, reformed criminal and media personality. In the past Buchan's wife always gave him an alibi. His new, middle-class girlfriend does the same.

GROWING PAINS
Shown: 22.3.90
Writer: Barry Appleton
Director: Philip Casson
CID go to an electronics factory where an intruder has been reported. Carver is injured by the intruder. Garfield thinks he has arrested an armed robber, but the suspect is only a fantasizing juvenile.

ONE OF THE BOYS
Shown: 27.3.90
Writer: Jonathan Rich
Director: Alan Wareing
Martella's first week in CID. Sent to bring in Sheena Rossi, prostitute, drug addict and vital witness, she loses her and chases her all over town – ruining her new outfit in the process. She brings Sheena in – only to learn that she is no longer needed as a witness.

BEGGARS AND CHOOSERS
Shown: 29.3.90
Writer: Steve Trafford
Director: Bob Hird
Sun Hill is inundated with down-and-outs, and Monroe has to deal with the problem. Meanwhile Brownlow delivers a speech on policing in the nineties that is not quite what his audience were expecting.

CITADEL
Shown: 3.4.90
Writer: J. C. Wilsher
Director: Bob Hird
Brownlow learns of the plans for Sun Hill's future. Turnham's colleagues are questioned about him by Special Branch.

BLUE EYED BOY
Shown: 5.4.90
Writer: Julian Jones
Director: Nick Laughland

Melvin is taking expensive holidays, turns up late for a court hearing and looks as if he may have kept a ring after a burglary. In fact he has acquired a rich older girlfriend.

FULL HOUSE
Shown: 10.4.90
Writer: Arthur McKenzie
Director: Julian Amyes
Sun Hill in the process of refurbishment. There has been an indecent assault on a six-year-old girl. On patrol, Hollis spots a man who fits the description of the culprit and brings him in.

BIG FISH, LITTLE FISH
Shown: 12.4.90
Writer: Patrick Harkins
Director: Nick Laughland
Burnside and Greig follow a bag of illicit guns as they are passed on. The ringleader is an ex-policeman. Stamp and Garfield stop a group of fishermen covertly bringing home the dead body of their friend.

INFORMATION RECEIVED
Shown: 17.4.90
Writer: Kevin Clarke
Director: Michael Simpson
In order to catch Mickey Owen, who runs a protection racket, Roach is forced to use his former snout the transvestite Roxanne. He is reluctant because he was the cause of Roxanne being beaten up. Pressure from the Flying Squad, who are also after Owen, adds to his problems.

CLOSE CO-OPERATION
Shown: 19.4.90
Writer: Garry Lyons
Director: Michael Simpson
When Billy Steen, a small-time drug-pusher arrested by Burnside, is beaten up in his Barton Street cell, the Sun Hill officers have to decide where their loyalties lie.

MIDDLEMAN
Shown: 24.4.90
Writer: J. C. Wilsher
Director: Michael Simpson
Operation Middleman, a combined operation between Sun Hill and the Drugs Squad, gets under way. There is rivalry between Burnside and DI Wray. When Middleman goes disastrously wrong, Burnside finds himself under Brownlow's scrutiny.

CORKSCREW (Part 2 of MIDDLEMAN)
Shown: 26.4.90
Writer: J. C. Wilsher
Director: Michael Simpson
Burnside reaches a reluctant truce with Wray as they mount Operation Corkscrew on a suspect policeman at Barton Street. The operation is a success. Only then does Burnside discover that Wray is his new guv'nor.

OBSESSIONS
Shown: 1.5.90
Writer: Peter Gibbs
Director: Julian Amyes
A woman is obsessed by a married man after having a fling with him. The man and his wife say that she is threatening violence and want her removed from outside their house. Martella believes the woman is dangerous, and her suspicions are confirmed when the woman tries to run the wife over.

SMALL HOURS
Shown: 3.5.90
Writer: Kevin Clarke
Director: Mike Vardy
Night shifts. A streaker causes Stamp to crash the Area Car. Carver is interested in Datta, but she is more concerned with some Vietnamese. She is later trapped when their flat is set on fire. Quinnan is injured by the man who started the fire.

VICTIMS
Shown: 8.5.90
Writer: Jonathan Rich
Director: Derek Lister
Tosh Lines sees a pattern in a series of attacks on women and puts pressure on Brownlow to get permission for a large-scale surveillance. A troublesome couple, the Cleghorns, complain that nothing has been done about their burglary.

SOMEBODY'S HUSBAND (Part 2 of VICTIMS)
Shown: 10.5.90
Writer: Jonathan Rich
Director: Derek Lister
The surveillance is under way. Ackland talks to Valerie Martin, who has a confused complaint about her husband, and realizes that the husband is the attacker. She warns Burnside, but his men are watching the wrong man, and it is Ackland who eventually catches the culprit.

CANLEY FIELDS
Shown: 15.5.90
Writer: Christopher Russell
Director: Mike Vardy
Two youths report seeing a man dragging a young boy into bushes skirting Canley Fields. Nothing is found, and Roach suspects it is a hoax; but then an alarmed mother reports her son as missing – and his description matches that of the boy seen being abducted.

THE NIGHT WATCH
Shown: 17.5.90
Writer: J. C. Wilsher
Director: Graham Theakston
Martella and Roach deal with an alleged rape; and Garfield and Young are called to a noisy party and discover a body.

TROJAN HORSE
Shown: 22.5.90
Writer: Pat Dunlop
Director: Graham Theakston
Melvin and Garfield pull in Kenny Wilkes, a car thief, driving a smart Jaguar. Melvin drives the car back to Sun Hill with Hollis. The car boot contains a bomb, and it explodes in the yard with Melvin at the wheel, killing him.

RITES (Part 2 of TROJAN HORSE)
Shown: 24.5.90
Writer: Jonathan Rich
Director: Derek Lister
Melvin's funeral. Burnside takes CID on a job, and they arrive late for the service.

ANSWERS
Shown: 29.5.90
Writer: Peter J. Hammond
Director: Christopher Hodson
Dashwood and Lines visit Phil Roth on the day he is planning to celebrate his first wedding anniversary with his second (pregnant) wife. Two years after the detectives interviewed Roth in connection with sexual attacks on women, his ex-wife has withdrawn the alibi she gave him.

A FRESH START (Part 2 of CANLEY FIELDS)
Shown: 31.5.90
Writer: Christopher Russell
Director: Derek Lister
The new Sun Hill is officially opened. In the midst of all the celebrations news comes that a child's body has been found.

A CASE TO ANSWER (Part 2 of NIGHT WATCH)
Shown: 5.6.90
Writer: J. C. Wilsher
Director: Stuart Burge
The committal hearing for the rape case dealt with in 'Night Watch'. DCI Wray arrives at Sun Hill and ruffles Burnside's feathers.

LINE UP
Shown: 7.6.90
Writer: Elizabeth-Anne Wheal
Director: Stuart Burge
Stamp arrests a vicious young mugger. Martella insists on an identity parade; the victim makes a positive identification; but at the last minute the forensic evidence falls down and the case is abandoned.

POLICE POWERS
Shown: 12.6.90
Writer: Julian Jones
Director: Gordon Flemyng
Sun Hill officers attend a football match. Cryer arrests a player who hits another player as they leave the field. He is backed by Peters but frustrated by Monroe and Brownlow.

ACTION BOOK (Part 3 of CANLEY FIELDS)
Shown: 14.6.90
Writer: Christopher Russell
Director: Graham Theakston
The inquiry into the murder of Jennie Price gets under way. Roach is assigned to run the Incident Room under the supervision of Superintendent Meadows.

TACTICS
Shown: 19.6.90
Writer: Arthur McKenzie
Director: Graham Theakston
A provisional force ask Sun Hill to set up raids on a team of villains active in the Midlands. Wray insists that Burnside remains with him at the station. They attend a senior officers' meeting where a good deal of political manoeuvring takes place.

SCORES
Shown: 21.6.90
Writer: Peter J. Hammond
Director: Gordon Flemyng
Trafford, a known villain, arrives in Sun Hill. Burnside wants him moved on. Roach is curious about Burnside's former dealings with Trafford's wife, Rikki.

WITCH HUNT
(Part 4 of CANLEY FIELDS)
Shown: 26.6.90
Writer: Christopher Russell
Director: Derek Lister
Tosh Lines has questioned a suspect on a murder inquiry and released him without a charge. A second murder has been committed. Was Lines right or wrong?

CLOSE TO HOME
Shown: 28.6.90
Writer: Christopher Russell
Director: Nick Laughland
Ackland and Cryer investigate a domestic incident in which a toddler has been badly burned. Cryer finds his own family problems influencing his judgement.

BREAKING POINT
Shown 3.7.90
Writer: Les Pollard
Director: Peter Barber-Fleming
Burnside and Dashwood go to arrest a burglary suspect. He escapes them and is finally brought to bay on a bridge where he threatens suicide. We learn that he has been under psychiatric care. Despite all efforts to save him, he jumps off the bridge and is killed.

JUMPING THE GUN
Shown: 5.7.90
Writer: David Hoskings
Director: Peter Barber-Fleming
After a vicious building society robbery Burnside is convinced that Kilby is responsible. Despite Kilby's sister's alibi Burnside is determined to arrest him for the job.

WHAT KIND OF MAN?
(Part 5 of CANLEY FIELDS)
Shown: 10.7.90
Writer: Christopher Russell
Director: Chris Lovett
A routine visit to a school gives Quinnan reason to suspect George Blake of the murder of Jennie Price and Graeme Butler. After a search Penny arrests him and listens to his confession as CID and Brownlow celebrate.

BEAT CRIME
Shown: 12.7.90
Writer: J. C. Wilsher
Director: Nick Laughland
In Burnside's absence, DCI Wray encourages closer co-operation between CID and uniform, but his encouragement of Ackland

goes further and he invites her out to dinner.

UNSOCIAL HOURS
Shown: 17.7.90
Writer: J. C. Wilsher
Director: Derek Lister
CID are mounting an observation on a restaurant – one to which Wray has taken Ackland. So there is much to gossip about.

INTERPRETATIONS
Shown: 19.7.90
Writer: Jonathan Rich
Director: Julian Amyes
A house occupied by Tamils is firebombed. Brownlow assumes it is a racist attack, but Roach discovers that an Asian racket lies behind it.

ANGLES
Shown: 24.7.90
Writer: Arthur McKenzie
Director: Roger Tucker
Burnside's 'pop and seize' operation is only a partial success.

WATCH MY LIPS
Shown: 26.7.90
Writer: Patrick Harkins
Director: Julian Amyes
A deaf man resists arrest and attacks Carver. The man is assumed to be James Doyle. WPC Ford interprets for him but finally realizes that he is not Doyle but has stolen Doyle's belongings.

FEELING BRAVE
Shown: 31.7.90
Writer: John Milne
Director: Richard Holthouse
A post office job goes wrong, leaving Carver looking down the barrel of a shotgun. Roach suspects an inside job.

COME FLY WITH ME
Shown: 2.8.90
Writer: Peter Gibbs
Director: Michael Kerrigan
A local travel agency goes bust. Stamp is among the angry customers demanding their money back. Then one of the firm's managers is found dead.

ATTITUDES
Shown: 7.8.90
Writer: Arthur McKenzie
Director: Richard Holthouse
A card game before the shift leads to the victimization of Young by Stamp and Garfield.

ROBBO
Shown: 9.8.90
Writer: Brian Finch
Director: Chris Lovett

Robbo Robbins is Tosh Lines's self-appointed snout, but he provides more aggravation than help.

GROUND RULES
Shown: 14.8.90
Writer: Geoff McQueen
Director: Michael Kerrigan
Dashwood and Roach question a suspect in a car, not realizing that the interview is being taped. They escape trouble when Monroe discovers that the suspect's tape-recorder is stolen property.

ONCE A COPPER
Shown: 16.8.90
Writer: Robin Mukherjee
Director: Frank W. Smith
Burnside visits Cooper, a former CID officer doing time for corruption, to get information about a villain. He makes a deal but doesn't intend to honour it.

VENDETTA
Shown: 21.8.90
Writer: Peter Brooks
Director: Graham Theakston
A vendetta between two criminal families is exploited by Sun Hill CID to aid the investigation into an armed robbery

MY FAVOURITE THINGS
Shown: 23.8.90
Writer: Arthur McKenzie
Director: Roger Tucker
Conway makes a routine check on the property store. When Monroe hears that a jemmy has gone missing he suspects Quinnan but orders a search of all the lockers.

WIN SOME LOSE SOME
Shown: 28.8.90
Writer: Jonathan Rich
Director: Jeremy Ancock
Carver and Martella set out to clean up a seedy nightclub; while Quinnan and Stringer seek stolen dustbin-lids.

UP THE STEPS
Shown: 30.8.90
Writer: Carolyn Sally Jones
Director: Jeremy Ancock
Giving evidence in court, Loxton and Young find themselves under fire in a 'trial within a trial'.

WHERE THERE'S A WILL
Shown: 4.9.90
Writer: Patrick Harkins
Director: Garth Tucker
Burnside becomes interested when he

discovers that a local burglar has made a violent criminal the heir to his entire estate; while Cryer is left some money in the will of an ex-prostitute and discovers an attempted fraud.

NEAR THE KNUCKLE
Shown: 6.9.90
Writer: Ayshe Raif
Director: Nick Hamm
A respectable doctor and his wife are brought in after a 'domestic'. Datta wants to charge the husband, but the issue turns out to be more complicated than expected.

BODY LANGUAGE
Shown: 11.9.90
Writer: Dick Sharples
Director: Nick Hamm
Stamp arrests a black youth who is later released without charge. The incident is used by the youth's solicitor to disrupt Brownlow's Police Consultative Committee meeting.

WHEN DID YOU LAST SEE YOUR FATHER?
Shown: 13.9.90
Writer: Barry Appleton
Director: Bob Gabriel
Some schoolchildren are in the station after their coach has crashed, and a little boy identifies an Identikit picture as his father.

EYE-WITNESS
Shown: 18.9.90
Writer: Christopher Penfold
Director: Graham Theakston
A black man is knifed in a squabble between black and white youths after a football match. Greig exposes a continuing race war.

SUFFICIENT EVIDENCE
Shown: 20.9.90
Writer: Rib Davis
Director: Garth Tucker
Investigating a disturbance at a party, Quinnan finds a stash of dope which he claims he saw a man place on a table. He asks Garfield to verify this, but Garfield is uncertain.

FORGET-ME-NOT
Shown: 25.9.90
Writer: Russell Lewis
Director: Frank W. Smith
A chauvinistic outburst by Quinnan in the canteen, the arrival of her ex-husband, DS Hooper, and a violent domestic incident give Cathy Marshall a trying day.

SOMETHING TO REMEMBER
(Part 6 of CANLEY FIELDS)
Shown: 27.9.90
Writer: Christopher Russell
Director: Laura Sims
Quinnan goes to Scotland Yard to receive a commendation for his quick thinking in the Canley Fields murder investigation; and Penny feels slighted because he was actually the arresting officer.

OFF THE LEASH
Shown: 2.10.90
Writer: Christopher Russell
Director: Christopher Hodson
Delia French, former typist, returns to Sun Hill as a WPC; and Tosh Lines pursues some 'steamers'.

FAMILY TIES
Shown: 4.10.90
Writer: Martyn Wade
Director: Chris Lovett
Ackland arrests a woman for stealing drugs, and discovers how far a mother will go to 'help' her child.

OLD FRIENDS
Shown: 9.10.90
Writer: Nick Collins
Director: Michael Kerrigan
Datta and Quinnan attempt to rescue a girl trapped in an underground pipe. Roach investigates an attack on the elderly mother of an old colleague, who eventually admits his guilt.

PRIDE AND PREJUDICE
Shown: 11.10.90
Writer: Tim Firth
Director: Laura Sims
Garfield and Stamp detain a respectable man on a charge of arson, and discover that he has been the victim of harassment since he was found HIV-positive.

HOUSEY HOUSEY
Shown: 16.10.90
Writer: John Chambers
Director: Bill Brayne
Early-morning eviction of squatters from a block of council flats. A distraught father attacks the bailiff and is arrested. Conway tries to sort things out with Councillor Judge.

CONNELLY'S KIDS
Shown: 18.10.90
Writer: Michael Cameron
Director: Chris Lovett
A villain Greig arrests for fencing turns out to be the father of three equally industrious children, and

subsequent investigation brings to light allegations of abuse.

ONE OF THOSE DAYS
Shown: 23.10.90
Writer: Roger Leach
Director: Nick Laughland
Ackland and Loxton attend an RTA which results in the young woman victim losing her baby. Following a conference at the Yard, Brownlow interviews all the women officers.

JACK-THE-LAD
Shown: 25.10.90
Writer: Michael Baker
Director: Bill Hays
Burnside is on the heels of an armed jewellery-shop robber; while Stamp and Datta find one woman viciously assaulting another.

BLUE MURDER
Shown: 30.10.90
Writer: Russell Lewis
Director: Stuart Urban
While involved in an operation to foil an armed robbery Cryer shoots one of the villains.

EFFECTIVE PERSUADERS
Shown: 1.11.90
Writer: J. C. Wilsher
Director: Nick Laughland
Sun Hill officers are on an interview training course; and practising role-play leads Carver and Quinnan into an angry confrontation.

A SENSE OF DUTY
Shown: 6.11.90
Writer: Julian Jones
Director: Bill Hays
While off duty Roach restrains a man in a restaurant. Stamp and Garfield arrive and take the man to Sun Hill, assuming that Roach has arrested him. Monroe insists that Roach should be at the station and sends for him.

LYING IN WAIT
Shown: 8.11.90
Writer: Chris Boucher
Director: Bill Brayne
Peters, Ackland and Garfield are called to a minor disturbance and discover a dead body; Stamp, enjoying a quiet moment by the canal, is called upon to save a child's life; and a set of stolen traffic lights causes problems.

PLATO FOR POLICEMEN
Shown: 13.11.90
Writer: Robin Mukherjee

Director: Christopher Hodson
Roach visits a familiar thief who is supposed to be going straight; Ackland and Hollis discover a traumatized victim; and Brownlow goes back to school and doesn't like it.

TESTIMONY (Part 2 of PLATO FOR POLICEMEN)
Shown: 15.11.90
Writer: Robin Mukherjee
Director: Christopher Hodson
Roach is investigating a case of aggravated burglary and rape. The suspect is a small-time burglar who is, apparently, a caring family-man.

DECISIONS
Shown: 20.11.90
Writer: Arthur McKenzie
Director: Tom Cotter
On his first day back at work after the shooting, Cryer deals with an old lady who has planted weapons all round her house in case burglars who took her purse with her house-keys in it return.

KNOW YOUR ENEMY
Shown: 22.11.90
Writer: Nick Collins
Director: Moira Armstrong
Roach goes to the defence of his occasional girlfriend Kim Jarvis when her ex-husband, whom she shopped, is released from prison.

LIES
Shown: 27.11.90
Writer: Brendan McDonald
Director: Roger Tucker
Greig leads a successful raid resulting in four arrests. Unfortunately they miss a handgun thrown by one of the villains. When a child is later injured playing with the gun, Greig must face the consequences.

OLD WOUNDS
Shown: 29.11.90
Writer: Ian Briggs
Director: Roger Tucker
Patrick Litton is out for revenge on the man who put his father in a police cell, where he died. And, if he can make fools of the police in the process, so much the better.

JUST FOR THE MOMENT
Shown: 4.12.90
Writer: Susan B. Shattock
Director: Tom Cotter
Stamp and Loxton bring in

Gary, a seemingly docile young man who, inexplicably, has assaulted his mother. In the hectic custody area, Gary is momentarily unattended. He grabs the knife that was brought in as evidence and holds Datta hostage.

MARKET FORCES
Shown: 6.12.90
Writer: Peter Brooks
Director: Sarah Pia Anderson
When a special cycle patrol to combat thefts from vehicles catches a seventeen-year-old in the act, it seems a straightforward case; but the inquiry takes an unexpected turn.

ONE FOR THE ROAD
Shown: 11.12.90
Writer: Michael Crompton
Director: John Strickland
There is a party at the pub to celebrate Cryer's twenty years' service. On his way home, Penny is stopped and breathalysed by two Barton Street PCs.

START WITH THE WHISTLE (Part 2 of ONE FOR THE ROAD)
Shown: 13.12.90
Writer: J. C. Wilsher
Director: John Strickland
Penny has to make important decisions in court after being positively breathalysed at Barton Street.

OUT OF THE BLUE
Shown: 18.12.90
Writer: J. C. Wilsher
Director: Moira Armstrong
Brownlow learns that Wray and Ackland are having an affair. Wray faces the consequences, and Ackland wrongly accuses Monroe of grassing on her.

STREET SMART
Shown: 20.12.90
Writer: J. C. Wilsher
Director: Sarah Pia Anderson
Hollis and Stamp plan revenge on Monroe; and the new DCI, Kim Reid, arrives at Sun Hill – with a prisoner!

SAFE AS HOUSES
Shown: 26.12.90
Writer: Russell Lewis
Director: Tom Cotter
Lennie Powell is due to give vital evidence against a group of villains. Dashwood, Carver, Martella and Lines are given the job of

'babysitting' for twenty-four hours.

FRIENDS AND NEIGHBOURS
Shown: 27.12.90
Writer: Christopher Russell
Director: Mike Dormer
Roach is cheated of a good arrest by Burnside, who claims the glory; and Carver moves into the section house after moving out of his girlfriend's flat.

GRIEF
Shown: 1.1.91
Writer: Arthur McKenzie
Director: Graham Theakston
Traffic lights, DAC Hicks, Hollis and a collapsed roof are all causing Brownlow grief; while Dashwood is getting grief from DCI Reid.

THE CHASE
Shown: 3.1.91
Writer: Carole Harrison
Director: Stuart Urban
When a petrol station is robbed, many of the Sun Hill officers become involved. Datta rescues a child from a car parked in the robbers' path; and Loxton, chasing the robbers in the Area Car, is involved in a serious POLAC.

THE ATTACK
Shown: 8.1.91
Writer: Philip Palmer
Director: John Black
Marshall is attacked, and Monroe investigates the case with particular diligence.

CROWN V. COOPER
Shown: 10.1.91
Writer: Jane Hollowood
Director: Michael Kerrigan
Loxton and Garfield are in court to give evidence against Cooper on a charge of assaulting a police officer, but find themselves accused of conspiring to pervert the course of justice.

THE GIRL CAN'T HELP IT
Shown: 15.1.91
Writer: Arthur McKenzie
Director: John Strickland
During the search for a girl missing from home and lured into prostitution, Quinnan learns the value of straight talking from Ackland's dealing with the girl and her father, and Conway irritates Brownlow by going on local radio without consulting him.

MACHINES
Shown: 17.1.91
Writer: Peter J. Hammond
Director: Bob Gabriel
In court a man charged with fraud is remanded on bail after claiming that he is dependent on a dialysis machine. Roach believes he is buying time and doesn't want him to get away with it.

LOOPHOLE
Shown: 22.1.91
Writer: Michael Baker
Director: John Strickland
CID join uniform to investigate burglaries on an estate; while Young's sick-leave provokes action on stress management.

BOTTLE
Shown: 24.1.91
Writer: Arthur McKenzie
Director: Graham Theakston
Following a disturbance at a pub, a drunk claims that the landlord shot him. Maitland's investigation causes concern to Roach, for the landlord is a snout.

SAMARITAN
Shown: 29.1.91
Writer: Brian Finch
Director: John Black
A man is arrested after stopping to 'assist' a woman apparently in distress. The woman has been molested. The man is considered a likely suspect, but Burnside fails to make a charge stick.

FEAR OR FAVOUR
Shown: 31.1.91
Writer: Christopher Russell
Director: Mike Dormer
When an alleged drug-dealer is arrested on the Jasmine Allen Estate, a mob gathers, and in the ensuing disturbance Ackland is hurt. Everton Warwick, her alleged assailant, is arrested and charged with GBH.

START TO FINISH
Shown: 5.2.91
Writer: Graham Ison
Director: Laura Sims
Tom Penny, now working as a security officer, turns up at Sun Hill – still trying to pretend he's a policeman.

NIGHT AND DAY
Shown: 7.2.91
Writer: Russell Lewis
Director: Michael Owen Morris
Called to a burglary, Stringer feels sympathy for the attractive young female victim; but Lines later arrests her as the

perpetrator. WPC French discovers that the cavalry don't always arrive when you need them.

FAVOURS

Shown: 12.2.91
Writer: Martyn Wade
Director: Bob Blagden
Roach and Dashwood investigate thefts from premises guarded by a security firm. Kemble, the head of the firm, is an ex-copper and a friend of Roach. Dashwood doesn't trust Kemble and, because of this, doesn't trust Roach.

IN CHAMBERS

Shown: 14.2.91
Writer: Carolyn Sally Jones
Director: Michael Owen Morris
A case on which Greig has spent months of careful work begins to disintegrate before his eyes.

KIDS DON'T CRY ANYMORE

Shown: 19.2.91
Writer: Barry Appleton
Director: Tom Cotter
Ackland notices some children playing. As she gets closer she realizes that they are playing make-believe drug-dealers. Dashwood's application to join the Fraud Squad is turned down.

TOO MANY CHIEFS

Shown: 21.2.91
Writer: Tony Etchells
Director: David Hayman
Quinnan and Marshall return Lynne Corby to Milford House bail hostel – only to see her run off again. When Caroline Bennett's suicide is discovered, Monroe begins to wonder if the two are connected.

EVERY MOTHER'S SON

Shown: 26.2.91
Writer: Patrick Harkins
Director: Laura Sims
Monroe mounts an operation to catch drug addicts who are threatening doctors on an estate; and Hollis has a great idea how to catch them.

FURTHERS

Shown: 28.2.91
Writer: Robin Mukherjee
Director: Brian Farnham
Dashwood is looking for Bailey, who has absconded from an open prison; but it becomes apparent that Bailey is out for revenge on

Dashwood.

CLOSING THE NET

Shown: 5.3.91
Writer: Robin Mukherjee
Director: Michael Brayshaw
Tosh Lines profiles a child molester. Is there a pattern which will narrow the field?

THE PUBLIC INTEREST (Part 2 of FEAR OR FAVOUR)

Shown: 7.3.91
Writer: Christopher Russell
Director: Sarah Pia Anderson
Pursuing her claim against the man who assaulted her, Ackland is forced to consider a private prosecution. A man is convicted of having an affair with a fifteen-year-old schoolgirl.

PHOTO FINISH

Shown: 12.3.91
Writer: David Hoskins
Director: Bob Blagden
From Tony's bedroom Datta and Garfield keep watch on a pub where a customer is suspected of drug-dealing. It leads to the arrest of Tony's friend Colin. Garfield discovers £200 in Tony's room and implies that the boy is a possible dealer.

JUST DESSERTS

Shown: 14.3.91
Writer: Christopher Russell
Director: Alan Bell
Kim Reid investigates the murder of a man who, by drunken driving, caused the death of another man's wife.

832 RECEIVING

Shown: 19.3.91
Writer: Barbara Coy
Director: Alan Bell
Ackland and French bring in a girl pickpocket, and her mother turns out to be claiming fraudulent benefit.

THE BETTER PART OF VALOUR

Shown: 21.3.91
Writer: Arthur McKenzie
Director: David Hayman
An attack on a security van brings problems for Sun Hill CID, and tension between Burnside, Roach and Reid.

DOUBLE OR QUITS

Shown: 26.3.91
Writer: Rib Davis
Director: Bill Pryde
A supplier of rent boys for

the Amsterdam sex trade is arrested, and Martella gets a result in court with a trick learned from Burnside.

WE COULD BE HEROES

Shown: 28.3.91
Writer: Tony Etchells
Director: John Strickland
A young woman is the victim of a hit-and-run driver; and Quinnan and Stamp find themselves in trouble with Monroe.

COLD TURKEY 1 (LIFELINE)

Shown: 2.4.91
Writer: J. C. Wilsher
Director: Gordon Flemyng
A drug addict seals himself off in a block of flats with a young boy and possibly an injured woman. Conway has to get him out.

COLD TURKEY 2 (LATE TURN SUNDAY)

Shown: 4.4.91
Writer: J. C. Wilsher
Director: Gordon Flemyng
The siege continues. Conway has to authorize the shooting of the drug addict.

NOW WE'RE MOTORING

Shown: p.4.91
Writer: J. C. Wilsher
Director: Michael Brayshaw
Hollis supervises the towing-away of a BMW, unaware that it is being stolen under his nose.

DEAD MAN'S BOOTS

Shown: 11.4.91
Writer: Julian Jones
Director: John Glenister
The job of Duty Sergeant falls vacant. Peters declines the job, and Cryer accepts it.

CAUGHT NAPPING (Part 2 of SAFE AS HOUSES)

Shown: 16.4.91
Writer: Russell Lewis
Director: John Strickland
The Serious Crime Squad arrive at Sun Hill to investigate the murder of Lennie Powell while in CID custody.

HAMMER TO FALL (Part 3 of SAFE AS HOUSES)

Shown: 18.4.91
Writer: Russell Lewis
Director: Richard Holthouse
The Lennie Powell investigation continues. The Drugs Squad combines

with Sun Hill officers on a raid.

CRY HAVOC

Shown: 23.4.91
Writer: Russell Lewis
Director: Stuart Urban
Peters is stabbed, and Stringer chases the suspect into a power station. The man falls to his death.

RULES OF ENGAGEMENT

Shown: 25.4.91
Writer: Elizabeth-Anne Wheal
Director: David Attwood
Martella is praised for her work in solving robberies of sound equipment; but her career is under threat when her current boyfriend turns out to be the mastermind behind the robberies.

DELIVERY ON TIME

Shown: 30.4.91
Writer: Jonathan Myerson
Director: David Attwood
A burglar posing as a delivery man threatens female occupants with violence.

BLACK MONDAY

Shown: 2.5.91
Writer: Peter J. Hammond
Director: Alan Bell
Lines sees a fraudster he thought had committed suicide five years earlier; while Carver investigates a supplier of stolen car parts.

JOB FOR THE BOYS

Shown: 7.5.91
Writer: Carolyn Sally Jones
Director: Alan Bell
A thief executes a major robbery from a supermarket and a minor robbery to avoid the maximum sentence for the major crime. Maitland makes the connection.

WITHOUT CONSENT

Shown: 9.5.91
Writer: Julian Jones
Director: Derek Lister
When prostitute Linda turns up at the front desk and claims that she has been raped, the male officers on duty treat her with derision. Only Ackland takes the case seriously – until Kim Reid weighs in.

SAINTS AND MARTYRS

Shown: 14.5.91
Writer: Christopher Russell
Director: John Glenister
Thieves posing as Water Board officials gain access to pensioners' homes; and

a fault in the air-conditioning in the custody suite causes problems

OBSERVATION

Shown: 16.5.91
Writer: Martyn Wade
Director: Sarah Pia Anderson
The Flying Squad and Sun Hill officers combine on a successful raid on hijackers.

THE GREATER GOOD

Shown: 21.5.91
Writer: David Hoskins
Director: Mike Dormer
Conway becomes involved when a friend of his, a respected Youth Community Centre worker, is suspected of a car insurance fraud.

THE BEST YOU CAN BUY (Part 3 of FEAR OR FAVOUR)

Shown: 23.5.91
Writer: Christopher Russell
Director: Moira Armstrong
Ackland's case against Everton Warwick for assault reaches court.

ADDICT

Shown: 28.5.91
Writer: Victoria Taylor
Director: Chris Lovett
Peters's first day back on active duty after being stabbed.

BLACK MARK

Shown: 30.5.91
Writer: Philip Palmer
Director: Bill Pryde
Dashwood's snout lodges a complaint of corruption against him, and MS15 investigate.

THE RIGHT THING TO DO

Shown: 4.6.91
Writer: Kieran Prendiville
Director: Brian Parker
Following a tip-off, Lines and Carver raid a pub and arrest a gospel rap band for possession of drugs; but Lines suspects it was a set-up.

THE HARDER THEY FALL

Shown: 6.6.91
Writer: Tony Etchells
Director: Chris Lovett
Loxton is assaulted by two men and blacks out. When he regains consciousness he cannot remember the incident. One of the men dies in hospital, and for a time Loxton is under suspicion.

SOMETHING PERSONAL
Shown: 11.6.91
Writer: Brendan J. Cassin
Director: Brian Parker
An investigation into the death of a young woman from a drugs overdose leads Dashwood and Carver to a video shop with a sideline in drugs and pornography.

HIJACK
Shown: 13.6.91
Writer: Philip Palmer
Director: Derek Lister
Three armed men hijack a lorryload of cigarettes.

WITH INTENT
Shown: 18.6.91
Writer: Carolyn Sally Jones
Director: Bill Pryde
A CPS lawyer comes to explain CPS procedures and the difficulty of proving intent. Carver, who has just returned from a frustrating morning in court, is not sympathetic.

INITIATIVE
Shown: 20.6.91
Writer: J. C. Wilsher
Director: Mike Dormer
Kim Reid initiates a pilot project on the Bannister Estate in her campaign to target street crime.

CARELESS WHISPERS
Shown: 25.6.91
Writer: Edward Canfor-Dumas
Director: Derek Lister
Burnside's raid on an estate is only a partial success

MINIMUM FORCE
Shown: 27.6.91
Writer: Simon Andrew Stirling
Director: Bill Brayne
Stringer and Datta discover that a householder has seriously assaulted an apparent burglar. At Sun Hill the drunken Annie makes sure the police look as if they have been unnecessarily violent.

SKELETONS
Shown: 2.7.91
Writer: Kevin Clarke
Director: Brian Farnham
Hollis finds a house full of skeletons, and Sun Hill CID think they are on the trail of a mass murderer.

TARGETS
Shown: 4.7.91
Writer: J. C. Wilsher
Director: Suri B. Krishnamma
An observation and a trap are set up for the juvenile perpetrators of street crime.

THE NEGOTIATOR
Shown: 9.7.91
Writer: Paul Bond
Director: Stuart Urban
Hollis suddenly finds himself held hostage at gunpoint in a shop's storeroom and has to keep his captor calm.

REPUTATIONS
Shown: 11.7.91
Writer: Simon Moss
Director: Suri B. Krishnamma
A man claims he was framed for a jewellery robbery. CID link the job to a security van robbery, but revenge motivated by jealousy is involved.

THE JUGGLER AND THE FORTUNE TELLER
Shown: 16.7.91
Writer: Barry Appleton
Director: Alan Bell
Forensic evidence for a rape case is stolen from Martella's car. It is recovered, but the victim refuses to give evidence and the case is withdrawn.

JOEY
Shown: 18.7.91
Writer: J. C. Wilsher
Director: Derek Lister
A badly executed street robbery by a young boy results in an arrest for Loxton; and the boy's confession is of interest to CID.

YOUR SHOUT
Shown: 23.7.91
Writer: Julian Jones
Director: Bill Pryde
Acting sergeant Cathy Marshall fails to note that she has inherited a case of child abduction from C Relief; and it reflects on her suitability for promotion.

LADYKILLER
Shown: 25.7.91
Writer: Steve Trafford
Director: Moira Armstrong
An investigation is mounted when a woman is burned to death in a car.

A CORPORAL OF HORSE
Shown: 30.7.91
Writer: Julian Jones
Director: Mike Vardy
Seconded to C Relief as acting sergeant, Cathy Marshall puts Sergeant Locket's career on the line.

CAUSE AND EFFECT
Shown: 1.8.91
Writer: Christopher Russell
Director: Jan Sargent
Animal liberationists take a hostage.

GETTING INVOLVED
Shown: 6.8.91
Writer: Stephen Churchett
Director: Richard Holthouse
A pub brawl between thieves in which one of the men is stabbed.

BENEFIT OF THE DOUBT
Shown: 8.8.91
Writer: Jonathan Myerson
Director: Mike Vardy
A barrister is arrested on suspicion of assaulting a prostitute, but he is eventually released as the evidence is only circumstantial – though the girl turns out to be HIV-positive.

CRACK-UP
Shown: 13.8.91
Writer: Barry Appleton
Director: Bill Brayne
A Barton Street officer is shot dead in a motiveless attack.

THE LAST LAUGH
Shown: 15.8.91
Writer: Duncan Gould
Director: Denny Lawrence
Quinnan solves the case of a stolen JCB excavator whose engine has been 'ringed'.

ACCESS
Shown: 20.8.91
Writer: Anthony Attard
Director: Brian Parker
CID are looking for bogus Gas Board officials who are robbing pensioners; and an estranged husband denied access to his son attacks his wife's lover with a meat-cleaver.

SIX OF ONE
Shown: 22.8.91
Writer:
Director: Sharon Miller
A girl jewel-thief escapes and dumps the stolen goods. One item is missing, and Stringer is suspected of taking it. (The girl is caught recovering it later.)

MARRIED TO THE JOB
Shown: 27.8.91
Writer: Roger Leach
Director: Brian Parker
Stamp is forced to choose between marriage and the Job.

DOMESTIC
Shown: 29.8.91
Writer: Philip Palmer
Director: Graham Theakston
A rape victim withdraws an allegation against her boyfriend and is then murdered by him.

STRESS RULES
Shown: 3.9.91
Writer: Robin Mukherjee
Director: Jan Sargent
Brownlow is promoting an anti-stress campaign; and Young is called to an estate stabbing connected with drugs

THEY ALSO SERVE
Shown: 5.9.91
Writer: Russell Lewis
Director: David Hayman
Sun Hill officers spend a boring afternoon in a van on standby duty for a major demonstration. Their presence is not required, and they make their way back to the station. Then there is a sudden eruption of violence.

INSIDE JOB
Shown: 10.9.91
Writer: Simon Moss
Director: Denny Lawrence
A shop assistant is attacked and robbed of the week's takings by thieves on a motorcycle.

BONES OF CONTENTION
Shown: 12.9.91
Writer: Susan B. Shattock
Director: Sarah Pia Anderson
Anonymous letters expose Stringer's affair in police time with a prisoner's wife. Meanwhile Conway is frustrated at a lack of promotion.

WIDE OF THE MARK
Shown: 17.9.91
Writer: David Hoskins
Director: Chris Lovett
A professional hired killer is active in Sun Hill.

HITTING THE MARK
(Part 2 of WIDE OF THE MARK)
Shown: 19.9.91
Writer: Steve Trafford
Director: Mike Dormer
Burnside hunts for the hired killer to prevent him making his next hit.

BENDING THE RULES
Shown: 24.9.91
Writer: Eric Deacon
Director: Alan Bell
A yob arrested for shoplifting turns out to be a respected police officer. Burnside unravels the story of his change in behaviour.

SKINT
Shown: 26.9.91
Writer: Brendan Martin
Director: Graham Theakston
Garfield's birthday party only adds to his money troubles.

FRIDAY AND COUNTING
Shown: 1.10.91
Writer: Barry Appleton
Director: Bill Pryde
Roach's investigation into a mugging becomes a murder inquiry when the woman victim dies.

LEST WE FORGET
Shown: 3.10.91
Writer: Victoria Taylor
Director: Bill Pryde
Brownlow is questioned by Yorkshire police with regard to a wrongful conviction that took place when Brownlow was in CID.

NUTTERS
Shown: 8.10.91
Writer: Philip Palmer
Director: Richard Holthouse
AMIP investigates a teenage murder.

DOWNTIME
Shown: 10.10.91
Writer: Peter J. Hammond
Director: Richard Holthouse
A woman schoolteacher is murdered by her lesbian lover when she ends their affair.

OUT OF ORDER
Shown: 15.10.91
Writer: Dave Simpson
Director: David Hayman
Young sexually assaults Datta.

EMPIRE BUILDING
Shown: 17.10.91
Writer: Philip Palmer
Director: Nick Laughland
Cryer sets up a major operation to arrest defaulters on fine-payments. Peters accuses him of empire-building.

LOSING IT
Shown: 22.10.91
Writer: Russell Lewis
Director: Jim Goddard
Young discovers a suicide. Later he visits Datta in the section house and attacks her.

INNOCENCE
Shown: 24.10.91
Writer: Victoria Taylor
Director: Sarah Pia Anderson
Two boys are reported missing. Abduction is suspected, but later the boys are found asleep after a blowout on a parent's booze money. Brownlow meets Davis, his old colleague, to

discuss the wrongful conviction about which he was interviewed.

SHOTS
Shown: 29.10.91
Writer: J. C. Wilsher
Director: Christopher Lovett
Loxton attends a firearms course, but decides not to continue. Conway and Cryer are also there.

THE SQUARE PEG
Shown: 31.10.91
Writer: Christopher Russell
Director: Jim Goddard
Young goes missing on his beat. Quinnan and Loxton find his body in his car: he has committed suicide.

A QUESTION OF CONFIDENCE
Shown: 5.11.91
Writer: Robin Mukherjee
Director: Sarah Pia Anderson
There are serial assaults on prostitutes by Hawkins, a prison escapee, in revenge for a pimp putting his daughter on the game; and a Citizen's Advice Bureau employee refuses to divulge information about Hawkins.

BALLS IN THE AIR
Shown: 7.11.91
Writer: J. C. Wilsher
Director: Sharon Miller
On his first day at Sun Hill, Sergeant Boyden demonstrates that he knows all the angles; and Roach ends up owing him a favour.

THE TASTE
Shown: 12.11.91
Writer: Julian Jones
Director: Alan Bell
Smollett wants to go back on the beat; a girl wants to sell a German bayonet for drugs; and Cryer stands in for Maitland and enjoys his old job.

TURNING BACK THE CLOCK
Shown: 14.11.91
Writer: Barry Appleton
Director: Aisling Walsh
A prisoner's release gives Burnside a chance to clear up a three-year-old case of robbery and murder.

DISCRETION
Shown: 19.11.91
Writer: Edward Canfor-Dumas
Director: Niall Leonard
On his first day as Home Beat Officer, Smollett investigates the mugging of an old lady.

CHAPTER AND VERSE
Shown: 21.11.91
Writer: Carolyn Sally Jones
Director: Aisling Walsh
Burnside wants to question a 'drunk and incapable' man in the cells about a missing girl; but Maitland is determined to uphold the rules of PACE.

THE WHOLE TRUTH
Shown: 26.11.91
Writer: Duncan Gould
Director: Duncan Gould
Datta is in court over a drink-driving case complicated by mouthwash; and Stringer is attacked by car thieves in a multistorey carpark.

PROFIT AND LOSS
Shown: 28.11.91
Writer: Tony Etchells
Director: Nick Laughland
An illegal Turkish immigrant coerced into prostitution to pay her boss's debts commits suicide.

THICKER THAN WATER
Shown: 3.12.91
Writer: Matthew Wingett
Director: Sarah Pia Anderson
Loxton and Stringer are called to a 'domestic'; but the man beating his wife is PC Mike Gibbs of Stafford Row, a friend of Loxton.

ON THE TAKE
Shown: 5.12.91
Writer: Steve Trafford
Director: Patrick Lau
Roach, investigating an armed robbery, finds evidence of police corruption that points to DS Lovell. Meadows is forced to bring in MS15.

CARING
Shown: 10.12.91
Writer: A. Valentine
Director: Aisling Walsh
Ackland and Smollett deal with Mrs Cook and her schizophrenic son.

THE SORCERER'S APPRENTICE
Shown: 12.12.91
Writer: Victoria Taylor
Director: Alan Bell
A juvenile prisoner lies about his age, then has an epileptic fit in his cell, causing problems for Roach.

IMPOSTERS
Shown: 17.12.91
Writer: Tony McHale
Director: Bill Hays
Maitland and Monroe investigate a pornography

racket; Marshall and Stamp look for a beggar who seduced a mentally retarded girl.

A WOMAN SCORNED
Shown: 19.12.91
Writer: Victoria Taylor
Director: Derek Lister
Reid discusses tactics with regard to Burnside with AC Renshaw. A dog digs up a corpse in a back garden.

VITAL STATISTICS (Christmas special: one hour)
Writer: Christopher Russell
Director: Jeremy Summers
The discovery that their arrest rate is inferior to that of B Relief stings A Relief into action.

DECENT PEOPLE
Shown: 26.12.91
Writer: Edward Canfor-Dumas
Director: Mike Dormer
Quinnan works undercover on a building site to investigate the theft of kitchen units.

BREAKOUT (New Year special: one hour)
Writer: Carolyn Sally Jones
Director: Frank W. Smith
A learner driver backs into a police prison van, and the prisoner escapes. South Yorkshire police ask Sun Hill to pick up Terence Otley on their behalf. 'Yorkie' Smith turns up again at Sun Hill: he is now a DC in the South Yorkshire force. Carver accompanies him back to Yorkshire with Otley

THE BEST POLICY
Shown: 2.1.92
Writer: Victoria Taylor
Director: Derek Lister
CID investigates an armed robbery, and Kim Reid plays political games with Burnside.

A FRIEND IN NEED
Shown: 7.1.92
Writer: Duncan Gould
Director: Bill Pryde
Quinnan is the subject of a civil complaint, and Stamp and Stringer become involved with care in the community.

WHOSE SIDE ARE YOU ON?
Shown: 9.2.92
Writer: Duncan Gould
Director: Bill Hays
Lines tries to get a mugging victim charged with the murder of his assailant.

LIP SERVICE
Shown: 14.1.92
Writer: Arthur Ellis
Director: Derek Lister
Lines becomes involved in a pub brawl and uncovers a loan-sharking business as a result.

ILLEGALS
Shown: 16.1.92
Writer: Christopher Russell
Director: Laura Sims
When a cellarful of illegal immigrants is discovered, Boyden takes a fancy to one of the females; but Lines realizes what he is up to and warns him off.

FAIR PLAY
Shown: 21.1.92
Writer: Mark Holloway
Director: Niall Leonard
Quinnan suspects a black boxer of the illegal sale of steroids; but Garfield, who is a friend of the boxer, doesn't believe it.

DINOSAUR
Shown: 23.1.92
Writer: Victoria Taylor
Director: Laura Sims
Kim Reid is concerned about a complaint against Sun Hill officers, but MS15 are interested in her applying to join them. Burnside's old-fashioned methods (like putting a snout's head down a toilet to get information) produce results.

JOYRIDE
Shown: 28.1.92
Writer: Mike Harris
Director: John Strickland
When a girl is seriously injured in a joyriding incident, Brownlow must decide whether he is prepared to risk a riot by sending officers into an estate to round up the culprits.

NOT WAVING
Shown: 30.1.92
Writer: Russell Lewis
Director: Richard Holthouse
When a student nurse is sexually assaulted, Burnside quickly arrests Shaun, a mentally retarded gypsy boy. When Shaun escapes from police custody his guilt seems confirmed – wrongly, as it happens.

MATES
Shown: 4.2.92
Writer: Philip Palmer
Director: Derek Lister
Operation Marlin to raid a brothel. Cryer works

undercover as a punter. His presence antagonizes Peters. Cryer sees Brownlow about giving up his job as Duty Sergeant.

LOST BOY
Shown: 6.2.92
Writer: Mark Holloway
Director: Nick Laughland
While searching for a missing thirteen-year-old boy Dashwood and Ackland become involved in an operation against ponces running rent boys at Victoria Station.

CHICKEN
Shown: 11.2.92
Writer: Julian Jones
Director: Chris Lovett
While trying to stop children playing 'chicken' on a railway line, Stringer sees one of them run down by a train. As a consequence of this incident Peters changes to Duty Sergeant, swapping jobs with Cryer.

SOMEBODY SPECIAL
Shown: 13.2.92
Writer: Christopher Russell
Director: John Strickland
Kim Reid is promoted out of Sun Hill to MS15. Acting DI Greig tries to recruit a hardened female thief as a snout.

PREVIOUS CONVICTIONS
Shown: 18.2.92
Writer: Tony Etchells
Director: Aisling Walsh
Investigating an apparent accident in which a man's hand is crushed in a car-breaker's yard, Maitland uncovers years of animosity, neglect and revenge.

BEGGAR MY NEIGHBOUR
Shown: 20.2.92
Writer: Jonathan Whitten
Director: Niall Leonard
The attempted murder of a tramp reveals drug-dealing and blackmail.

IT'S A SMALL WORLD
Shown: 25.2.92
Writer: Barry Appleton
Director: Bill Pryde
Dashwood applies for a job in a firm of security consultants and uncovers their fraudulent activities.

LICENCE
Shown: 27.2.92
Writer: Neil Mackay
Director: Gordon Flemyng
The probation service fails to notify Sun Hill that a

convicted murderer who strangled his wife has been released on licence. They learn of his presence only when his son causes a disturbance.

COMEBACK
Shown: 3.3.92
Writer: Julian Jones
Director: John Darnell
Smollett's community police station on the Kingsmead Estate is blown up. Loxton and Datta have their Area Car stolen.

FIREPROOF
(Part 2 of COMEBACK)
Shown: 5.3.92
Writer: Julian Jones
Director: Mike Dormer
The investigation into the fire gets under way. Smollett's popularity on the estate is important in leading him to the culprit.

THE PADDY FACTOR
Shown: 10.3.92
Writer: J. C. Wilsher
Director: Chris Lovett
Carver and Martella have a car thief under observation, and see him shot as he gets into a car. Inquiries reveal IRA involvement.

THE WILD ROVER
(Part 2 of THE PADDY FACTOR)
Shown: 12.3.92
Writer: J. C. Wilsher
Director: Chris Lovett
Sun Hill officers are drawn into the world of the IRA; and army weapons are sold to robbers for profit.

COINCIDENCE
Shown: 17.3.92
Writer: Peter J. Hammond
Director: Patrick Lau
Investigating a small boy's claim of assault by a man in an adventure playground, Ackland and Maitland discover that the molester is the child's 'honorary' uncle.

GOING SOFT
Shown: 19.3.92
Writer: Barry Appleton
Director: Derek Lister
Visiting a magistrate with a Bible to obtain a warrant, Dashwood is taken prisoner by two hooded burglars.

RE-HAB
Shown: 24.3.92
Writer: Tony Etchells
Director: Derek Lister
DCI Meadows, on his first day at Sun Hill, becomes involved with a father suspected of murdering his drug-addict son. In fact the boy died from an overdose.

ACTING DETECTIVE
Shown: 26.3.92
Writer: Mark Holloway
Director: Nick Laughland
A Nigerian woman who collapsed at Heathrow is found to be carrying drugs in her stomach. Burnside gets French to take her place in an operation to discover the dealer.

STOPOVER
Shown: 31.3.92
Writer: Peter J. Hammond
Director: Aisling Walsh
A woman whose husband is in prison, and who runs a hotel, keeps reporting an intruder on the premises. Smollett gives her support. His colleagues think he is wasting his time, but an intruder is eventually arrested.

SUSPECTS
Shown: 2.4.92
Writer: Philip Palmer
Director: Richard Holthouse
Greig arrests Bartlett for armed robbery, but is proved wrong. Someone else did it.

ALL THE KING'S HORSES
Shown: 7.4.92
Writer: Duncan Gould
Director: John Darnell
A lorry overturns and sheds its load outside a school, burying a girl and a boy. Loxton rescues both of them, but the boy later dies.

PARTY POLITICS
Shown: 9.4.92
Writer: Susan B. Shattock
Director: Alan Bell
Burnside and Roach attend a party given by crooked businessman 'Big George'. Burnside is tempted by George's offer of a job, but ends up arresting a villain at the party instead.

TRIALS AND TRIBULATIONS
Shown: 14.4.92
Writer: A. Valentine
Director: Chris Lovett
When Marshall, a vital witness in a murder trial, has her flat ransacked and her car vandalized, Sun Hill suspect that someone is trying to intimidate her.

A CAN OF WORMS
Shown: 16.4.92
Writer: Duncan Gould
Director: Charles Beeson
A traffic accident draws Sun Hill's attention to a minicab firm whose owner is using young boys as thieves.

TIMING
Shown: 21.4.92
Writer: Russell Lewis
Director: Aisling Walsh
A series of arson attacks is investigated by Meadows; while Roach and Dashwood track down an escaped prisoner.

A NICE LITTLE LINE IN PLASTIC
Shown: 23.4.92
Writer: Margaret Simpson
Director: Sarah Pia Anderson
A simple arrest by Quinnan and Datta uncovers a major racket involving stolen credit cards.

TRIAL AND ERROR
Shown: 28.4.92
Writer: Edward Canfor-Dumas
Director: Alan Bell
George Hannah, an armed robber who put an innocent bystander in a wheelchair, has twice been acquitted of the crime; but the victim's son takes the law into his own hands by firebombing Hannah's house.

OWNING UP
Shown: 30.4.92
Writer: Martyn Wade
Director: Charles Beeson
Loxton and Stringer's investigation of a mugging is nearly ruined when it collides with an investigation by Greig and Meadows.

UP BEHIND
Shown: 5.5.92
Writer: J. C. Wilsher
Director: Sarah Pia Anderson
Martella investigates a series of artifice burglaries involving pensioners and finds herself locked in a room by one of the victims, who then calls the police!

APPEARANCES
Shown: 7.5.92
Writer: Simon Moss
Director: Patrick Lau
Following an argument with a pub customer, a young barman is hit by a car and later dies. Quinnan and Stringer have their suspicions about the customer, but there are no witnesses.

PRINCIPLED NEGOTIATION
Shown: 12.5.92
Writer: J. C. Wilsher

Director: Gordon Flemyng
Burnside and Roach look favourably on an ex-villain with a loan-shark problem; but they expect favours in return.

SIGN OF OUR TIMES
Shown: 14.5.92
Writer: David Squire
Director: Laura Sims
An armed robber admits that redundancy and the repossession of his house made him take to crime to solve his problems.

PRIORITIES
Shown: 19.5.92
Writer: Neil McKay
Director: Anya Camilleri
When Stringer and Loxton investigate a robbery at an old people's home, they begin to suspect that the ex-copper who runs the home is ill-treating his residents.

USERS
Shown: 21.5.92
Writer: Simon Moss
Director: Laura Sims
When Martella arrests Maria Saunders for drug-dealing, Burnside suspects that she is using teenage girls as couriers by offering them free holidays in Spain.

MAN OF THE PEOPLE
Shown: 26.5.92
Writer: Christopher Russell
Director: Richard Holthouse
Stringer wins the election for Federation rep, beating Hollis by fifty-eight votes to two; and Brownlow decides to eat in the canteen with the other ranks – much to their discomfort.

RUNAWAY
Shown: 28.5.92
Writer: Christopher Russell
Director: Udayan Prasad
When a girl is found badly beaten up in a pipe on waste ground, Roach interviews the boyfriend she says beat her and discovers that he is responsible for a series of murders being investigated by AMIP.

EXPOSURES
Shown: 2.6.92
Writer: Mark Holloway
Director: Richard Holthouse
When Martella investigates a fourteen-year-old girl's claim that she was sexually assaulted during a photographic session, she discovers that the girl invented the story to stop her ambitious mother from forcing her to become a model and to hide the fact that she had posed for pornographic photos.

BETTER THE DEVIL
Shown: 4.6.92
Writer: Russell Lewis
Director: Jeremy Silberston
Marshall is on attachment to the Domestic Violence Unit at Stafford Row; and Stringer discovers a horrifying case of parental cruelty in a devoutly religious black family.

PRISONERS
Shown: 9.6.92
Writer: Victoria Taylor
Director: Chris Lovett
The night shift at Sun Hill. A drunk who swallows his own vomit is resuscitated by Hollis; an Asian man who understands no English is brought in; and Boyden is sympathetic towards a prostitute called Gloria.

WORLD TO RIGHTS
Shown: 11.6.92
Writer: Russell Lewis
Director: Graham Theakston
A woman's house is wrecked after her husband is convicted of beating her up; and Marshall, at the Domestic Violence Unit, makes an error of judgement and is attacked by a woman's husband.

DO THE RIGHT THING
Shown: 16.6.92
Writer: Marianne Colbran
Director: Christopher Hodson
Stringer is mugged by a gang; and Marshall follows a cheque-card fraudster who links up with the very same gang.

HIDING TO NOTHING
Shown: 18.6.92
Writer: Jonathan Rich
Director: Graham Theakston
Stamp is ambushed by youths on the Jasmine Allen Estate; in trying to rescue him Ackland makes an error of judgement and crashes the Area Car – much to Loxton's delight. Later Loxton is ambushed by the same gang, and Ackland saves him.

PUNCHING JUDY
Shown: 23.6.92
Writer: Russell Lewis
Director: Moira Armstrong
Greig and Meadows interview Keith Smith, who has carried out a brutal attack on his wife. When

CASEBOOK

• •

Smith's wife dies, Marshall decides to abandon the Domestic Violence Unit and return to the beat.

VICIOUS CIRCLES
Shown: 25.6.92
Writer: Duncan Gould
Director: Christopher Hodson
Hollis arrests a woman in the park for being drunk in charge of a baby, and attempts to help her twelve-year-old daughter who is struggling to cope with an alcoholic mother.

UP ALL NIGHT
Shown: 30.6.92
Writer: Tony Etchells
Director: Mike Dormer
Garfield is beaten up by a burglar he was pursuing. Boyden should have come to his assistance, but he was having sex with Jackie, the wife of a convict and also Roach's snout and lover. Boyden's action brings hostility from the relief and trouble for Roach.

PART OF THE FURNITURE
Shown: 2.7.92
Writer: Christopher Russell
Director: Udayan Prasad
It is Dashwood's last day at Sun Hill. He has transferred to the Art and Antiques Squad. Roach hands him a burglary at an infants' school as a wind-up, but it develops into a case that allows Dashwood to show the others a thing or two.

SNAKES AND LADDERS (Part 2 of UP ALL NIGHT)
Shown: 7.7.92
Writer: Tony Etchells
Director: Michael Simpson
It is Garfield's first day back on duty after the attack. The relief place bets on the likelihood of Garfield punching Boyden. Garfield does eventually take his revenge.

STREET CLEANING (Part 3 of UP ALL NIGHT)
Shown: 9.7.92
Writer: Christopher Russell
Director: Laura Sims
Cryer gets the relief to put the Garfield-Boyden affair behind them and get back to work – in this case sorting out the takeover of genuine beggars' pitches by violent professional thieves.

HANDS UP
Shown: 14.7.92
Writer: Christopher Russell
Director: Michael Simpson
Conway takes to the streets and arrests a drunk for criminal damage, but finds it harder than expected to make the charge stick. A building society robber turns out to be a woman who wants the money to provide for pensioners.

A SCANDALOUS ACT
Shown: 16.7.92
Writer: A. Valentine
Director: Anya Camilleri
Garfield brings in a young girl alone, and she accuses him of sexually assaulting her. Kim Reid, now with MS15, arrives to investigate.

RAIDERS
Shown: 21.7.92
Writer: Rib Davis
Director: Brian Parker
CID arrive at a ram-raid and find the passenger dead. As they investigate, a well-organized family business is revealed.

TALK OUT
Shown: 23.7.92
Writer: Peter J. Hammond
Director: Brian Parker
An enigmatic couple, Mr and Mrs Chamberlain, come to the front desk and report their female neighbour missing. Ackland's misgivings are justified when the neighbour turns up and Mrs Chamberlain admits that she contrived the situation to avoid a repetition of the circumstances eighteen years ago when her husband committed murder in Yorkshire.

TRUE CONFESSIONS
Shown: 28.7.92
Writer: Edward Canfor-Dumas
Director: Jeremy Silberston
Roach is put under pressure in court when Lawson, convicted of stabbing and robbing an Asian shopkeeper, retracts his confession and accuses the police of oppression.

PRIVATE ENTERPRISE
Shown: 30.7.92
Writer: Carolyn Sally Jones
Director: Patrick Lau
Meadows tackles CID about passing information to the Collator; but Roach is reluctant to share information relating to his current operation involving money-laundering, a

minicab, and evidence in its boot of murder.

GETTING THROUGH
Shown: 4.8.92
Writer: Carolyn Sally Jones
Director: Andrew Higgs
The night shift are saddled with a feud between two violent men (one a former boxer) who come to the front desk to lay a complaint of GBH against each other and end up fighting.

LAST NIGHT OF FREEDOM
Shown: 6.8.92
Writer: Lizzie Mickery
Director: Chris Clough
When someone is stabbed on his stag night, Mickey Johnson can't remember a thing about it but he is a likely suspect. A prostitute gives him an alibi but loses him his intended bride.

CUTTING LOOSE
Shown: 11.8.92
Writer: Steve Trafford
Director: Chris Clough
A woman teacher comes forward as an eyewitness four months after a robbery took place but fails to identify the chief suspect, Harding, at an identity parade. Returning Harding to prison, Burnside and Lines are ambushed by Harding's gang and Harding is freed. Meadows discovers that the teacher helped to set it up.

SOFT TARGET
Shown: 13.8.92
Writer: Roy Macgregor
Director: Laura Sims
A local villain is driving people out of their flats and reletting the properties to squatters without the council's knowledge. Meanwhile at Sun Hill civilian typist Sonya Gifford is discovered to be having an affair with a known villain. It poses an ethical dilemma for Cryer and Monroe.

I'VE NEVER BEEN TO HARROGATE
Shown: 18.8.92
Writer: Christopher Russell
Director: Moira Armstrong
Greig and Woods detain a man who thinks he is helping elderly lonely people with nothing to live for by killing them – and who takes their possessions as his 'reward'.

HUMAN RESOURCES
Shown: 20.8.92
Writer: Robert Jones
Director: Andrew Higgs
Lack of manpower for Roach's operation against con-men places Martella in danger and makes it necessary for Roach to rescue her.

EXIT
Shown: 25.8.92
Writer: Peter J. Hammond
Director: Tom Cotter
A young woman identifies the assailant of a loan-shark, but she strings Greig along and eventually disappears; and the loan shark withdraws his complaint when asked to supply a list of clients.

LOYALTIES
Shown: 27.8.92
Writer: Duncan Gould
Director: Tom Cotter
Acting on information from snout Jazzer Osborne, Burnside mounts a raid on crack-houses. The raid is abortive, and the search is on for the person who leaked details. But in fact Jazzer told the dealers about the raid in order to protect himself.

SNAP SHOT
Shown: 1.9.92
Writer: Tony Etchells
Director: Mike Dormer
A complaint over loud music quickly escalates into an armed siege and the shooting of the complainant.

LETTING GO
Shown: 3.9.92
Writer: Joanne Maguire
Director: Chris Lovett
Greig winds up the incident room on the unsolved murder of a barrister only to find that his last visit to the victim's wife leads to the discovery that she and her lover hired someone to commit the murder.

TRAVELLING LIGHT
Shown: 8.9.92
Writer: Rod Lewis
Director: Sheree Folkson
AMIP are two weeks into a murder inquiry, and Donna Harris is drafted in to re-enact the last moments of the victim's life. Burnside's instinct as to the identity of the murderer proves correct.

RADIO WAVES
Shown: 10.9.92
Writer: Simon Moss

Director: Chris Lovett
A routine arrest of teenage joyriders leads Woods and Carver to a security firm partnership which is disabling alarm systems, stealing car stereos and selling them back to their unsuspecting customers.

A BLIND EYE
Shown: 15.9.92
Writer: Julian Jones
Director: Mike Dormer
Stamp delays intervention when he sees a 'mugger' being beaten up by local vigilantes; but he then discovers that the 'mugger' is an off-duty policeman who went to help an old lady who had fallen over.

SYMPATHY FOR THE DEVIL
Shown: 17.9.92
Writer: Edward Canfor-Dumas
Director: Sheree Folkson
CID are surprised to find that an armed robber they trap carrying out a raid on a building society is a man in his sixties.

FORCE IS PART OF THE SERVICE
Shown: 22.9.92
Writer: J. C. Wilsher
Director: Anya Camilleri
Loxton uses what he considers 'reasonable force' in making an arrest, and then finds himself facing a complaint of wrongful arrest and assault from the prisoner, who turns out to be the wrong man.

ON THE RECORD, OFF THE RECORD
Shown: 24.9.92
Writer: David Hoskins
Director: Anya Camilleri
A warehouse robbery looks like an inside job, but an employee with a criminal record proves to be innocent as he points the finger at the security man, a bent ex-copper who organized the raid.

STONING THE GLASSHOUSE
Shown: 29.9.92
Writer: A. Valentine
Director: David Attwood
Cryer is asked by a keen Neighbourhood Watch man to have a word with his son whom he has found in possession of drugs. Cryer sends Garfield and Stringer undercover to catch the dealer, who turns out to be the man's son.

119

TIP-OFF
Shown: 1.10.92
Writer: Sebastian Secker Walker
Director: John Darnell
A convicted burglar offers Lines information in return for a transfer to a prison near where his wife lives. The tip-off leads to the arrest of a robbery gang, but the prisoner is beaten up for grassing.

OPEN TO OFFERS
Shown: 6.10.92
Writer: Russell Lewis
Director: Roger Gartland
When a suspect in an extortion racket, in an attempt to have the charge dropped, attempts to blackmail Quinnan by revealing that he moonlights as an electrician, Quinnan is forced to confess to his superiors to save his career.

PLAYING GOD
Shown: 8.10.92
Writer: Margaret Phelan
Director: Roger Gartland
Greig's early cautioning of Patten, suspected of the euthanasia of his wife, proves ill-judged when it transpires that Patten is likely to be innocent.

CRACK OF DOOM
Shown: 13.10.92
Writer: Gregory Evans
Director: John Darnell
A suspected drug-dealer allows his house to be used as an observation-post to monitor a street crack-market, but the plan goes awry when his teenage daughter returns home early and warns her boyfriend, one of the traders.

SPIT AND POLISH
Shown: 15.10.92
Writer: Robert Jones
Director: Frank W. Smith
Loxton and Quinnan deal with a man driving a Mercedes dangerously. He has stolen the car from his wife, and in the boot is the body of his wife's lover whom he has murdered.

OVERDUE
Shown: 20.10.92
Writer: J. C. Wilsher
Director: Chris Lovett
While Burnside faces a promotion board at Scotland Yard (unsuccessfully, as it turns out), Meadows takes over one of his cases and quickly learns a lot about his methods.

WE SHOULD BE TALKING
Shown: 22.10.92
Writer: Duncan Gould
Director: David Attwood
There is trouble for both Ackland and Garfield when Sun Hill's radio system breaks down.

REASONABLE GROUNDS
Shown: 27.10.92
Writer: Julian Spilsbury
Director: Colm Villa
Stringer and Stamp pursue a man who, for no obvious reason, keeps running away. Around the corner a seven-year-old child has gone missing. Is there a connection?

DISCIPLINE
Shown: 29.10.92
Writer: Joanne Maguire
Director: Colm Villa
CID's investigation of a small-time racketeer is hampered by a former AMIP colleague of Meadows, Ken Haines, who has been suspended for corruption and has good reason to believe that the racketeer set him up.

MINEFIELD
Shown: 3.11.92
Writer: Carolyn Sally Jones
Director: Jean Stewart
Maitland finds himself in the the wrong when he discovers that the dangerous and possibly psychopathic Osborne has been arrested twice for the same offence. Osborne is released.

GAMERS
Shown: 5.11.92
Writer: Jonathan Myerson
Director: Frank W. Smith
A simple case of shoplifting leads to an investigation of an Asian gaming club.

**OCCUPATIONAL HAZARD
(Part 2 of MINEFIELD)**
Shown: 10.11.92
Writer: Carolyn Sally Jones
Director: Jean Stewart
CID are anxious to nail Osborne, suspected of several vicious attacks on women and whom they were previously forced to release. When another woman is attacked, it seems they have grounds to arrest him; but his solicitor decides not to press charges when Osborne attacks him.

JUST SEND SOME FLOWERS
Shown: 12.11.92
Writer: Michael Jenner
Director: Chris Lovett
A woman's house is burgled while she is at her husband's funeral, and evidence suggests that it is one of a string of burglaries linked to a florist's van.

WAIFS AND STRAYS
Shown: 17.11.92
Writer: Jonathan Rich
Director: Haldane Duncan
When a blood-stained book belonging to a missing girl is found, inquiries are intensified; and the girl's brother reluctantly leads Lines and Smollett to the squat where she is hiding.

HAPPY FAMILIES
Shown: 19.11.92
Writer: David Hoskins
Director: Andrew Higgs
When CID attempt to arrest Daniel Batt for a stabbing, they have to arrest his father, too, for assaulting Lines.

WELL OUT OF ORDER
Shown: 24.11.92
Writer: Steve Trafford
Director: Peter Smith
Smollett has set up a police office in the community centre on the Tankeray Flats Estate. Meadows and Burnside want to go in with troops to root out the criminal elements, but Brownlow is committed to a softer approach.

**INTO THE MIRE
(Part 2 of WELL OUT OF ORDER)**
Shown: 26.11.92
Writer: Steve Trafford
Director: Peter Smith
CID receive information that leads to the arrest of a prolific handler of stolen goods on the Tankeray Flats Estate. This in turn enables Burnside to arrest a corrupt council housing official who controls illegal squatting on the estate, but the youths on the estate fight back.

MASTER OF THE HOUSE
Shown: 1.12.92
Writer: Christopher Russell
Director: Derek Lister
A son confesses to killing his tyrannical father; but he is covering for his mother, who actually committed the murder.

FIREWORKS
Shown: 3.12.92
Writer: Duncan Gould
Director: Nick Laughland
Stamp tackles the problem of children playing with British Rail detonators.

COLD SHOULDER
Shown: 8.12.92
Writer: Tony Etchells
Director: Haldane Duncan
When a local villain is stabbed in the centre of a densely populated housing development without anyone apparently witnessing the crime, Meadows sets out to reassert the supremacy of the law over the rule of the vigilante.

SAFETY FIRST
Shown: 10.12.92
Writer: Mick Duffy
Director: Nick Laughland
Sun Hill confronts the problems caused by the widespread ownership of shotguns.

COUNTING THE COST
Shown: 15.12.92
Writer: A. Valentine
Director: Lawrence Moody
Ackland takes up the cause of a man who prevented a robbery, and was severely injured in the process, but has received no compensation.

COMPASSION
Shown: 17.12.92
Writer: Frank Kippax
Director: Chris Lovett
Investigating the murder of a prostitute, Burnside comes into conflict with a hostile probation officer; but her husband turns out to be the murderer.

FINDERS KEEPERS
Shown: 22.12.92
Writer: Christopher Russell
Director: Derek Lister
Dashwood, now with the Art and Antiques Squad, takes a case away from Carver and gets a result.

**RETURN MATCH
(Part 2 of FINDERS KEEPERS)**
Shown: 24.12.92
Writer: Christopher Russell
Director: Derek Lister
When a collection of valuable dolls is stolen, Dashwood again turns up at Sun Hill, wrong-foots Lines and once more gets a result.

HIGH PLACES
Shown: 29.12.92

Writer: Peter J. Hammond
Director: Jeremy Silberston
An ex-criminal who used to be part of a high-wire act is found dead, apparently from a fall; but the pathologist says he died elsewhere. Then reports of a series of bizarre burglaries come in.

WHEN PUSH COMES TO SHOVE
Shown: 31.12.92
Writer: Tony Etchells
Director: Matthew Evans
Ackland is relaxing in a pub with Quinnan and Loxton when some troublemakers arrive. She tries to calm the situation, but Quinnan and Loxton provoke a fight. However, it is Ackland who has to face the consequences.

**DYING BREED
(first of thrice-weekly episodes)**
Shown: 5.1.93
Writer: Chris Ould
Director: Chris Clough
While buying a watch, Carver becomes involved in an armed robbery.

FACT OF LIFE
Shown: 7.1.93
Writer: Julian Jones
Director: Derek Lister
The law allows a burglar to go free, but Greig and Quinnan try to pin him down again.

ALL THROUGH THE NIGHT
Shown: 8.1.93
Writer: J. C. Wilsher
Director: Jeremy Silberston
What Stamp believed was going to be a dull evening escorting an Environmental Health Officer on the party patrol turns into something more to his liking when she invokes the full might of the law to seize some party sound equipment.

NEW TUNE, OLD FIDDLE
Shown: 12.1.93
Writer: J. C. Wilsher
Director: Lawrence Moody
When Conway learns that Inspector Cato from Barton Street is to be posted to Sun Hill as Community Liaison Officer, he feels that he has been overlooked and applies for the post himself – without telling Brownlow.

DELINQUENT
Shown: 14.1.93
Writer: Victoria Taylor

Director: Chris Lovett
A persistent young offender is arrested for burgling his parents' house. His father is furious with him but takes it out on Smollett, attacking him during the interview.

BRINGING UP BABY
Shown: 15.1.93
Writer: Edward Canfor-Dumas
Director: Matthew Evans
A 'missing' newborn baby has in fact been sold by its mother for illegal adoption.

RAINY DAYS AND MONDAYS
Shown: 19.1.93
Writer: Trevor Wadlow
Director: Sarah Pia Anderson
The warden of a hostel for homeless girls calls the police when one of the girls claims to have been sexually assaulted by the night security man; but he makes counter-claims about the warden, who has been putting some of the girls on the game and using them to steal for her.

SUPPLY AND DEMAND
Shown: 21.1.93
Writer: Joanna Maguire
Director: Chris Clough
A complaint about a 'pornographic' home video leads to a result for the burglary team.

ON THE CARDS
Shown: 22.1.93
Writer: Gregory Evans
Director: Jan Sargent
Taken off a murder investigation to work on a case involving obscene phone calls, Martella stumbles on to evidence that leads her to the killer.

SHOCK TO THE SYSTEM
Shown: 26.1.93
Writer: Christopher Russell
Director: David Attwood
When the news breaks that Conway is the new Community Liaison Officer and Cato is his replacement, Sun Hill goes into a state of shock.

LIVING IT DOWN
Shown: 28.1.93
Writer: Ron Rose
Director: David Attwood
The search for a missing victim of abuse uncovers a child pornography ring.

HEAT OF THE MOMENT
Shown: 29.1.93
Writer: Edward Canfor-Dumas
Director: Sarah Pia Anderson
A woman admits to killing her husband, but insists she did it in the heat of the moment. Martella believes her, but Meadows is convinced that the crime was premeditated. Both are wrong. The woman is protecting her daughter, who actually committed the murder.

SHAKE RATTLE 'N' ROLL
Shown: 2.2.93
Writer: Susan B. Shattock
Director: George Case
A cocky landlord gets his comeuppance when Monroe organizes a highly successful raid on his pub, which is a den of vice. At Sun Hill, Cato's appointment continues to cause anxiety.

NO THANKS TO YOU
Shown: 4.2.93
Writer: Candy Denman
Director: Jan Sargent
Garfield fails to save the life of a glue-sniffer and then, through no fault of his own, allows a bail absconder to escape.

A BETTER LIFE
Shown: 5.2.93
Writer: Roy Mcgregor
Director: Andrew Higgs
Greig is convinced that Darren Hancock has committed a burglary, but the victim herself insists that he is not the culprit.

ECHO
Shown: 9.2.93
Writer: Peter J. Hammond
Director: Bill Pryde
CID suspect Holt of murdering a missing girl – until another man walks into another station and confesses.

FAGINS
Shown: 11.2.93
Writer: Julian Jones
Director: Brian Farnham
Greig closes down a jeweller who is fencing stolen goods, and Operation Bumblebee has a surprise success arising from the murder of another fence.

CRIED TOO LATE
Shown: 12.2.93
Writer: Matthew Wingett
Director: Chris Lovett
A woman victim of domestic violence is reluctant to let Datta into her flat. She has murdered her husband by throwing an electric fire into the bath.

GONE FOR A SOLDIER
Shown: 16.2.93
Writer: Steve Trafford
Director: Brian Farnham
Ackland is teamed up with Dakin of the military police. He has come to Sun Hill to find a soldier who has gone AWOL with a gun to find his girlfriend who is pregnant by another man.

PERSUASION
Shown: 18.2.93
Writer: Marianne Colbran
Director: Richard Holthouse
A woman drug-dealer is attacked by another dealer to get her off his patch.

HARD MAN
Shown: 19.2.93
Writer: Carolyn Sally Jones
Director: Andrew Higgs
Following a stabbing, Greig uncovers a nasty DSS fraud at a bed-and-breakfast establishment.

MISSIONARY WORK
Shown: 23.2.93
Writer: Steve Trafford
Director: Bill Brayne
As Community Liaison Officer, Conway has to decide which of two bids for a grant he should recommend to the Commissioner – his own or that of Brownlow and Cato.

HYPOCRITICAL OATH
Shown: 25.2.93
Writer: Matthew Bardsley
Director: Andrew Higgs
CID fail to uncover the new drug-couriers on the Cockcroft Estate until a boy's overdose enables Lines and Carver to link registered addicts to a doctor.

TRIVIAL PURSUITS
Shown: 26.2.93
Writer: Len Collin
Director: Brian Parker
Loxton dismisses a domestic argument between homosexual lovers as a waste of time – until he is called back to the same address and finds himself staring down the barrel of a gun.

OUT OF THE MOUTHS
Shown: 2.3.93
Writer: Duncan Gould
Director: Graeme Harper
When Hollis takes the Bumblebee message into a local school, he uncovers some interesting information.

KEEPING IN TOUCH
Shown: 4.3.93

Writer: A. Valentine
Director: George Case
Sun Hill's concern about the activities of a private security firm is confirmed when one of its employees is arrested for assault on an elderly blind woman.

IF IT ISN'T HURTING
Shown: 5.3.93
Writer: Tony Etchells
Director: Paul Unwin
CID trainee investigator WPC Suzi Croft learns some old-style policing methods from Burnside.

KEEPING OUT OF TROUBLE
Shown: 9.3.93
Writer: Michael Jenner
Director: Brian Parker
A woman claims to have inside information about a series of raids on petrol stations. In fact she is prepared to grass on her boyfriend's mates in order to stop him joining them.

SCHOOL OF HARD KNOCKS
Shown: 11.3.93
Writer: Robert Jones
Director: Graeme Harper
While Terry Larch was in prison, his ex-wife married his partner, Bill O'Brien. Burnside has targeted O'Brien. When Larch appears to abduct his own son from outside O'Brien's house, it gives Burnside an excuse to increase his pressure on O'Brien.

A LITTLE FAMILY BUSINESS
Shown: 12.3.93
Writer: Steve Trafford
Director: Michael Simpson
When a family business is hit by recession, the son arranges a burglary to claim the insurance; but in the course of the robbery his father is hit by one of the robbers and dies of a heart-attack.

BREAKING THE CHAIN
Shown: 16.3.93
Writer: Jonathan Myerson
Director: Bill Pryde
CID target juvenile offender Ricky Blackwell, and Ricky has to grass on his mates to save his skin.

THE FORTRESS
Shown: 18.3.93
Writer: Philip Palmer
Director: Bill Pryde
Maitland arrests the owner of an off-licence for using unreasonable force on a young shoplifter.

IN BROAD DAYLIGHT
Shown: 19.3.93
Writer: Roy Macgregor
Director: Richard Holthouse
On the trail of two rapists Jo Morgan puts herself at risk and incurs Meadows's anger.

CREDIBLE WITNESS
Shown: 23.3.93
Writer: Joanne Maguire
Director: Diane Patrick
Stringer feels discredited when his description of a thief fleeing from a jeweller's conflicts with that of the main witness, who works in the shop.

THE PRICE OF FAME
Shown: 25.3.93
Writer: Lizzie Mickery
Director: Haldane Duncan
When CID suspect that a modelling agency is a scam, Polly Page finds herself going undercover as a model.

THE SHORT STRAW
Shown: 26.3.93
Writer: Russell Lewis
Director: Bill Brayne
Martella turns up late for a briefing, and Burnside excludes her from a CID operation against armed raiders. When she decides to help Stamp with routine inquiries concerning a handbag-snatcher, events take a shocking turn and she is shot dead by one of the raiders.

MISSING
Shown: 30.3.93
Writer: Christopher Russell
Director: Roger Gartland
A mentally retarded young man goes missing, and Burnside has to deal with the consequences for the parents.

GOODS RECEIVED
Shown: 1.4.93
Writer: Julian Spilsbury
Director: Diana Patrick
The investigation of a burglary links up with the case of a missing schoolboy.

DOUBLE ENMITY
Shown: 2.4.93
Writer: David Hoskins
Director: Paul Unwin
When a woman is in the market for a hit-man to murder her husband, Alan Woods goes undercover to pose as a contract killer.

HARD EVIDENCE
Shown: 6.4.93
Writer: Tony Etchells
Director: Laurence Moody
Woods's former guv'nor, Corby, arrives at the head of an AMIP murder team; and Meadows becomes uneasy at Corby's exploitation of Woods's loyalty to get a result regardless of the real evidence.

HIGH HOPES AND LOW LIFE
Shown: 8.4.93
Writer: Roy Macgregor
Director: John Darnell
A promising young boxer is attacked and has his hands maimed. His trainer seeks revenge and is arrested for attempted murder.

ON THE LOOSE
Shown: 9.4.93
Writer: Candy Denman
Director: Laurence Moody
A raid on an illegal dog-fight leads to a receiver of stolen goods.

OUT OF COURT
Shown: 13.4.93
Writer: Mark Holloway
Director: Jim Goddard
A woman is acquitted of attacking an Asian minicab-driver, but then she is knocked down in a pub carpark. The jury foreperson admits that she accidentally ran the woman over, but Carver thinks it was deliberate.

BEDFELLOWS
Shown: 15.4.93
Writer: Christopher Russell
Director: Jan Sargent
Cato's arrest of two Bengali youths leads to a protest outside Sun Hill.

CAT AND MOUSE
Shown: 17.4.93
Writer: Sebastian Secker Walker
Director: John Darnell
A woman's desire to get rid of her burglar boyfriend and his fence, with whom she has been having an affair, provides Burnside with two arrests.

BROTHERS
Shown: 20.4.93
Writer: Christopher Lang
Director: Roger Gartland
Two brothers deserted by their mother fend for themselves by committing burglaries.

PLAYING AWAY
Shown: 22.4.93
Writer: Chris Ould
Director: Ed Braman
Ackland arrests a fifteen-year-old boy for shoplifting, and finds herself investigating his relationship with a woman twenty years his senior.

COMING TO TERMS
Shown: 24.4.93
Writer: Roy Macgregor
Director: Jeremy Silberston
Parents of a young man awaiting trial for the murder of a child are distressed when their home is broken into and they receive threatening phone calls.

RETURN TO SENDER
Shown: 27.4.93
Writer: Michael Jenner
Director: Jeremy Silberston
A young postwoman has been beaten up, but the motive is unclear and she seems unwilling to talk.

STICKS AND STONES
Shown: 29.4.93
Writer: David Lane
Director: Betsan Morris Evans
When Lines hits the jackpot during a raid on the home of an armed robber, it makes an already difficult court-case for Greig even harder.

TANGLED WEBS
Shown: 1.5.93
Writer: Ron Rose
Director: David Attwood
A mysteriously unmotivated break-in at a garage leads to a web of sexual deception and a jealous husband's rampage.

RECRUITING OFFICER
Shown: 4.5.93
Writer: Len Collin
Director: Ed Braman
Maitland enlists McCann's help in reassuring a young black applicant whose wife has serious misgivings about the Job, but McCann is discovering racism within the force for himself.

GIVE 'EM AN INCH
Shown: 6.5.93
Writer: Duncan Gould
Director: Ken Horn
Despite being warned that a Town Hall demonstration could be hijacked by racists, Cato allows it to go ahead. When it turns ugly, he is forced to reverse his previous orders.

BY HOOK OR BY CROOK
Shown: 8.5.93
Writer: A. Valentine
Director: Haldane Duncan
Disgusted when a judge halts the trial of a man accused of crippling a police officer, Roach sets about 'helping' the man to secure his own conviction.

HOME TO ROOST
Shown: 11.5.93
Writer: Julian Spilsbury
Director: Chris Clough
When Sun Hill officers accompany some children to Chessington, Datta loses one of her charges, who is later found with his father who has returned from the Middle East.

IN SAFE HANDS
Shown: 13.5.93
Writer: Steve Trafford
Director: Chris Clough
When Lines and Morgan arrest two members of a shoplifting team, they discover that one of them has been sexually abused by her stepfather.

PUNCH DRUNK
Shown: 15.5.93
Writer: Edward Canfor-Dumas
Director: Michael Simpson
Called to a fight in a pub, Stamp and Quinnan find that one of the participants is Roach. When he also punches Monroe in the face, matters become even more serious. Burnside tries to help Roach, but Roach decides to resign.

FALL OUT
Shown: 18.5.93
Writer: Carolyn Sally Jones
Director: A. J. Quinn
Roach's departure leaves a valuable informant open to threat, as Burnside and Morgan quickly discover.

AWAYDAYS
Shown: 20.5.93
Writer: Peter J. Hammond
Director: Laurence Moody
An elderly ex-copper on a visit to London for the first time in years, in order to find his estranged daughter, claims he has been robbed at his hotel. As Lines helps him it becomes clear that the two men have very different values.

PRIDE AND JOY
Shown: 22.5.93
Writer: Chris Ould
Director: Betsan Morris Evans
When a young woman's car is stolen with a baby on board, the CID fear an abduction; but the girl's father has taken the baby.

FAST FOOD
Shown: 25.5.93
Writer: Margaret Phelan
Director: Ian White
Carver and Woods uncover a drugs operation at a takeaway; while Loxton and Maitland are in trouble when Loxton is accused of stealing some money from a drunk in the cells.

SOFT TOUCH
Shown: 27.5.93
Writer: Robert Jones
Director: A. J. Quinn
Stamp fails to stop a runaway road-roller, Jarvis finds a revolver in a rubbish-bin, and a murder investigation quickly develops.

WE GAVE HIM ALL OUR LOVE
Shown: 29.5.93
Writer: Michael Russell
Director: David Attwood

HEARTS AND MINDS
Shown: 1.6.93
Writer: Tony Etchells
Director: Derek Lister
Burnside and Conway have different attitudes towards dealing with a young offender.

CRY BABY
Shown: 3.6.93
Writer: Edward Canfor-Dumas
Director: Derek Lister
Page and Monroe attend what appears to be a cot death, but the baby has a head injury.

A WILLING VICTIM
Shown: 5.6.93
Writer: Isabelle Grey
Director: Jim Goddard
Garfield introduces a friend, who seems set for a successful boxing career, to a business manager; but Pearce already has the same business manager under investigation.

RANK OUTSIDER
Shown: 8.6.93
Writer: Susan B. Shattock
Director: Roger Gartland
Working alone in an under-staffed CAD room, and under the eye of Cato (on a tour of inspection), Polly Page makes a mistake that leads to the release of Loxton's prisoner, who should have been held. Loxton and Jarvis have the task of getting him back before Cato finds out.

TENDER MERCIES
Shown: 10.6.93
Writer: Jane Woodrow
Director: Ken Horn
Datta becomes involved with an Asian woman whose husband has disappeared, Lines uncovers an Asian loan-sharking operation, and suddenly the husband's disappearance starts to look more sinister.

DOUBLE TAKE
Shown: 12.6.93
Writer: A. Valentine
Director: Haldane Duncan
'Stolen' property is found in a garden shed, but who actually put it there?

MOUTH AND TROUSERS
Shown: 15.6.93
Writer: Len Collin
Director: Michael Simpson
Two warring families, the Mullens and the Kennedys, fight out their differences; while Stringer, as Federation rep, tries to contest the ban on overtime.

USES AND ABUSES
Shown: 17.6.93
Writer: Joanne Maguire
Director: Michael Simpson
A woman blinds a young man by spraying him with oven cleaner, but was it self-defence or assault?

PICKING A WINNER
Shown: 19.6.93
Writer: Michael Jenner
Director: Haldane Duncan
Quinnan goes undercover and joins the crew of a refuse-cart to investigate a series of robberies.

BROKEN
Shown: 22.6.93
Writer: Roy Macgregor
Director: John Bruce
Monroe deals with the case of Ken Farley, an alcoholic ex-miner who tries to organize exploited workers and is assaulted – and later dies.

INSIDER DEALING
Shown: 24.6.93
Writer: Julian Spilsbury
Director: John Strickland
When a desperate prisoner admits to crimes he didn't commit in order to gain a transfer, he enables CID to uncover one way in which drugs are being smuggled into the prison.

TO HAVE AND TO HOLD
Shown: 26.6.93
Writer: Edward Canfor-Dumas
Director: Sarah Pia Anderson
A woman complains that

her estranged husband has raped her, but he insists that she consented.

HONOUR AMONG THIEVES
Shown: 29.6.93
Writer: Joanne Maguire
Director: John Strickland
When Burnside questions three robbers after a botched getaway, he encounters a mass of recriminations and conflicting stories concerning the missing money.

SOMEBODY TO LOVE
Shown: 1.7.93
Writer: Marianne Colbran
Director: Ian White
Datta tries to help a woman break free from her husband, but discovers that it is another man who has beaten her up.

MORNING HAS BROKEN
Shown: 3.7.93
Writer: Gregory Evans
Director: Sarah Pia Anderson
There is a major operation to thwart a raid on a supermarket; while Meadows has to deal with robbers who have taken the wife of a building society manager hostage.

SWAPS
Shown: 6.7.93
Writer: Duncan Gould
Director: Laurence Moody
Loxton swaps jobs with Garfield and finds himself having to deal with the new screen-phones in the CAD room; while Garfield attends a fatal RTA which involves an exchange of cars between father and son.

TRUST
Shown: 8.7.93
Writer: Marianne Colbran
Director: Aisling Walsh
Greig suspects that his female snout may not be playing straight, but it becomes clear that she is being fed false information to mislead CID.

DIVIDED WE FALL
Shown: 10.7.93
Writer: Ron Rose
Director: James Cellan Jones
Members of the relief respond to Billy Staggers, a paranoid schizophrenic, in different ways as he tries to remake broken connections with his family.

A DUTY OF CARE
Shown: 13.7.93

Writer: Philip Palmer
Director: Indra Bhose
Cryer and Garfield attend a warehouse where a seventeen-year-old boy has fallen from a fork-lift to his death. Investigation reveals that it was not a simple accident: the boy's workmates forced him on to the lift even though they knew he was afraid of heights.

FAMILY VALUES
Shown: 15.7.93
Writer: James Stevenson
Director: Graham Theakston
A lorry full of dresses is hijacked, and in the process the driver is hit on the head and dies.

A MATTER OF LIFE AND DEATH
Shown: 17.7.93
Writer: Christopher Lang
Director: Aisling Walsh
An elderly man is arrested for beating his wife, but the couple have a bigger secret to hide. They were involved in a hit-and-run in which a boy was killed and a girl seriously injured.

KITH AND KIN
Shown: 20.7.93
Writer: Isabelle Grey
Director: Indra Bhose
When a woman is taken to hospital, her son burgles her house and steals money, and his sister starts to strip the house of its contents. Both resent a young absconder who looks after their mother, and to whom she has left her house in her will.

PART OF THE FAMILY
Shown: 22.7.93
Writer: Clive Hopkins
Director: Michael Offer
The theft of a necklace reveals a case of domestic violence against a young Bangladeshi woman.

MIGHTY ATOMS
Shown: 24.7.93
Writer: Neil Clarke
Director: Alex Kirby
Persistent offender Lee Gibson holds the clue to the whereabouts of missing teenager Danny Finnegan, a dedicated athlete; but the missing boy is in much deeper trouble than the notorious Gibson.

A MALICIOUS PROSECUTION
Shown: 27.7.93
Writer: Julian Jones

Director: James Cellan Jones
A civil action is brought against Garfield and Marshall for wrongful arrest, malicious prosecution and false imprisonment; and the verdict goes against them.

OUTBREAK
Shown: 29.7.93
Writer: Stephen C. Handley
Director: Michael Offer
A remand prisoner escapes from hospital, and Morgan and Croft's questioning of the apparently embarrassed prison officers who fell asleep while guarding him reveals that it was an inside job.

UNRELIABLE WITNESS
Shown: 31.7.93
Writer: Steve Griffiths
Director: Chris Lovett
A timid music teacher is intimidated by a violent ex-pupil, and Garfield is the subject of a complaint.

SWEET CHARITY
Shown: 3.8.93
Writer: Len Collin
Director: Chris Clough
Mother and daughter fall out over a shared boyfriend; while Cryer pursues bogus charity workers.

DAVID AND GOLIATH
Shown: 5.8.93
Writer: Duncan Gould
Director: Chris Lovett
Jarvis feels compelled to act on an abused boy's behalf when his mother refuses to testify against her husband.

WHAT A PAIR
Shown: 7.8.93
Writer: Lizzie Mickery
Director: John Bruce
A man working for an illegal escort agency seems to be stealing cash and credit cards from his female clients, but Ackland discovers that it is his daughter who was robbing them to put women off him.

DESIRABLE PROPERTY
Shown: 10.8.93
Writer: Mark Holloway
Director: John Bruce
A series of break-ins are linked to the estate agency through which the properties were sold.

BLIND SPOT
Shown: 12.8.93
Writer: Roger Davenport
Director: Matthew Evans
Jarvis and McCann attempt to charge villain Paul

Jeffries with assault, but the incident occurred just outside their field of vision. Should they pretend they saw it? Danny Pearce seems to think they should.

CARRYING THE LOAD
Shown: 14.8.93
Writer: Michael Jenner
Director: Matthew Evans
A lorry-hijack investigation takes a surprise turn when the husband of the depot's owner is beaten up.

DEADLY WEAPON
Shown: 17.8.93
Writer: Graham Harvey
Director: Haldane Duncan

ALL THE WRONG CONNECTIONS
Shown: 19.8.93
Writer: Roy Macgregor
Director: Haldane Duncan
The girl accused of running over a young woman has an alibi and the support of a bent solicitor.

GIVE AND TAKE
Shown: 21.8.93
Writer: Elizabeth-Anne Wheal
Director: John Strickland
Polly Page sees Stafford Row WDS Sally Johnson plant drugs on a known dealer. Should she say something? And to whom?

DESPERATE MEASURES
Shown: 24.8.93
Writer: Candy Denman
Director: Sue Dunderdale

TO CATCH A THIEF
Shown: 26.8.93
Writer: Lyndon Mallett
Director: Sue Dunderdale

NATURAL REACTION
Shown: 28.8.93
Writer: Tom Needham
Director: Michael Simpson
Carver and Lines question a thirty-year-old man about his relationship with a fourteen-year-old girl. Lines is convinced that he is guilty but knows it will be difficult to prove.

DESPERATE REMEDIES
Shown: 31.8.93
Writer: Barry Simner
Director: Andrew Higgs

BRIGHT LIGHTS
Shown: 2.9.93
Writer: Peter J. Hammond
Director: Michael Simpson
CID investigate attempts at sexual assault by an electrician who turns out to have connections with the local psychiatric hiospital.

BARE FACED LIES
Shown: 4.9.93
Writer: Lizzie Mickery
Director: Alex Kirby

BUT NOT FORGOTTEN
Shown: 7.9.93
Writer: Russell Lewis
Director: David Attwood

PUSH
Shown: 9.9.93
Writer: Mark Holloway
Director: John Strickland

BAD REACTION
Shown: 10.9.93
Writer: Joanne Maguire
Director: Moira Armstrong

COMPLIMENTS OF THE SERVICE
Shown: 15.9.93
Writer: A. Valentine
Director: Derek Lister

GAME OF TWO HALVES
Shown: 16.9.93
Writer: Robert Jones
Director: Andrew Higgs
Croft, partnered with McCann, is back in uniform for the day – much to Meadows's chagrin and Cato's satisfaction.

THE KNOWLEDGE
Shown: 18.9.93
Writer: Michael Russell
Director: Chris Clough
An Asian minicab firm becomes involved with black cabs in a battle for customers.

NO PLACE LIKE HOME
Shown: 21.9.93
Writer: Tony Etchells
Director: Graham Theakston
When a resident of the Greenfield Estate is battered by an absconder from a nearby unit for young offenders, the other residents protest at her very presence in their midst.

CUSTOMER CARE
Shown: 23.9.93
Writer: Trevor Wadlow
Director: Derek Lister
Haines deals with a young Italian man accused of rape; and two children left alone by their mother steal £100 from a neighbour.

THE RIGHT MAN FOR THE JOB
Shown: 25.9.93
Writer: Chris Ould
Director: Jeremy Silberston
A case of joyriding which ends with a crash reveals an insurance fraud.

A LIFE IN THE DAY OF
Shown: 28.9.93
Writer: Edward Canfor-Dumas
Director: Moira Armstrong
Loxton fails to stop a young man from committing suicide; while Quinnan deals with an irate woman who illegally parks her car with Loxton's permission – only to have it clamped fifteen minutes later.

HAVING WHAT IT TAKES
Shown: 30.9.93
Writer: Isabelle Grey
Director: Gill Wilkinson
When the youngest member of the notorious Draper family comes in to Sun Hill to confess to a three-year-old murder, Meadows believes he will be able to clear up a case he left behind when he was demoted from AMIP; but he does not get the result he had expected.

PLAY THE GAME
Shown: 2.10.93
Writer: Philip Palmer
Director: Aisling Walsh
Haines is convinced that the assailant in a pub fight was protecting himself against a knife which no one else saw. The man is charged, but on his release he is stabbed to death by his injured opponent.

UNLUCKY FOR SOME
Shown: 5.10.93
Writer: Julian Spilsbury
Director: David Attwood
Following an armed robbery at a bingo hall, one of the employees reveals that it was an inside job; but she discovers that the perpetrator was her own son.

GIFT OF THE GAB
Shown: 7.10.93
Writer: A. Valentine
Director: Ted Clisby
Pearce has to use some smart talking to prevent a man suspected of stealing an old lady's pension money from being released on bail.

A CLASS ACT
Shown: 9.10.93
Writer: Trevor Wadlow
Director: Jeremy Woolf
A CID raid on an alleged crack dealer turns up two suspects – but no crack.

DANGEROUS TRADE
Shown: 12.10.93
Writer: Graham Harvey
Director: Jeremy Woolf
A tragic car injury to a little boy leads Page and Quinnan to an illegal trade in imported alcohol.

CHEATING HEART
Shown: 14.10.93
Writer: Scott Cherry
Director: Nick Mallett
A man persuades two women to lend him money for a bar in Spain. When they find out about each other, one woman attacks the other, and the other woman attempts suicide.

SOMEWHERE TO HANG MY HAT
Shown: 16.10.93
Writer: Neil Clarke
Director: Ted Clisby
An old man has been pushed down the stairs of a run-down house; and Endicott, the intimidating landlord, wants the property emptied of its sitting tenants.

NO COMMENT
Shown: 19.10.93
Writer: Christopher Russell
Director: Jeremy Silberston
An old man is killed in his flat, and his money is stolen. Meadows has two black suspects, but they claim their right to silence.

SHRINKAGE
Shown: 21.10.93
Writer: Duncan Gould
Director: Nick Mallett
Cryer convinces Brownlow of the virtues of an arrest referral scheme offering counselling to those arrested on drugs charges.

STREET LEGAL
Shown: 23.10.93
Writer: James Stevenson
Director: Chris Lovett
Loxton's investigation into an assault uncovers a major car-theft operation.

THE GREEN EYED MONSTER
Shown: 26.10.93
Writer: Christopher Lang
Director: Laura Sims
Haines, with AMIP, investigates the murder of Sally Evan, and her husband's jealousy comes to light.

BEHIND CLOSED DOORS
Shown: 28.10.93
Writer: Sebastian Secker Walker
Director: Gill Wilkinson
An Indian woman has been beaten by her husband. An Asian community leader fails to secure his release so that he can be dealt with by the family 'in their own way'.

LINKS IN THE CHAIN
Shown: 30.10.93
Writer: Duncan Gould
Director: Laura Sims
A break-in at a storage warehouse points to a desperate drug-dealer, and Cryer helps Meadows in the arrest of both him and his pressing supplier.

CARE IN THE COMMUNITY
Shown: 2.11.93
Writer: Jane Hollowood
Director: Chris Lovett
Quinnan and Garfield investigate a case of 'granny-dumping'; while Jarvis arrests a man for assault only to discover that the youth he assumed to be drunk is in fact suffering from a diabetic 'hypo'.

YOU DON'T ALWAYS GET WHAT YOU WANT
Shown: 4.11.93
Writer: Stephen C. Handley
Director: Chris Clough
A raid on Tony Gaines and his girlfriend Lizzie reveals a relationship based on fear and forced drug abuse: Tony feeds Lizzie's habit to keep her with him.

REASON TO BELIEVE
Shown: 6.11.93
Writer: Joanne Maguire
Director: Ian White
Haines works with AMIP on a murder inquiry; but does a witness who comes forward – too eagerly, in Morgan's opinion – hold the key to the case?

LET SLIP
Shown: 9.11.93
Writer: Lyndon Mallett
Director: Riita Leena Lynn
Page and Jarvis are called to a shopping centre terrorized by two Rottweilers.

UNTIL PROVEN GUILTY
Shown: 11.11.93
Writer: Sebastian Secker Walker
Director: Derek Lister
Meadows is obliged to bail a cunning and brutal loan-shark without charge for the fourth time. The CPS advise dropping the case, but Meadows secures the co-operation of a lesser villain to ensure a result.

THE HARD SELL
Shown: 13.11.93
Writer: Michael Jenner
Director: Derek Lister
Quinnan suspects that a squatted shop is also being used as an auction-house for stolen goods.

CONSEQUENCES
Shown: 16.11.93
Writer: Marianne Colbran
Director: Riita Leena Lynn
Meadows tackles a drug-dealer who is laundering money through car sales; and an illegal immigrant asks Steele to get her three-year-old boy adopted in England when she is returned to Brazil.

A QUESTION OF IDENTITY
Shown: 18.11.93
Writer: David Lane
Director: Ian White
An HIV-positive addict is signing for heroin and state benefits at two clinics under two names.

CUTTING EDGE
Shown: 20.11.93
Writer: Terry Hodgkinson
Director: Michael Simpson
There is a lot of blood at the scene of an aggravated burglary, but it has not come from the victim. The trail leads to a villain in a private hospital. The victim's husband had used his National Service Malayan knife to cut off three of the villain's fingers.

PUT DOWN
Shown: 23.11.93
Writer: Edward Canfor-Dumas
Director: Michael Simpson
An invalid is found dead in bed. Was it suicide or euthanasia?

LEFT BEHIND
Shown: 25.11.93
Writer: Judith Johnson
Director: Frank Smith
When convicted wife-beater Malcolm Clay is released from prison, he, his wife and his son all end up at Sun Hill on suspicion of violent assaults.

REAL VILLAINS
Shown: 27.11.93
Writer: Gregory Evans
Director: Chris Clough
Sun Hill has to deal with vigilante activity on the Whitegate Estate where parents are fearful for their children in the face of growing lawlessness.

QUESTIONABLE JUDGEMENT
Shown: 30.11.93
Writer: Candy Denman

Director: Paul Unwin
The death of a dosser in a night shelter becomes a murder inquiry when the post-morten shows that he was suffocated.

TAKING CARE OF BUSINESS
Shown: 2.12.93
Writer: Steve Griffiths
Director: Christopher Hodson
When one of the suspects in a shop burglary is beaten up, suspicion falls on his partner; but in fact the shop's owner has taken the law into his own hands.

THE LAW IN THEIR HANDS
Shown: 4.12.93
Writer: Len Collin
Director: Graeme Harper
Stuart Giggs is beaten up by a father and son who believe he burgled their house; but Loxton and Quinnan catch a thief who owns up to the burglary for which Giggs was blamed.

CAUSE FOR COMPLAINT
Shown: 7.12.93
Writer: Edwin Pearce
Director: Frank W. Smith
Monroe investigates a complaint about an unattended emergency call when an Asian is beaten up. The Asian attributes the police delay to racial prejudice; but Monroe discovers that Loxton took the call from the man's wife and, unable to understand the woman's accent, mistook the address.

BLOOD COUNTS
Shown: 9.12.93
Writer: Andy Garrett
Director: Paul Unwin
Carver and Pearce suspect an ex-con of stealing a mailbag from a postman, but his sons provide the answers.

HURTING INSIDE
Shown: 11.12.93
Writer: Harry Duffin
Director: Peter Cattaneo
An ex-addict and convicted burglar absconds while on day release from prison to attend a rehabilitation centre. He wishes to dissuade his daughter, who is living with a drug-dealer and taking drugs, from following in his footsteps.

CORROBORATION
Shown: 14.12.93
Writer: Margaret Phelan

Director: John Bruce
Carver and Jarvis are in court, but the poor identification evidence of a witness needs corroboration and the CPS don't seem to be trying hard enough.

DEATH OF A LADIES MAN
Shown: 16.12.93
Writer: Marianne Colbran
Director: Chris Lovett
When Alex Kennedy goes missing, Greig learns that he is a bigamist and an armed robber – and his wives are not what they seem, either.

AN ILL WIND
Shown: 18.12.93
Writer: Graham Harvey
Director: Laurence Moody
A bizarre suicide involving toxic gas and car exhaust fumes poses a health threat to both police and public.

KEEP ON TRUCKING
Shown: 21.12.93
Writer: Duncan Gould
Director: Graeme Harper
The Bumblebee team deal with a spate of senior citizens' holiday break-ins with the assistance of Garfield and his knowledge of tachographs. A driver at the Big Trippa Coach Company sells passengers' addresses to a burglar.

A FAMILY TRAIT
Shown: 23.12.93
Writer: Candy Denman
Director: Aisling Walsh
CID find themselves in pursuit of two members of the same family for different crimes.

PAID IN FULL
Shown: 24.12.93
Writer: Elizabeth-Anne Wheal
Director: John Bruce
Boyden foils a smash-and-grab at a hi-fi shop and takes a free gift for his trouble. But Monroe finds the hi-fi equipment, and Boyden has to get himself off the hook.

CAUSE FOR CONCERN
Shown: 28.12.93
Writer: Julian Spilsbury
Director: Christopher Hodson
Datta and Stamp attend a 'domestic' which ends with a Thai wife stabbing her husband; but her predecessor, her sister, lies buried in the garden – murdered by her husband.

NOTHING VENTURED
Shown: 31.12.93
Writer: Edward Canfor-Dumas
Director: Nick Laughland
When an informant tips off Haines about an LSD factory, Haines is keen to set up the bust; but Meadows has other plans for him, which result in Haines deciding to leave Sun Hill and rejoin the Drugs Squad.

GAMES
Shown: 4.1.94
Writer: Len Collin
Director: Andrew Higgs
The search for a nine-year-old boy uncovers the world of computer pornography.

SECOND SIGHT
Shown: 6.1.94
Writer: Elizabeth-Anne Wheal
Director: David Attwood
DI Johnson picks up on a robbery investigation by Croft, and their combined enthusiasm results in quick progress.

DARKNESS BEFORE DAWN
Shown: 7.1.94
Writer: Sebastian Secker Walker
Director: Nick Laughland
On a quiet night shift Page and Boyden are called to a 'domestic' in a tower-block and discover that a woman and her baby have fallen to their death.

HE WHO WAITS
Shown: 11.1.94
Writer: Neil Clarke
Director: Douglas MacKinnon
The AMIP team suspect that Freddy Longden has been killed during an interrupted burglary; but Garfield, on duty outside the murder scene, thinks otherwise.

MIX AND MATCH
Shown: 13.1.94
Writer: Chris Ould
Director: Charles Beeson
Trakbak, a private security firm, informs Sun Hill that a stolen Mercedes has been traced to their ground. Their representative is keen to recover it, but Steele and Pearce see an opportunity for a larger operation.

DEALER WINS
Shown: 14.1.94
Writer: Duncan Gould
Director: Charles Beeson
At family court, Johnson uses her relationship with Jackie Garrett to bring about a string of drug-dealing arrests, and in return she helps Jackie to fight a care application on her daughter.

NO JOB FOR AN AMATEUR
Shown: 18.1.94
Writer: Candy Denman
Director: Riita Leena Lynn
The suspect for an assault in a nurses' home turns out to be a man known to have beaten up several prostitutes; and Ackland realizes that the victim, a student nurse, has been moonlighting on the game.

JUDGE AND JURY
Shown: 20.1.94
Writer: James Stevenson
Director: Bill Pryde
Carver's blinkered investigation of a street robbery leaves him with egg on his face; and a trusted duty solicitor betrays his professional ethics when he attempts to defend his troubled wife for making off without paying for petrol and driving her car straight at the garage proprietor.

THE MOURNING AFTER
Shown: 21.1.94
Writer: Mark Holloway
Director: Chris Lovett
The body of a young man is found in Canley Fields, and Morgan is sent to break the news to his mother, who is blind. However, there has been a mistake with the identification, and the blind woman's son turns out to be the murderer, not the victim.

JUST SAY NO
Shown: 25.1.94
Writer: Nigel Baldwin
Director: Jan Sargent
Conway wins the confidence of a fifteen-year-old girl drug addict who claims to have information about a murder.

MUD STICKS
Shown: 27.1.94
Writer: Isabelle Grey
Director: Peter Cattaneo
The chairman of the action committee formed to rid Jessup Street of prostitutes is a racist and is involved in a series of muggings. When the man's Thai wife is found beaten unconscious it emerges that his real fear is that his wife had been a prostitute in Thailand before he married her.

ONE BAD TURN
Shown: 28.1.94
Writer: A. Valentine
Director: Laurence Moody
A call for Cato to clamp down on prostitution leads to a drug dealer being arrested and an informant, a pregnant prostitute, being badly beaten.

FAITH IN THE SYSTEM
Shown: 1.2.94
Writer: Matthew Wingett
Director: Bill Pryde
Carver chances to witness the arrest of a young man for criminal damage by Boulton, an off-duty CID officer from Barton Street. The young man files a complaint for assault, and Boulton turns to Carver for support – and not for the first time.

KEEPING MUM
Shown: 3.2.94
Writer: Lizzie Mickery
Director: Michael Simpson
When Greig and Croft arrive at the Paley house to arrest Joe for theft, they discover that his mother has been assaulted.

DOUBLE VISION
Shown: 4.2.94
Writer: Neil Clarke
Director: Chris Clough
Pearce takes the credit for information leading to the arrest of the Bennet twins for hijacking, but Johnson and Loxton discover that the original robber was Titch Lineker.

NO ACCESS
Shown: 8.2.94
Writer: Isabelle Grey
Director: Riita Leena Lynn
The disappearance of eleven-year-old Denny Atkin directs Morgan's attention to a men's group that has been involved in helping divorced men to abduct their own children.

WAYS AND MEANS
Shown: 10.2.94
Writer: Jane Woodrow
Director: Jan Sargent
Boyden receives a tip-off about a gang of shoplifters. Datta tries to get a man locked up for breaking his bail conditions and intimidating his wife, but the magistrates release him – with disastrous consequences.

CUTTING IT
Shown: 11.2.94
Writer: Michael Jenner
Director: Brian Parker
When Sergeant Kegan of B Relief is accused of sexual harassment by probationer WPC Karen Beavis, the Federation sergeants' rep, Steele, faces a clash of loyalties.

SECRETS
Shown: 15.2.94
Writer: Neil McKay
Director: Douglas MacKinnon
When a thirteen-year-old girl is reported missing, Boyden and Loxton's investigation leads them to a convicted sex-offender living in the neighbourhood.

BIN-MEN
Shown: 17.2.94
Writer: Roger Davenport
Director: Ian White
Investigating a case of assault, Stamp and Page uncover a small-time brothel a man is running from his flat.

DUCKING AND DIVING
Shown: 18.2.94
Writer: Barry Purchese
Director: Chris Clough
When McCann is badly beaten during a warehouse burglary, Garfield, as Federation rep, complains to Cato that the relief was undermanned.

GONE AWAY
Shown: 22.2.94
Writer: Isabelle Grey
Director: Ian White
Johnson runs a joint operation with Customs to find the dealer supplying Sun Hill with heroin.

DEAD MEN DON'T DRIVE CARS
Shown: 24.2.94
Writer: Rob Gittins
Director: John Bruce
Loxton and Quinnan encounter a man taking driving tests and acquiring licences under false names; but the man's criminal activities turn out to be much wider.

SATURDAY NIGHT'S ALL RIGHT
Shown: 25.2.94
Writer: Len Collin
Director: John Bruce
A rent party ends in tragedy when a man is attacked by thugs, and there are twenty-eight suspects.

RANKS AND FILES
Shown: 1.3.94
Writer: Edward Canfor-Dumas
Director: Derek Lister
Stamp tries to process a juvenile before the end of his shift to win a bet with

Quinnan, and Johnson tries to locate vital papers that have not been seen since the departure of Roach.

BUSINESS AS USUAL
Shown: 3.3.94
Writer: Philip Palmer
Director: Indra Bhose
Quinnan and Ackland investigate a burglary at a clothes shop that turns out to be an inside job.

ROOT OF ALL EVIL
Shown: 4.3.94
Writer: Joanne Maguire
Director: Indra Bhose
Johnson and Woods have plenty of suspects when they investigate an arson attack, but can a loan shark help them to make sense of everything?

MAN TO MAN
Shown: 8.3.94
Writer: Trevor Wadlow
Director: Derek Lister
John Howard confesses to murder, but Johnson is convinced that his wife incited him to murder her lover.

MENACE
Shown: 10.3.94
Writer: Tom Needham
Director: Brian Parker
As CID investigate malicious phone calls, their suspect has surprising information which helps to trap a sex offender.

KILLJOYS
Shown: 11.3.94
Writer: Gregory Evans
Director: Laurence Moody
Jarvis and McCann are assigned to help close down a pirate radio station; but Pearce and Croft believe the pirates can lead them to a drug dealer.

ONE OF THEM
Shown: 16.3.94
Writer: Chris Lang
Director: Nick Laughland
A seemingly motiveless attack on a popular youth worker makes no sense to Carver until he learns that the man has been homosexually involved with a sixteen-year-old boy from the club.

DAY OF RECKONING
Shown: 17.3.94
Writer: Julian Spilsbury
Director: Diana Patrick
When Meadows's snout Bannon gives him an opportuniy to nail Grieve over a drugs haul, Grieve's

revenge leads to Bannon's death but enables Meadows to charge Grieve with murder.

SLEEPING WITH THE FISHES
Shown: 18.3.94
Writer: Julian Jones
Director: Laurence Moody
A small boat is found floating down the Thames. Cryer discovers that a teenage lark has ended with two boys and a girl being drowned, with another boy racked with guilt because he did not dive in to help.

FAIR EXCHANGE
Shown: 22.3.94
Writer: Chris Lang
Director: Diana Patrick
An arson attack on a known villain appears to be part of a long-running feud, but it is his daughter who has the strongest reason for wanting him dead.

LAST RIGHTS
Shown: 24.3.94
Writer: Candy Denman
Director: Nick Laughland
A terminally ill old lady's attempt to kill herself goes wrong when her daughter visits. Her doctor advises against forceful interference by the police, and Stamp gently persuades the woman to go into hospital.

MEAN STREAK
Shown: 25.3.94
Writer: James Stevenson
Director: Michael Offer
Morgan catches only one of a gang of milk-depot raiders, but Quinnan's investigation of a burglary turns up a weak villain who can provide the information she needs.

PIG IN THE MIDDLE
Shown: 30.3.94
Writer: Jonathan Myerson
Director: Carol Wilks
Carver and Woods find themselves being used by one drug dealer on the Brontë Estate to eliminate a rival.

HOUSE ARREST
Shown: 31.3.94
Writer: Barry Simner
Director: Carol Wilks
Investigation of a robbery leads Meadows and Woods into the stormy relationship between ex-con Ronnie Lee and his daughter Lorraine. Unknown to Ronnie, Lorraine masterminds robberies.

CLUBBING TOGETHER
Shown: 1.4.94
Writer: Sebastian Secker Walker
Director: Brian Farnham
A nightclub doorman is arrested for assault, but his victim won't say why it happened.

PALS
Shown: 6.4.94
Writer: Mark Holloway
Director: Aisling Walsh
After a piece of foul play during a rugby match, Jarvis is interviewed by Area Complaints.

SOLD OUT
Shown: 7.4.94
Writer: Stephen C. Handley
Director: Michael Offer
Morgan finally nails Harry Burton for handling stolen car spares, but only after his accomplice is found badly beaten.

LAST ORDERS
Shown: 8.4.94
Writer: Michael Jenner
Director: Chris Lovett
Investigating a series of violent keg-thefts, Meadows finds himself working alongside brewery security officer Chivers.

ALL THE COMFORTS OF HOME
Shown: 13.4.94
Writer: Lyndon Mallett
Director: Aisling Walsh
A teenage girl is found sleeping rough. She has obviously been beaten up, but won't talk about it; then Ackland and Quinnan are called to a disturbance at the home of a woman who turns out to be the girl's mother.

WILD JUSTICE
Shown: 14.4.94
Writer: Nigel Baldwin
Director: Graeme Harper
In trying to break an alibi Greig, Croft and Johnson uncover an elaborate scheme of revenge.

GIVE AWAY
Shown: 15.4.94
Writer: Len Collin
Director: Brian Farnham
Morgan and Lines want to nail David Knox, a vicious bully who manages to get people to give him things; while Boyden and Hollis get their hooks into some stolen Koi carp.

NOWHERE TO RUN
Shown: 19.4.94
Writer: Simon Frith

Director: Chris Lovett
Following a break-in at a women's refuge, a burglar is nailed; but will Elaine and her child ever be safe?

FINAL STRAW
Shown: 21.4.94
Writer: Tom Needham
Director: Gwennan Sage
Greig suspects a caretaker of burgling his own school. The caretaker's attempted suicide makes the case a delicate one.

BODYGUARD OF LIES
Shown: 22.4.94
Writer: Elizabeth-Anne Wheal
Director: Gwennan Sage
When Ackland uncovers a series of muggings, Johnson is unimpressed; but Monroe organizes a stakeout on a pub, and a mugging gang preying on building workers is arrested.

FRIENDS LIKE THAT
Shown: 26.4.94
Writer: Tony Etchells
Director: Roger Gartland
When the socially inadequate Mark Abbot, whose life is falling apart, recognizes Quinnan as the PC who nicked him in his youth, Quinnan finds himself drawn into Abbot's problems.

DISCLOSURES
Shown: 28.4.94
Writer: Carolyn Sally Jones
Director: Graeme Harper
Greig and Ackland are confident of their case against Michael Henessey for burglary and assault – until a witness arrives at the court and alleges that Ackland did not record her complete statement.

BIG EAGLE DAY
Shown: 29.4.94
Writer: Terry Hodgkinson
Director: A. J. Quinn
Following a complaint of loud music being played at three in the morning, Boyden, Garfield, Page and Stamp arrive at the house to find two known villains and a couple of girls swimming in champagne and thousands of pounds in banknotes.

BOTTLENECK
Shown: 3.5.94
Writer: J. C. Wilsher
Director: David Richards
Conway arranges a party which will give him a chance to sound out DAC Hicks about changes to the

upper ranks; Meadows, Cato and Brownlow also seize the same opportunity – but Meadows also wishes to be present when an escaped prisoner is arrested.

HONOUR AND OBEY
Shown: 5.5.94
Writer: Lizzie Mickery
Director: Roger Gartland
Skase's low opinion of women's abilities is made very plain to Croft when she works with him to solve some wedding-present thefts.

HOT OFF THE PRESS
Shown: 6.5.94
Writer: Edwin Pearce
Director: A. J. Quinn
A campaign to rid the streets of illegally parked cars uncovers a seventeen-year-old distributor of racist literature.

KILLING TIME
Shown: 10.5.94
Writer: Mark Holloway
Director: Jeremy Silberston
A fifteen-year-old burglar takes an army revolver from a house. Can the police catch him before he uses it?

BUTTER WOULDN'T MELT
Shown: 12.5.94
Writer: Neil Clarke
Director: David Richards
Quinnan thinks that Mick Sweeting, an ageing hippie, is inciting Jason Shelley to steal car radios; but the real thief is Tony Phelan, who is manipulating Sweeting.

ALL THINGS NICE
Shown: 13.5.94
Writer: Ron Rose
Director: David Attwood
A drugs raid on a pub discovers the body of an eighteen-year-old man in the toilet. He has been murdered by four girls.

NO WAY TO TREAT A LADY
Shown: 17.5.94
Writer: Scott Cherry
Director: Ian White
Carver uses Billy Gowers to catch villain Ted Knight, and Cato is outraged that Steele has included some casual remarks in the minutes of a meeting.

THE PRICE
Shown: 19.5.94
Writer: Roy Macgregor
Director: Jeremy Silberston
The prosecution of a local thug is jeopardized when a

key witness goes missing.

OLD SCORES
Shown: 20.5.94
Writer: David Hoskins
Director: Ian White
When an anonymous caller offers evidence that could convict a local villain, Boyden suspects that he has been set up. When MS15 turn up at the pick-up point, his suspicions are confirmed.

BRANDED
Shown: 24.5.94
Writer: Barry Simner
Director: David Attwood
An investigation of arson attacks on two cars leads to a convicted sex offender and his father, who is struggling to come to terms with his son's crimes.

GOOD FRIENDS
Shown: 26.5.94
Writer: Marianne Colbran
Director: June Howson
When one of her snouts is given as a false alibi for a burglary, Johnson discovers that both the burglary and the snout are not what they seemed.

RTA
Shown: 27.5.94
Writer: Philip Palmer
Director: Douglas MacKinnon
Investigating a traffic accident in which the woman passenger died, Monroe begins to suspect that the driver deliberately crashed the car in order to kill both himself and his wife.

NO MARKS
Shown: 31.5.94
Writer: Robert Jones
Director: June Howson
When young John Samson is sent by his mother from Devon to stay with his father in Sun Hill because he has misbehaved, he finds himself stumbling out of the frying-pan and into the fire.

SWEETNESS AND LIGHT
Shown: 2.6.94
Writer: Ron Rose
Director: David Attwood
A gang of bikers is intimidating a group of mothers at their club. One of the mothers has an idea how to tackle them; but one of the fathers has a more old-fashioned approach.

HEY DIDDLE DIDDLE
Shown: 3.6.94

Writer: Gerry Huxham
Director: Nick Laughland
A solicitor delivers a tape to Sun Hill in which the recently deceased Ralph Towner posthumously confesses to the murder of his former business partner.

FUNNY MONEY
Shown: 7.6.94
Writer: Duncan Gould
Director: Graham Dixon
A high-quality counterfeit ten-pound note leads Meadows and Lines to a couple of clever forgers.

TILL DEATH US DO PART
Shown: 9.6.94
Writer: Harry Duffin
Director: Chris Clough
When Loxton and Quinnan are called by a familiar tramp to the scene of an attack on a DSS inspector beside the canal, they suspect that he may be more involved than he is saying.

ALL ALONG THE WATCHTOWER
Shown: 10.6.94
Writer: Stephen C. Handley
Director: Sue Dunderdale
Conway and Monroe have to deal with the aftermath of a near-fatal traffic accident caused by a fourteen-year-old joyrider.

SNOWBLIND
Shown: 14.6.94
Writer: Steve Griffiths
Director: Douglas MacKinnon
Skase's preoccupation with crack dealers makes him fair game for a set-up.

LESSON TO BE LEARNED
Shown: 16.6.94
Writer: Roy Mitchell
Director: Andrew Higgs
When a teacher at Canley Comprehensive School is savagely assaulted, a young black student seems the obvious suspect, but the teachers have something to hide.

DEAR JOHN
Shown: 17.6.94
Writer: Lyndon Mallett
Director: Brian Farnham
A man appears to have fallen from a block of flats, but there is a knife-wound in his back. Investigation leads to a second body.

WITHIN LIMITS
Shown: 21.6.94
Writer: Brian B. Thompson

Director: Christopher Hodson
While investigating an assault, Boyden meets an old flame and helps her deal with her violent husband.

TAILS YOU LOSE
Shown: 23.6.94
Writer: Maxwell Young
Director: Christopher Hodson
Skase is compromised when his concern to protect his snout leads him to discover the true extent of her criminal activities.

GATE FEVER
Shown: 24.6.94
Writer: Isabelle Grey
Director: Jim Goddard
When lifer Chris Perry is released from prison on licence, the parents of his murder victim cannot accept that their other daughter has befriended him while in prison.

THE ROAD NOT TAKEN
Shown: 28.6.94
Writer: Ron Rose
Director: Jim Goddard
A drugs raid brings Page a surprise reunion with an old schoolfriend whose life has gone down a different route.

FALLEN ANGEL
Shown: 30.6.94
Writer: Rob Gittins
Director: Graham Dixon
Woods uncovers a customer's scheme to take revenge on a cowboy builder, and takes great satisfaction in placing the builder in the hands of the VAT man.

A TOUCH OF BRAID
Shown: 1.7.94
Writer: Edwin Pearce
Director: Frank Smith
Johnson's raid on a flat on the Cockcroft Estate goes wrong when a young boy falls from the third-floor balcony while fleeing.

MASQUERADE
Shown: 5.7.94
Writer: Julian Spilsbury
Director: Frank Smith
When Greig realizes that a house has been burgled twice he finds a new criminal in the area: 'Mr Memory', who is currently helping entertaining Sun Hill's pensioners at the Community Centre – assisted by Conway.

GOOD DAYS
Shown: 7.7.94
Writer: Peter J. Hammond
Director: Michael Simpson

John Joseph Monk, wanted for questioning about an armed robbery, is on the run. Lines and Woods discover that his lady-friend, Grace Walsh, has murdered him.

BANNED
Shown: 8.7.94
Writer: Michael Baker
Director: Sam Miller
Johnson makes problems for herself when she removes an aggressive solicitor's clerk from a robbery-suspect interview.

PARENTAL GUIDANCE
Shown: 12.7.94
Writer: Richard Stoneman
Director: Chris Lovett
Trevor, an aspiring police officer, provides useful clues for an investigation of DIY detoxification that takes Lines ominously close to home.

SETTLING THE SCORE
Shown: 14.7.94
Writer: Tom Needham
Director: Baz Taylor
Carver realizes that snout Jeff Price gave him false information to set up Matt Hardy and clear the way for an affair with his wife.

HIGH DRIVERS
Shown: 15.7.94
Writer: Nigel Baldwin
Director: Sam Miller
A fatal collision between a Spanish lorry and a domestic car creates problems for Monroe when it turns out that the Spaniard arrested isn't the driver and the dead boy's identity is mistaken.

PERSONAL SPACE
Shown: 19.7.94
Writer: Carolyn Sally Jones
Director: Moira Armstrong
Croft, fresh from an interview course, criticizes Woods's methods in trying to obtain a confession from a man suspected of abducting a girl.

PUBLIC SPIRIT
Shown: 21.7.94
Writer: Simon Frith
Director: Sue Dunderdale
A young crack-dealer is fatally injured in a street-fight. Morgan finds a witness, but how does she persuade him to talk?

DIRTY LAUNDRY
Shown: 22.7.94
Writer: Elizabeth-Anne Wheal
Director: Moira Armstrong

An apparently motiveless shooting of a black youth reminds CID of how far from being on top of the crack problem they really are.

PAYING THE PRICE
Shown: 26.7.94
Writer: Robert Jones
Director: John Bruce
Conway clips the wing-mirror of a car in a narrow street and soon finds himself listening to William Swift's confession to an attempted armed robbery.

BEST INTERESTS
Shown: 28.7.94
Writer: James Stevenson
Director: Brian Farnham
Determined to track down a boy who has been abducted by his father, Morgan breaks the rules and finds herself in trouble.

EASY PREY
Shown: 29.7.94
Writer: Mark Holloway
Director: Baz Taylor
Fry, a recluse since being disfigured in a crash, is found unconscious in his flat. He appears to have been assaulted during a burglary; but even when it emerges that Fry may have taken an overdose the circumstances are no less suspicious.

UNFINISHED BUSINESS
Shown: 2.8.94
Writer: David Hoskins
Director: Jeremy Silberston
The arrival of Chris Deakin, the new DS, is delayed while he gives evidence in court. Meanwhile Johnson attempts to track down a violent escaped prisoner.

WAR OF NERVES
Shown: 4.8.94
Writer: Edwin Pearce
Director: Danny Hiller
Differing attitudes at Sun Hill towards domestic violence give Datta an awkward time and bring her into conflict with Cato.

LEGACY
Shown: 5.8.94
Writer: Chris Ould
Director: Laurence Moody
Deakin inherits a snout and gets information that Johnson badly needs to solve her case. He shares the information but on his own terms.

DEATH AND TAXES
Shown: 9.8.94

Writer: Jonathan Myerson
Director: David Yates
Cryer unearths extortion within the world of the young homeless; while Ackland and Quinnan investigate a break-in at a chemist's that turns out to be an inside job.

IN TOO DEEP
Shown: 11.8.94
Writer: Roy Macgregor
Director: Nick Mallet
A young windscreen-washer is found lying critically injured from a bullet wound. Meadows and Deakin discover that the shooting is linked to a local drug-dealer.

YOU BELONG TO ME
Shown: 12.8.94
Writer: Marianne Colbrann
Director: Jeremy Silberston
When Datta investigates the disappearance of a seventeen-year-old girl, she finds that both the girl's half-sister and her brother-in-law have something to hide.

LOOKING FOR MR RIGHT
Shown: 16.8.94
Writer: Barry Simner
Director: Danny Hiller
The stabbing of Yussuf Ali involves Morgan in the marital problems of Shobana Lal and Farida Khan, and exposes Ali as a paid 'bounty hunter'.

SKINNING CATS
Shown: 18.8.94
Writer: Duncan Gould
Director: Nick Mallet
Meadows and Conway clash over how to handle a crack problem on the Abelard Estate.

FULL CONTACT
Shown: 19.8.94
Writer: Steve Griffiths
Director: David Yates
Meadows is not impressed when a truckload of tobacco is hijacked on Sun Hill's ground. Meanwhile, a fight in a pub car park turns out to be more than just a squabble over the landlady's favours.

PARTNERS
Shown: 23.8.94
Writer: Simon Moss
Director: John Bruce
Deakin and Croft pick through the pieces of four interwoven friendships to find out who shot a jeweller.

ON THE LATCH
Shown: 25.8.94
Writer: Michael Jenner
Director: Gill Wilkinson
The seemingly violent death of an old soldierr on the run-down Antrim Green Estate immediately creates ripples, but what crime are Meadows and Morgan investigating - manslaughter, aggravated burglary or what?

WALL OF SILENCE
Shown: 26.8.94
Writer: David Hoskins
Director: Gill Wilkinson
A telesales girl is found injured and Johnson's and Deakin's enquiries reveal a sordid background of sexual harassment and office cover-ups.

BUSINESS OPPORTUNITIES
Shown: 30.8.94
Writer: Isabelle Grey
Director: Dominic Allan
McCann finds Tony Wright sleeping rough on a bench, yet learns that he owns a house just around the corner. His curiosity leads to an investigation by Pearce of the Irish roofer, Samuel o'Rourke, who has targetted Tony, depressed and alone, for large weekly payments for roofing work he has never carried out.

A LITTLE LEARNING
Shown: 1.9.94
Writer: Michael Jenner
Director: Chris Lovett
When a teacher seems reluctant to bring a charge of indecent assualt against a pupil, Woods has to question her motives. Is Stephanie telling the truth, or is she being used to get at the boy?

RIGHT WAY, WRONG WAY
Shown: 2.9.94
Writer: Nigel Baldwin
Director: Simon Meyers
Aggro between the West Indian and Chinese communities threatens to escalate as Steele and McCann investigate.

INSTANT RESPONSE
Shown: 6.9.94
Writer: Joanna Maguire
Director: Nick Laughland
A stolen car leaves a trail of destruction through Sun Hill; can Stamp and Quinnan, in the Area Car, stop it before someone gets killed?

WASHBACK
Shown: 8.9.94
Writer: Anthony Valentine
Director: Chris Clough
Investigating a sawn-off shotgun found in a house fire, Lines is led to Lee Ruddick, a crack dealer. When Lines and Johnson team up to raid him, Ruddick eats the evidence, with fatal consequences.

KICKBACK (Part 2 of WASHBACK)
Shown: 9.9.94
Writer: Anthony Valentine
Director: Laurence Moody
When Lee Ruddick dies at St Hugh's, CIB is called in and DI Johnson is accused of manslaughter. Claudia Morris, the complainant and chief witness, later withdraws her allegation, but just as Johnson seems to be in the clear, Ruddick's family serves her with a private prosecution for manslaughter.

BIRTHRIGHT
Shown: 13.9.94
Writer: Peter J. Hammond
Director: Aishling Walsh
Ackland and Datta are drawn into the past when a couple are pestered by a young woman claiming to be a long-lost daughter. Meanwhile , a death message to an old lady reveals a relative she had forgotten she had.

THREATS AND PROMISES
Shown: 15.9.94
Writer: Gregory Evans
Director: Michael Simpson
When a young man is stabbed by Warren Judd, youngest brother in a notorious family of criminals, witnesses are too scared to speak. Morgan and Lines draw a blank until they realize that Diane, Warren's fiancée, may not be as respectable as she appears.

INSIDE
Shown: 16.9.94
Writer: Mark Holloway
Director: Gwennan Sage
A man holds a woman hostage in a flat. Jarvis is faced with the task of talking him out. As Jarvis builds a rapport with him, the investigation led by Monroe constructs a worrying picture of the hostage-taker. Can he be talked out or will force be necessary?

SAVING FACE
Shown: 20.9.94
Writer: Scott Cherry
Director: Dominic Allan
Carver ends up leading 'Operation Cock-up', and is determined not to look an idiot in front of Deakin.

OUT IN THE COLD
Shown: 22.9.94
Writer: David G. McDonagh
Director: Gwennan Sage
Jarvis, Loxton, Page and Cato deal with a trio of squatters and a violent landlord.

LIVING LEGEND (linked to INQUEST)
Shown: 23.9.94
Writer: Helen Leadbeater
Director: Brian Farnham
When Meadows arrests notorious robber Kenny Stone in a drugs-for-money exchange, Stone isn't in possession of the drugs. Meadows fails to detain Stone long enough to charge him, but he dies in his cell as he is about to be released.

THE SIXTH AGE
Shown: 27.9.94
Writer: Ron Rose
Director: June Howson
Loxton and Quinnan are drawn into a world of romance, intrigue and violent affections when called to attend an incident at the local tea dance.

DOWN AND OUT
Shown: 29.9.94
Writer: Simon Frith
Director: Laura Sims
Johnson's seeking vital information concerning a gang of payphone thieves. She comes into conflict with Custody Sergeant Boyden when she asks to speak to a prisoner with a history of mental illness.

INQUEST
Shown: 30.9.94
Writer: Margaret Phelan
Director: Brian Farnham
Sun Hill are at the Coroner's Court for the inquest on Stone, who died in custody. Did the Great Bullion Robber die of natural causes or are Sun Hill officers in some way to blame for his death?